Fashioning Japanese Subcultures

Fashioning Japanese Subcultures

Yuniya Kawamura

B L O O M S B U R Y

LONDON • NEW DELHI • NEW YORK • SYDNEY

Bloomsbury Academic

An imprint of Bloomsbury Publishing Plc

50 Bedford Square	175 Fifth Avenue
London	New York
WC1B 3DP	NY 10010
UK	USA

www.bloomsbury.com

English edition first published in 2012 by Berg
Reprinted by Bloomsbury Academic 2013

British Library Cataloguing-in-Publication Data
A catalogue record for this book is available from the British Library.

ISBN: HB: 978-1-8478-8948-5
PB: 978-1-8478-8947-8

Library of Congress Cataloging-in-Publication Data
Kawamura, Yuniya, 1963–
Fashioning Japanese subcultures / Yuniya Kawamura.
pages cm
Includes bibliographical references and index.
ISBN 978-1-84788-948-5 (hardback)—ISBN 978-1-84788-947-8—
ISBN 978-0-85785-216-8 1. Fashion—Japan. 2. Fashion design—Japan.
3. Subculture—Japan. 4. Japan—Social life and customs. I. Title.
GT1560.K35 2012
391.00952—dc23 2012004413

Typeset by Apex CoVantage, LLC, Madison, WI, USA.
Printed and bound in Great Britain

To My Family

Contents

List of Plates and Tables

PLATES

TABLES

Acknowledgments

My appreciation goes to the Fashion Institute of Technology (FIT) of the State University of New York for granting me a sabbatical leave and relieving me of my teaching duties during the spring 2010 semester to work on this project. I have been working on this topic since 2004, and I needed the time to concentrate on my fieldwork in Tokyo so that I could start writing a book. I am grateful to Valerie Steele, director and chief curator of the Museum at FIT, for giving me the opportunity to contribute an article, "Japanese Fashion Subcultures," to her exhibition catalog *Japan Fashion Now!* (Yale University Press, 2010) and to give a presentation at the exhibition symposium in November 2010.

I am thankful to all my colleagues in the Social Sciences Department who are supportive of my work: Yasemin Celik, Paul Clement, Luis Zaera, Ernest Poole, Spencer Schein, Meg Miele, Joseph Maiorca, Roberta Paley, Praveen Chaudhry, Emre Ozsoz, Dan Benkendorf, and Jung-Whan (Marc) de Jong. Students in my Clothing and Society and Cultural Expressions of Non-Western Dress/Fashion classes provided a valuable sounding board for the development of my ideas.

My gratitude also goes to Hiroshi Ishida, my former professor at the Graduate School of Arts and Sciences, Columbia University, who is now at the Institute of Social Science, Tokyo University, for sponsoring my residence there as a visiting fellow from January to August 2010. He also gave me the opportunity to speak at his Contemporary Japan Study Group in June 2010. The feedback I received from the audience was constructive and encouraging. While I was in Japan, Reiko Koga of Bunka Women's University and Takashi Machimura of Hitotsubashi University also invited me to present my research in their graduate classes.

Discussions with my former classmates in graduate school, Takeshi Wada of Tokyo University, and Tsutomu Nakano of the Graduate School of Business at Aoyoama Gakuin University, have been very productive.

I have given a number of presentations on Japanese fashion and subcultures at several academic conferences, such as at the European Sociological Association conference in Milan; the First Global Conference: Urban Popcultures in Prague, Czech Republic; and the Dressing Rooms: Current Perspectives on Fashion and Textile conference, in Oslo, Norway. I am grateful to the Center for Excellence in Teaching and Scott Stoddart, dean of liberal arts at FIT, for funding many of my conference trips.

I thank all the organizations and museums that invited me to give a presentation on my book even before its completion: Asia Society in New York; Parsons the New School for Design; the Museum of Arts and Design in New York; the University of California, Los Angeles; Potsdam University in Germany; the Textile Museum in Washington, D.C.; the Japanese-American Association of New York; the Japanese-Americans, Japanese in America in New York; Copenhagen Business School in Denmark; and the Centre for Fashion Studies in Sweden.

This is the fourth book that I am publishing with Berg, and it is always a pleasure working with their efficient and professional editorial team. I am grateful to Julia Hall, Anna Wright, Emily Medcalf, Noa Vazquez, Agnes Upshall, and Ian Buck at Berg.

I am thankful for the gracious assistance provided by the library staff at the Fashion Institute of Technology, Columbia University, and Bunka University.

My appreciation also goes to my friends in Tokyo—Yutaka Ishibashi, Takuo Tsuchida, Hideki Shimizu, and Satoko Iye—whom I called and e-mailed whenever I needed a distraction from writing.

I am eternally indebted to all the members of the Japanese subcultures who sat down with me and told me their candid stories and experiences. This book would not have been possible without their contributions. I am especially thankful to Momo Matsuura, Zuki, Haru, Yusuke Arai, Sphere, Ayumi Saito, Yutaka Toyama, Mayumi Abe, Sara, and Silvia Nodari for allowing me to use their original pictures.

I dedicate this book to my family, Yoya, Yoko, and Maya Kawamura, who have always been there for me whenever I needed them. I could not have completed this book without their love and encouragement. I am who I am today because of them.

Yuniya Kawamura
New York and Tokyo

I: INTRODUCTION

Japanese street fashion and youth subcultures have been topics of interest for many journalists, editors, bloggers, museum curators, and photographers both in and outside Japan (Aoki 2001, 2006; Evers, Macias, and Nonaka 2007; Godoy 2007, 2009; Keet 2007; Narumi 2010; Yoshinaga and Ishikawa 2007), who provide fascinating accounts as well as photographs that capture everyday clothes worn by ordinary but fashionable Japanese boys and girls on the streets. Japanese youth dress is indeed visually appealing, but more than that, it is vital to the theoretical understanding of subcultures to which many of the youth belong. My intention in writing this book is to provide theoretical frameworks within which the Japanese subcultural phenomenon can be analyzed. My study will make a contribution as a case study to subcultural studies and theories in general. The scholarly literature on Japanese fashion often focuses on major Japanese designers (English 2007, 2011; Fukai et al. 2010; Kawamura 2004; Koda 2008; Kondo 1997; Mears 2010; Mitchell 2006), such as Issey Miyake, Rei Kawakubo, and Yohji Yamamoto, or traces the cultural and social history of Japanese kimono or textiles (Brandon et al. 2005; Dalby 2001; Imperatore and Maclardy 2001; Munsterberg 1996; Slade 2010), and they do not pay much attention to Japanese youth fashion.

Thus, the purpose of this book is to fill the void between academic and non-academic perspectives since Japanese youth subcultures and their unique stylistic expressions as a research topic deserve scholarly and intellectual considerations just as punks, goths, mods, skinheads, and hippies in the West are studied in scholarship on youth subcultures (Baron 1989; Brake 1980; Haenfler 2006, 2009; Hebdige 1979; Hodkinson 2002; Issitt 2009, 2011; Muggleton 2000). My focus is not on any street fashion, which is a term used loosely to indicate any type of youth fashion. My attention is specifically on the members of different subcultural communities in Tokyo and their outward appearances. Like many other subcultures in the West, I argue that the Japanese subcultural phenomenon is an ideological one. By popularizing a subcultural style as a fashion trend, the legitimate taste in fashion is transforming and expanding with the help of the related industries, and they together constitute an institution and establish an alternative fashion system that goes against the mainstream system of fashion.

Fashioning Japanese Subcultures is a study of Japanese youth subcultures in Tokyo based on my empirical research between 2004 and 2010. I wanted to explore what these Japanese subcultures are. Why do the youth in these subcultures dress so differently from the mainstream? Is it just fashion for them? Do they want attention? What is their lifestyle? To what extent are they involved in the group? What does it meant to them to shop in these districts and not buy items online? What elements do they share or not share with the subcultures in the West? I was eager to identify and uncover any latent functions that these subcultures may have. My task, as a researcher, is to discern the hidden messages inscribed in code on the surfaces of style, to trace them as symbols that represent the very contradictions they struggle to resolve or conceal.

In addition, this research is partly an analytical extension and application of my previous work on high fashion within the French fashion system (Kawamura 2004), which consists of various macro-structural factors as well as micro-interactionist individual social networks in transforming clothing into fashion and legitimating designers' creativity. I compare and contrast youth fashion subcultures with high-fashion communities and examine theoretically their systemic similarities and differences in promoting and diffusing fashion. I attempt to show how the youth fashion subcultures are created/produced, disseminated, maintained, reproduced, and perpetuated with the help of fashion institutions.

To answer my research questions, this study crosses disciplinary boundaries. I draw on different theoretical perspectives, such as diffusion theories, micro- and macro-level sociological theories, subcultural theories, and media/textual studies. Furthermore, I point out that empirical research on subcultures in general often neglects the girls' and women's perspectives and ignores a non-Western or a multicultural focus. It is necessary to pose to what extent the components found in U.S. and British subcultures can be found in other, non-Western cultures, such as Japan.

My interests in Japanese youth fashion began in 2003, when I was visiting Sydney with an old friend from college. As we were strolling down the streets of Sydney talking about our days in college, we happened to pass by the Powerhouse Museum, which was holding a photography exhibition called FRUiTS. I first thought it was an exhibition about Australian produce and did not think much of it since at the time I did not know anything about the magazine *FRUiTS*. A huge poster of a Japanese boy and girl wearing flashy clothes hung in front of the museum building. Initially, it did not appear to be all that interesting. My friend insisted on going inside, so I reluctantly followed her.

Inside were about a hundred life-size photographs of boys and girls dressed in very creative and fashionable outfits taken in Harajuku, one of the major youth fashion districts in Tokyo. I was fascinated by these images. They were new, fresh, and different. This was the first time I had become aware of what the Japanese youth wore on the streets of Tokyo. The timing was also appropriate since I had just finished writing my book on Japanese designers in Paris, and I was searching for a new topic to delve into. I immediately knew what my next research topic was going to be. *FRUiTS*, a monthly magazine published by photographer Shoichi Aoki, contains only pictures taken in Harajuku and has no text.[1] Aoki explained to me why he started this project: "I started taking pictures of young people in Harajuku to keep a record of what is happening on the streets of Harajuku." My work on Japanese youth and subcultures evolved and developed from that experience in Sydney. It took me another few years before I decided to focus on different subcultures in different districts.

I later came across two books written in Japanese by members of a Japanese subculture: *The Anthropology of Gyaru and Gyaru-o*[2] (2009) by Yusuke Arai, who was a leader of the *Gyaru-o* gang in Shibuya, and *The World, Myself and Lolita Fashion*[3] (2007) by Momo Matsuura, a Lolita herself. The stories these authors tell in their books are partially autobiographical since the authors either are or were insiders to the group. Nonetheless, the authors make an attempt to write about their own world as objectively as possible.[4] I have met both of them at different occasions and interviewed them extensively about the group to which they belong. They gave me their contacts and became an important source of information to begin my fieldwork in Tokyo.

Angela McRobbie (1991: xv) explains her interest in subcultures as follows:

> There are two reasons why I have been interested in subcultures: first, because they have always appeared to me ... as popular aesthetic movements, or "constellations" ... and second, because in a small way they have seemed to possess the capacity to change the direction of young people's lives, or at least to sharpen their focus by confirming some felt, but as yet unexpressed intent or desire. Subcultures are aesthetic movements whose raw materials are by definition, "popular" in that they are drawn from the world of the popular mass media. It is not necessary to have an education in the *avant-garde* or to know the history of surrealism to enjoy the Sex Pistols or to recognise the influence of Vivienne Westwood's fashion. This kind of knowledge (of pop music or fashion images) is relatively easy to come by and very different from the knowledge of the high arts or the literary canon found in the academy.

I share many of McRobbie's views. Indeed, subcultures are "aesthetic movements." Nonetheless, while I personally find the different styles emerging out of Japanese subcultures extremely original and creative, I have come to discover that others take them as an offense to a good taste in fashion since subcultures are not considered part of high culture.[5] The devaluation of

Japanese subcultures as a group and their styles was one of my unexpected findings on which I will further elaborate in the subsequent chapters.

While Tokyo as a fashion city is still marginal from a global perspective (despite the efforts made by the fashion trade organization in Japan), the Japanese youth play a crucial role in forming a separate fashion community and producing the latest styles that express their subcultural affiliation and identity. Youth fashion in Japan—in Tokyo in particular—is geographically and stylistically defined. Subcultures are defined by where they congregate, the music they listen to, the celebrities they worship and idolize, the magazines they read, and, most importantly, the way they dress.

The study of Japanese youth subcultures needs to be conducted both theoretically as well as empirically, and thus my research is based on in-depth ethnographical fieldwork in various fashion districts in Tokyo. A visual investigation of Japanese youth subcultures focusing on their outward appearances is the first step to understanding their worldview, values, and norms, which have changed drastically over the past few decades. The way they dress serves as a marker of social background and subcultural allegiance. Fashion always reflects the prevailing ideology of a society, and today's Japanese youth are the case in point. When the Japanese media started to pay attention to youth subcultures in the mid-1990s, there were only two or three groups, and they were easily recognizable because of their distinct styles. Since that time, these subcultures have branched out intricately in different areas and into many smaller sub-subcultures; their social networks are becoming very complex.

I examine several different areas of Tokyo, and I am aware that each chapter on a district could be expanded into one book. But my goal here is to introduce various youth subcultures and their stylistic expressions and show the common threads across all the subcultures mentioned in this book as well their uniqueness in each group. I pay particular attention to the subcultures in which the members treat their appearance or image making very seriously, and make it one of the key components of their group membership. Dick Hebdige (1979) called British punks "a spectacular subculture," implying the crucial significance of their external appearance, while I call Japanese subcultures "fashion subcultures."

I investigate the nature of the Japanese subcultures found in different districts in Tokyo and explore its relationship to the structural problems of a wider socioeconomic structure. I argue that there is an ironic correlation between Japan's economic slump and the increase in the youth's creativity. The style and imagery of the subculture need a hermeneutic perspective that considers the meaning the subculture may have for potential members and for society at large. I also make an analysis of mass media's mediation of the nature of the subculture. Furthermore, in comparison with or in contrast to high fashion, I analyze the social organization of subcultural fashion. The values, norms, symbols, images, and behavior of the subculture need to be considered in terms of their social and economic contexts. The subculture is unlikely to remain unaltered, and the shifting boundaries of the subculture as well as its changing form need to be considered as well. Methodological strategies used in my research are explained in subsequent chapters.

OUTLINE OF THE BOOK

This book is divided into three parts. Part I is comprised of three chapters. Chapter 1 provides an overview and the historical background of subcultural studies and revisits Dick Hebdige's classical work on the punk subculture. I trace a brief history of cultural studies that emerged out of the Centre for Contemporary Cultural Studies at the University of Birmingham in England in the 1950s, which was started by Richard Hoggart, a British literary critic, and refer to different studies on subcultures that emerged in the West. Chapter 2, "Placing Tokyo on the Fashion Map," is reproduced from *World's Fashion Cities* (Kawamura 2006c) edited by Christopher Breward and David Gilbert, explaining two ways to place Tokyo as a fashion city in the urban hierarchy. Chapter 3 addresses the social, economic, cultural, and political transformations that Japan has gone through to understand what today's Japanese youth are facing, since a fashion phenomenon is never independent of its external surroundings. I refer to suicide rates, divorce rates, marriage rates, and other statistics to explain the changing structure of Japan's economy, labor market, and employment systems.

Part II examines geographically and stylistically defined subcultures in Tokyo since the mid-1990s. Chapters 4 through 8 cover each district and the specific fashion subcultures that are affiliated with the district; specifically, Shibuya, Harajuku, Akihabara/Ikebukuro, Shinjuku, and Kouenji. Chapter 9 analyzes the growing subcultural trends in Japan among the youth and examines institutional and individual networks within the subcultural system. I investigate the similarities and the differences among these subcultures and also make a systematic comparison between high fashion and youth fashion.

Part III discusses the influential power of the Japanese youth, and the trickle-up/bubble-up theory of fashion is revisited. Chapter 10 explores the deprofessionalization of various occupations in the Japanese fashion industry and the growing number of street photographers and amateur models, as more and more magazines include pages on ordinary, but very fashionable, kids on the streets. The line between professional and amateur is becoming blurry. At the same time, young consumers are becoming increasingly sophisticated such that they themselves can become the producers of fashion without any professional training or education. Chapter 11 investigates the globalization of Japanese fashion subcultures that have become extremely popular and are spreading to other parts of Asia, Europe, and the United States. I also discuss the future possibilities and limitations of Japanese subcultural fashion in terms of its diffusion.

Understanding Subcultural Studies:
Dick Hebdige Revisited

Before I introduce various subcultural groups found in different districts in Tokyo, it is important to understand what a subculture is and how it is studied by scholars. I first explain how the term *subculture* is defined and used in social sciences and other areas. I then trace the subcultural studies within the context of British cultural studies and, finally, review some of the subcultures in the United Kingdom and the United States to explore some of the key determinants that exist in these subcultural groups so that I can later look for these traits and characteristics in my research on Japanese subcultures. Methodological strategies in subcultural studies are also discussed by referring to recent research on subcultures. Additionally, I raise two issues or components that are often neglected in subcultural studies: girls' and women's perspectives, and non-Western cultural/subcultural contexts.

THE ORIGIN OF THE TERM *SUBCULTURE*

What is a subculture? How is it different from a culture? These are difficult questions to answer because sometimes the terms are used interchangeably. Some groups definitely constitute a subculture, but why can't we call those groups a culture?

According to the *Sage Dictionary of Cultural Studies* (2004), the signifier *culture* in subculture has traditionally referred to a "whole way of life" or "maps of meaning" that make the world intelligible to its members. The prefix *sub* implies notions of distinctiveness and difference from the dominant or mainstream society. Therefore, a subculture is constituted by groups of individuals who share distinct values and norms that are against dominant or mainstream society. Members often create their own symbols (verbal or nonverbal) that are comprehensible only to the inside members. If you are not dominant, you are subordinate; if you are not in the mainstream, you are on the periphery. Subcultures have been seen as spaces for deviant communities to claim their position or space, metaphorically and literally, for themselves. In many subcultural analyses, the notion of resistance to the dominant culture is the primary focus.

Brake (1980: 5) explains that the earliest use of the term *subculture* in sociology seems to be its application as a subdivision of a national culture by Alfred McLung Lee (1945) and Milton M. Gordon (1947), both of whom emphasized the effects of socialization within the cultural subsections of a pluralist society. On the other hand, Chris Jenks (2004: 7) remarks that definitions and versions proliferate and origins are obscure, and it has been argued by Marvin E. Wolfgang and Franco Ferracuti (1967) that the term *subculture* is not widely employed in the social science literature until after World War II. In 1955 Albert Cohen used the term and explored working-class youth who rejected the dominant values of society by creating their own subcultures. He further explained that, in the gang subculture, the core values of the straight world, such as sobriety, ambition, and conformity, were replaced by their opposites, such as hedonism, defiance of authority, and the quest for excitement. Cohen's definition is probably the closest to how we currently understand a subculture.

Phil Cohen (1972) defined subculture as a compromise solution between two contradictory needs: the need to create and express autonomy and difference from parents and the need to maintain the parental identification. More recently, Ken Gelder (2007) has argued that subcultures are social, with their own shared conventions, values, and rituals. He described different forms and practices of subculture and explained that the members' negative relations to work and class; a specific geographical territory, such as the street, the hood, and the club; and excessive exaggerated stylistic expressions are some of the identifying points of a subcultural affiliation.

Subcultures are often related to youth and deviance. According to *Contemporary Youth Culture: An International Encyclopedia* (2006), youth is shaped by macro-social forces such as ideology. Youth create their sense of self and group expression. Identity plays an essential role in the development of young men and women through every generation. Identity is what an adolescent insists on having, and he or she continually searches for it through music preferences, physical looks, sexuality, relationships, and so on. Some analysts see this as expressing an opposition to the dominant culture. Subcultures, by their very existence, suggest that there are alternative forms of cultural expression that reflect a plurality in a group that seems, on superficial examination, to dominate the members of a society.

Subcultural groups project a certain image, which is composed of costume, accessories, hairstyle, jewelry, artifacts, and a distinct vocabulary. One of the universal characteristics that sets one culture off from another is the verbal mode of communication—that is, language. The language barrier tends to exclude outsiders and reinforces collective identity through a distinctive frame of communication. Just as institutions, clothing, appearance, and social rituals serve to identify and integrate all members of youth subcultures, the insiders use their own slang and the language sets apart members from nonmembers.

Subculture is a system of values, attitudes, modes of behavior, and life-styles of a social group that is distinct from but related to the dominant culture of a society. In modern society, there is a great diversity of such subcultures.

SUBCULTURES WITHIN BRITISH CULTURAL STUDIES

Up to the middle of the twentieth century, popular culture, including fashion and subcultures, was seen as shallow, trivial, and not worthy of intellectual consideration. Richard Hoggart and Raymond Williams overthrew and dismissed such views and proposed the need to understand popular culture, which was seen as a product of working-class experience. Therefore, it is not an overstatement to say that the tradition of cultural studies is marked by Williams and Hoggart. Hoggart's 1957 work, *The Uses of Literacy*, is a seminal text in cultural studies. In it, he discussed that traditional ideas and attitudes were being challenged by the impact of mass publications, such as tabloid newspapers, paperback novels, and glossy magazines, and there were major changes in working-class culture (Hoggart 1957: 11). His major contribution was to place working-class culture in the academic arena and apply the methods of literary criticism, such as close reading, to the materials and textual analysis of popular culture. Similarly, Williams provided a new theoretical model in cultural studies. He focused on mass culture and working-class culture in his 1958 work, *Culture and Society*. His data sources came primarily from novels. In *The Long Revolution* (1961), Williams gave a more sociological analysis of culture. He saw literature and art as one kind of culture and looked at it more broadly as an entire way of life.

THE CENTRE FOR CONTEMPORARY CULTURAL STUDIES

In 1964 the Centre for Contemporary Cultural Studies (CCCS) at the University of Birmingham in the United Kingdom was established, with Hoggart as director.[1] In 1968 another prominent scholar, Stuart Hall, became director of the center.

British cultural studies is interdisciplinary in research topics and theoretical frameworks, and applies the works of prominent theorists such as Richard Hoggart, Raymond Williams, Louis Althusser, Antonio Gramsci, Michel Foucault, Jacques Lacan, and Jacques Derrida. These scholars draw on postmodern theory, postcolonial theory, conflict theory, queer theory, and feminist theory, among others, and because there is a great deal of Marxist influence, they tend to focus on the relationships between culture, power, and class.

In the 1970s two seminal works on British youth subcultures emerged from the CCCS—*Resistance through Rituals* (1976), by Stuart Hall, and *Subculture: The Meaning of Style* (1979), by Dick Hebdige. Cultural theorists then argued that subcultures are best understood through the lens of Marxian cultural theory due to the specific class structures of British society at the time, so they studied working-class youth subcultures. Both works offer semiotic accounts of the social codes of youth subcultures in the United Kingdom and explain that the subcultures challenge the hegemony of the dominant culture through their spectacular appearance as a tool to express rebellion. The researchers studied the routine practices of the subcultural groups, such as their activities, dress codes, and drug use, as a culture of resistance grounded in class relations. The studies are structured around the neo-Marxist explanation of a stratified, capitalist society, and the subcultures are considered subversive. As far as the theoretical frameworks are concerned, I have been immensely influenced by Hebdige's analysis of subcultures. It is a classic for anyone who studies subcultures. There are many parallels between the punk subculture in London in the 1970s and early twenty-first-century Japanese subcultures.

More recently, some of the most provocative and intriguing studies on subcultural groups came out of British cultural studies. In his 1993 work *The Black Atlantic: Modernity and Double Consciousness*, Paul Gilroy offers the new concept of the black Atlantic diasporas. Angela McRobbie (1984, 1991) is perhaps the most important scholar in subcultural studies and often talks about the relationship between gender and culture/subculture. Hilary Pilkington's (1994, 1996, 2002, 2010) focused interest is on contemporary Russian society and youth. Chris Griffin (2008, 2011) studies the relationships between youth, class, gender, and a partying lifestyle. The trend in British cultural studies looks at the ways of life of various marginal or minority groups and sets about interpreting their social world. What makes this tradition distinctive from conventional ethnography is that everyday action tends to be interpreted within a political framework. Social activities are often conceptualized as acts of resistance to a dominant social order or as creative responses to oppression and injustice. These themes are central to the studies of youth subcultures by the CCCS.

HEBDIGE'S STUDY ON PUNK SUBCULTURE

Hebdige's study on punk is probably the most striking example of a group that has all the determinants of what defines a subculture. No subculture has sought with more grim determination than the punks to detach itself from the taken-for-granted landscape of normalized forms, or to bring down upon itself such vehement disapproval (Hebdige 1979: 19). Barnard (1996: 44) explains clearly that the example of punk may be understood as a more explicitly ideological phenomenon, and it is an ideological assault on the aesthetic values of dominant classes. Punks create their definition of an aesthetic taste by using as adornment objects such as chains, bin liners, and safety pins, which are not used as fashion items by the dominant classes. Aesthetic tastes are, after all, socially constructed, and thus any style, any fashion, any item can become good taste, even if it appears to be vulgar and in bad taste for some groups of people. As Hebdige (1979: 18) said: "Style in subculture is … pregnant with significance. Its transformations go 'against nature', interrupting the process of 'normalization'." Subcultural members receive both positive and negative attention by symbolically violating the social order, and such violation comes from their awareness of the dominant ideologies. "Subcultural codes might appear senseless, offensive, or infantile to outsiders, but they can be interpreted as an intelligent and creative moment that confronted, mocked, and inverted mainstream norms and values" (Hebdige 1979: 18).

HEGEMONY, CLASS, AND SUBCULTURE

The concept of class is a critical variable in defining the different subcultural options available to middle-class and working-class boys (McRobbie and Garber 1991: 2–3). Within any stratified society, there are class cultures, and subcultures can be conceptualized as subsets of these larger cultural configurations. Although subcultures share elements of the larger class cultures (sometimes called the parent culture) they are also distinct from them (Brake 1980: 7). For writers of cultural studies in the 1970s, subcultures were seen as symbolic representations of the structural problems of class.

Discussions on subculture and class are automatically related to the idea of hegemony and dominant ideology. *Hegemony* is a term used by Antonio Gramsci ([1929–1933] 1992) to describe how the domination of one class over others is achieved by a combination of political and ideological means. In modern democratic societies, certain ideologies are produced, achieved, and maintained through consent. Hegemony is achieved by ideological means. According to Hebdige (1979: 11), ideology, by definition, thrives beneath consciousness, and it is at the level of "normal common sense" that ideological frames of reference are most firmly solidified, because it is here that their ideological nature is most effectively concealed.

Modern Marxists frequently explain the political passivity of subordinate classes as the consequence of ideological incorporation. They interpret Marx as claiming that the ruling class everywhere is dominant in society, and that this indoctrinates subordinates who uncritically accept it as true. The thesis has been criticized both on theoretical grounds—that it is not a correct interpretation of what Marx actually believed—and empirically—that throughout history, subordinate groups have developed their own beliefs and frequently rejected those of the dominant classes. As Hebdige (1979: 17) says: "the challenge to hegemony which subcultures represent is not issued directly by them. Rather, it is expressed obliquely, in style. The objections are lodged, the contradictions displayed ... at the profoundly superficial level of appearances: that is, at the level of signs." This is evidenced in various studies of subcultures, including the phenomenon of Japanese subcultures.

AESTHETIC TASTE IN SUBCULTURES

According to Herbert Gans (1974: 10–11), there are taste cultures that function to entertain, inform, and beautify life, among other things, and that express values and standards of taste and aesthetics. Ordinary consumer goods also express aesthetic values or functions.

Fashion and the way individuals dress is an area where taste is contested. Depending on how items of clothing are coordinated and put together, certain styles can be a form of defiance, and dress code in different situations and contexts regulates and defines acceptable and unacceptable behavior. The rise of new youth lifestyles since the emergence of rock and roll in the 1950s offered opportunities to subvert the values and meanings of the dominant culture. Similarly, punk uses fashion and clothing to challenge the dominant ideology and to contest the distribution of power in the social order. Different ideas and beliefs about aesthetics are expressed by means of fashion and clothing (Barnard 1996: 44).

How we make sense of our surroundings and create meanings is up to us. Culture is the practice and process through which we share meanings. Different meanings can be ascribed to the same thing, and therefore meaning is always the site and the result of struggle. Denzin (1970: 93) explains that what is central to understanding behavior is the range and variety of symbols and symbolic meanings shared, communicated, and manipulated by interacting selves in shared situations.

BIASES IN SUBCULTURAL STUDIES: MALE DOMINANCE AND EURO-AMERICENTRISM

After reviewing various past and recent research studies on subcultures, I argue that there are two biases: male dominance and Euro-Americentrism.

This study on Japanese subcultures attempts to fill that gap. First, as explained in Part II, most of the subcultures in Japan are female dominant—one exception is found in Shibuya, *Gyaru-o*, a group from which male members must retire as they graduate from college. This has been pointed out by a number of women scholars (Leblanc 1999; McRobbie and Garber 1991). Second, Japan is obviously a non-Western nation, and there are no scholarly youth subcultural studies about it. We can question whether Japanese subcultures have the same or similar determinants as those in the West, and also investigate to what extent existing subcultural theories are applicable to explain the Japanese phenomenon.

MALE DOMINANCE IN SUBCULTURAL STUDIES

The concept of subculture and the work of the early subcultural theorists have been criticized for focusing almost exclusively on working-class young men and as uncritically accepting particular definitions of crime and delinquency.

Hebdige (1988: 27) explained that girls have been relegated to a position of secondary interest within both sociological accounts of subculture and photographic studies of urban youth, and the masculinist bias is evident in the subcultures themselves. The objective and popular image of a subculture is likely to be one that emphasizes male membership, male focal concerns, and masculine values (McRobbie and Garber 1991: 4). Very little seems to have been written about the role of girls in youth cultural groupings. "They are absent from the classic subcultural ethnographic studies, the pop histories, the personal accounts and the journalistic surveys of the field. ... How do we make sense of this invisibility? Are girls really not present in youth subcultures? Or is it something in the way this kind of research is carried out that renders them invisible?" (McRobbie and Garber 1991: 1).

Men scholars acknowledge that criticisms of subcultural studies by women scholars such as McRobbie and Garber (1991) and Smart (1976) have indicated the apparent absence of girls in the research. According to Brake (1980: 2), this is not surprising because an examination of the studies reveals not only a sexist perspective but also that the subcultures traditionally have been a place to examine centrally variations on several themes concerning masculinity.

> On the whole, youth cultures and subcultures tend to be some form of exploration of masculinity. These are therefore masculinist, and I have tried to consider their effect on girls, and one distinct sign of the emancipation of young girls from the cult of romance, and marriage as their true vocation, will be the development of subcultures exploring a new form of femininity. (Brake 1980: vii)

Are subcultures inherently masculine and male dominant? Do girls always play a marginal role if they want to be a member of a subculture? Do we never find any subcultures that are initiated by girls and dominated by girls? Recently, more scholars have begun studying the position of women in subcultures, such as Haenfler's work on girls as goth (2009), Harris's feminist perspectives on subculture (2007), Jeffreys's empirical research on tattooing from a feminist viewpoint (2000), and Reddington's (2004) and Raha's (2005) analysis on female punk. But the subcultural groups that the scholars focus on are still very much in the men's world.

Lauraine Leblanc (1999) pursues these questions and issues further. Her main research question is: How do punk girls reconcile a subcultural identity that is deliberately coded as masculine with the demands of femininity? She found that the girls use the punk subculture to construct various strategies of resistance to both mainstream and subcultural norms of femininity, strategies that hold broader implications for our thinking about girls' lives. Hebdige also briefly touched on this issue and said that conventional ideas of prettiness were jettisoned along with the traditional feminine lore of cosmetics (Hebdige 1979: 107).

Leblanc (1999: 6) explains the male-dominated gender dynamics in the punk subculture and how the punk subculture gives girls a place to be both assertive and aggressive. It also gives them self-liberation and empowerment. She writes:

> Girls in male-dominated youth subcultures such as punk continually confront ideologies of gender that remain largely invisible, perhaps even tacitly accepted, in many young women's everyday lives. Punk girls struggle to construct their gender within the confines of a highly male-dominated and therefore "masculinist" context. The punk subculture highly valorizes the norms of adolescent masculinity, celebrating displays of toughness, coolness, rebelliousness, and aggressiveness. Girls are present in the subculture, but the masculinity of its norms problematizes their participation. Thus, gender is problematic for punk girls in a way that it is not for punk guys, because punk girls must accommodate female gender within subcultural identities that are deliberately coded as male. (Leblanc 1999: 8)

Girls and women in the studies of Western subcultures have a distinct place and play a distinct role in often male-dominant subcultural groups. A subcultural female identity is unique and is different from the mainstream female identity. Girls and women in Western subcultures share some of the typical components found in male-dominant subcultures, such as rebellion, aggression, and resistance, instead of establishing a subculture that is totally unique and separate.

Leblanc draws on Simone de Beauvoir's provocative and groundbreaking work on women, *The Second Sex* (1949), which says that women are not simply born female but become women; that is, girls *learn* the qualities and social expectations of being a woman, such as femininity and feminine values and norms. Further, girls and women learn to appear weak, infantile, submissive, subordinate, vulnerable, docile, and fragile. Any self-assertion diminishes a woman's femininity and attractiveness (Beauvoir 1949). Women thus mold themselves to the impossible ideal of femininity (Leblanc 1999: 11).

However, it is girls who play a major role in Japanese subcultures. They spend a great deal of resources on clothes and makeup. Fashion is of the utmost importance because they want to stand out and be noticed; some may wish to rebel against the formal and traditional ways. They generally hang out in large groups around train stations and chat. The girl teens who belong to the street subcultures are sometimes treated as deviants by the rest of Japanese society, but they are bound by their strength in numbers and are always with friends who dress in a similar style. Instead of finding a place within the male-dominant subcultures, these Japanese girls have created and maintain their own autonomy and independence despite their expression of excessive cuteness and femininity.

One commonality between male-dominant subcultures in the West and female-dominant subcultures in Japan is that both are very much gender-specific. One emphasizes masculinity while the other values excessive femininity, which can be a new definition of femininity that is not always appreciated or welcomed by the opposite sex. This is discussed further in subsequent chapters.

EURO-AMERICENTRISM IN SUBCULTURAL STUDIES

While female scholars have pointed out the lack of female roles in Western subcultures, no scholar has discussed another bias evident in subcultural studies: the Euro-Americentric focus. Almost all of the significant subcultural studies conducted by European and U.S. scholars pay attention to Western societies only. In order for subcultural theories to be more complete, the studies need to be more diverse and inclusive, not merely including racial minorities living in the West (Jones 2007; Mills and Huff 1999; Rahn 2002). Only recently have scholars started to study subcultural phenomena in non-Western countries. Because much of this type of study requires an ethnographic task, moving into the area, getting used to the environment, and speaking the language, it is understandable that time and financial constraints have prevented many scholars and researchers from engaging in this type of study.

This bias occurs not only in subcultural studies but also in fashion and dress studies. Many fashion scholars have presumed that fashion is a product of Western society. There has been a shift from equating fashion with the lifestyles of social elites in the West and the rise of a mass fashion industry throughout the course of the twentieth century. Furthermore, fashion and dress from non-Western cultures were collected in Europe from the late sixteenth century onward as visual evidence of the existence of so-called exotic, mysterious peoples. Taylor (2004: 67) explains that, by the late nineteenth century, the collection and examination of garments and body ornaments was included within the emerging academic discipline of anthropology, and they were treated as cultural artifacts, such as tools or weapons. Still, in the early twenty-first century, studies and museum collections on ethnic dress are limited.

Similarly, few fashion scholars in academic circles pay attention to youth or subcultural fashion in non-Western cultures because such fashions are perceived as Western imitations. Indeed, there are subcultures that were directly imported to Japan from the West, such as hip-hop, goth, and punk. However, the subcultures discussed in this book are uniquely Japanese. A recent exhibition, *Japan Fashion Now!*, curated by Valerie Steele at the Fashion Institute of Technology in New York between September 2010 and April 2011, was probably one of the few exhibitions that displayed Japanese subcultural fashion.[2]

Some of the classical theorists, such as J. C. Flugel (1930) and Ferdinand Toennies ([1909] 1961), have argued that fashion originated in the West and is a Western product. Toennies explained the differences between fixed costume found in simple societies and modish costume found in complex societies, implying that costumes that change frequently exist only in the so-called civilized West. Such a statement seems to confirm the idea that fashion first started in the West, although some fashion scholars, such as Aubrey Cannon (1998), argue that fashion is found in traditional cultures as well. In the study of fashion and dress by European and U.S. scholars, fashion and Western dress generally have enjoyed privileged positions (Baizerman, Eicher, and Cerny 2008: 123). These scholars are less interested in ethnic dress or the fashion phenomenon of non-Western cultures. Researchers of dress and fashion need to focus more on cultural pluralism and multiculturalism and conduct more in-depth research on non-Western fashion phenomena so that we can acquire more facts and evidence to present convincing findings. Museums across the United States and Europe need to collect and conserve youth fashion as well as ethnic costumes so that they can be used in material culture studies. Fashion and dress studies broaden the intellectual base.

There should be no field of study in academia where the idea of diversity, multiculturalism, pluralism, or transnationalism is not included, because modern societies are becoming increasingly heterogeneous and culturally mixed. Any subcultural phenomenon is placed in those contexts, and many of them, including Japanese subcultures, are transcending cultural boundaries so that they are known worldwide.

METHODOLOGICAL STRATEGIES IN SUBCULTURAL STUDIES

The best methodological strategy to discover acts and accounts of resistance among small groups or subcultures within complex societies is ethnography, also known as fieldwork, which involves observation and participant observation.[3] It is a data collection and interpretation method widely used by qualitative sociologists and anthropologists. The method allows researchers to study people's lives, actions, and behaviors at close range, and it can lead to some of the most meaningful findings. It also provides both subjective and objective aspects of lives. Ethnographic approaches were adopted by earlier scholars, such as William Foote Whyte (1943), Elliot Liebow (1967), and Herbert Gans (1975), in the study of youth subcultures. To make a deeper analysis, there needs to be methodological rigor, such as in-depth observation and interviews. But like any methods, there are weaknesses to ethnography. It is sometimes considered too subjective, not generalizable, too narrow, partial, and incomplete in scope.

The study of subculture in Britain grew out of a tradition of urban ethnography that can be traced back at least as far as the nineteenth century to the work of Henry Mayhew (1812–1887); he published *London Labour and the London Poor* (1851), which is based on his interviews with prostitutes, laborers, market traders, and so on. A more scientific approach to subculture including participant observation did not emerge until the 1920s, when a group of sociologists and criminologists in Chicago began collecting evidence on juvenile street gangs and deviant groups. In 1927, Frederick Thrasher produced a survey of over a thousand street gangs, and later William Foote Whyte (1943) described at length in *Street Corner Society* the rituals, routines, and occasional exploits of one particular gang.

British researchers focused on symbolic cultural aspects of youth subcultures, such as music, language, and especially dress. In doing so, they constructed semiotic readings of the cultural artifacts of youth subcultures, analyzing these as sign systems, codes, and conventions, and focusing especially on the homology, or symbolic fit between these elements. Birmingham school theorists posited that resistance to cultural norms is primarily conducted through the construction of such distinctive styles. These styles, they held, constitute resistance to the dominant culture, with Dick Hebdige (1979) arguing that subcultural adolescents engage in "semiotic guerilla warfare" through their construction of style. Examining a variety of spectacular postwar subcultures such as Teddy boys, Mods, punks and skinheads allowed such theorists to elaborate how such varied clothing styles constituted challenges to the dominant order. (Leblanc 1999: 14–15)

Observation, participant observation, and interview produce intriguing accounts from the subculture members, while ethnography is treated as a marginal method in the positivist tradition of quantitative sociology since it lacks any analytical or explanatory framework. The picture and the perspective of a subculture based on various stories, anecdotes, and experiences told by the members provide only one picture and not the whole, and thus, are not generalizable. However, no methods in social sciences are perfect, but what is important is the awareness of their flaws and limitations so that they can be minimized during fieldwork.

RECENT ETHNOGRAPHIC STUDIES ON SUBCULTURES

More recent subcultural studies are also ethnographic in nature, and the researchers themselves are often insiders or long-time members of these groups. In such cases, the issue of insider versus outsider needs to be taken into consideration. There are both pros and cons to an insider.

When meeting punks, I always identified myself primarily as a researcher, or, as I became known in San Francisco, "the lady that does the interviews." Throughout this period, my appearance retained elements of my past involvement with the subculture, including dyed hair, punk clothes, and tattoos (one of which is on my wrist and therefore often visible even in the coldest weather). When I began my research, I still had a punk haircut (long on top, shaved on the sides and back), but as I allowed this to grow out ... , I sought out more dramatic hair coloring, finally settling on a cranberry shade achieved with considerable chemical effort. ... This eased my establishment of rapport with punks. (Leblanc 1999: 22)

Hodkinson (2002) conducted in-depth qualitative research on the goth scene in Britain for a number of years. His research goal was to focus on the norms, meanings, motivations, and social patterns of those involved as well as the voluntary and commercial events, media, and consumables that appeared to enable the goth scene to exist and survive on such a small scale (2002: 4). He combined various qualitative methods, such as participant observation, in-depth interviews, media analysis, and a questionnaire. There are several interesting ethnographic studies on goth, but Hodkinson's study best articulates the research process and methodologies that many researchers tend not to explain clearly in their work.

Hodkinson himself is part of the goth subculture. Therefore, he is completely an insider. He explains the transition in chapter 1 of his book, "From Participant to Researcher." He knows how he should dress, which music to listen to, and which magazines and novels to read to be part of the subculture. But he is aware that a researcher must take a few steps back to critically and objectively evaluate and assess the outcome of the research.

Similarly, Muggleton (2000) clearly explains his research strategies in his study on youth subcultures in the United Kingdom. He gives fieldwork details and an interview schedule in the appendix at the end of his book. He interviewed a total of fifty-seven people.

> The interview can best be described as semi-structured, often conversational, and the order of the questions was not always strictly adhered to. Informants would sometimes initiate the discussion and provide a more promising line of inquiry to be followed, or they might pre-empt my intended order of questioning. Nor was the wording of the questions particularly important, for I treated them as areas for discussion. After each fieldwork session the questions were slightly revised to take account of new themes and hypotheses generated inductively from the data. . . . All interviews were taped and transcribed. The duration of the interviews varied considerably, from twenty minutes to one and a half hours, with the typical time taken being around forty minutes. (Muggleton 2000: 171–72)

Regarding researchers who are insiders to the groups they research, we should keep in mind Bourdieu's (1992) idea of reflexivity in conducting research. Researchers in social sciences must at all times conduct their research with conscious attention to the effects of their own position, their own set of internalized structures, and how these are likely to distort or prejudice their objectivity. In conducting my research on Japanese youth subcultures, I am in a unique position, because I am a scholar who lives and works in New York, but I am of Japanese ancestry and go to Tokyo both for vacations and to conduct research. I am partially an insider to the culture but not completely. I see this as an advantage, and I had no problem communicating with the Japanese youth who think I am Japanese American. I can certainly remain an objective researcher as a bystander to the subcultures.

When ethnographers arrive at a new place, they usually wander around the location they plan to use as the research setting. I was already familiar with Tokyo. It did not take me long to familiarize myself with the locations of hangouts and stores where the youth shop and wander around. But getting entry into a subculture was a different story. Unlike Leblanc, Hodkinson, and Muggleton, I am not and never was a member of any of the subcultures I studied. I knew the snowballing method of gathering data would be most effective because I had used it in my previous research on Japanese designers in

Paris (Kawamura 2004). Every time I met an individual who was related to my work, at the end of the interview, I asked him or her to refer me to some of his or her friends. Some would invite me to their parties and events. In this way, the research and my contacts began to snowball. The process of developing relationships is part of gaining entry into a research area and community. Participant observation is the foundation of ethnographic research. It involves establishing rapport in a new culture and community, learning to act so that people go about their business as usual when you are there, and removing yourself every day from cultural immersion so you can continue to objectively observe what you see and hear.

CONCLUSION

Subcultural groups are often determined by class, gender, and age and are expressed in the creation of styles in order to construct members' identities. Subcultures exist in relation to dominant cultures, and at the same time, they attempt to maintain their autonomy, resist hegemony, exist in opposition to the establishment, and construct a cohesive group identity while forming new values and norms that may be valid only within their groups. Subcultural research always uses case studies in the West, and the subcultures are rarely studied transnationally. Subcultures are increasingly becoming global, and thus case studies in non-Western countries, such as Japan, should not be neglected—although, admittedly, ethnographic fieldwork, one of the primary methodological tools used in these studies, is time-consuming and costly.

Placing Tokyo on the Fashion Map:
From Catwalk to Street Style

This chapter focuses on the evolution of Tokyo as a fashion city. The history of Western clothing in Japan is still new. Ever since it first appeared in Japan in the mid-nineteenth century, the Japanese have been fascinated by Western dress. One hundred and fifty years later, that fascination persists, but Japan's position in the global order of fashion is in transition. Tokyo is emerging from its history as a city of consumption, where people competed with one another to purchase expensive Western brands for status, to becoming a city of production, where some of the most innovative designers in the world are establishing themselves. It is also attracting attention as a city that creates a unique form of street fashion.

There is a significant contrast between the idea of Tokyo as a new fashion center in the 1970s and 1980s that worked through the exoticization of Japanese designers in established Western centers and the new street fashion in the 1990s. Two different ways of placing Tokyo in fashion's world order are thus discussed. Also discussed in this chapter is the practice of purchasing brands that originated from major fashion centers in the West (Paris in particular) among women in Tokyo. French fashion is universally believed to be the epitome of high fashion, because of the system of Haute Couture, which exists only in France. Paris has always represented modernity in fashion, and it holds an exclusive symbolic status in the minds of Japanese consumers. Yet Tokyo today holds a unique position in the urban hierarchy of fashion, where consumption and production take place simultaneously with much intensity, making Parisian models less relevant. Tokyo is no longer just a city in which Western fashion is widely appreciated and consumed; it is becoming a center that produces innovative fashion ideas in its own right.

WESTERN CLOTHING IN JAPAN AS A SYMBOL
OF MODERNIZATION SINCE 1868

After a long period of isolation from foreign and neighboring countries, Japan opened its doors and moved toward Westernization during the Meiji era (1868–1912). This was a period of radical economic, social, and political reforms. The emperor supported and encouraged the modernization and military buildup of Japan. The government's new slogan was "Civilization and Enlightenment," following Western patterns. The most visible transformation was seen in clothes. This new cultural phenomenon, a shift from kimonos to Western styles, was a sign of sophistication and membership of the upper class. Western clothing styles were first adopted for men's military uniforms, and French- and British-style uniforms were designed for the Japanese army and navy since this was the style that Westerners wore when they first arrived in Japan. After 1870, government workers, such as police officers, railroad workers, and postal carriers, were required to wear Western-style men's suits. The emperor and the empress took the initiative and wore Western clothing and hairstyles at official events. By the end of the nineteenth century, the court had adopted Western clothes and formal imperial kimonos were worn only in traditional ceremonies.

During the Taisho period (1912–1926), wearing Western clothing continued to be a sign of sophistication and an expression of modernity. Working women, such as bus conductors, nurses, and typists, started wearing Western clothes as occupational uniforms. After World War II, fashion information from the United States and Europe began to spread throughout Japan. People in metropolitan centers in Japan—especially in Tokyo—began to consume Western fashion at a rapid pace in the 1950s and 1960s; whatever trend was popular in the West was imported to Japan, or exact copies were reproduced locally.

However, no matter how fashionable Japanese consumers became, Tokyo was not included in the global hierarchy of fashion centers, nor did it receive any recognition as a fashion city in the same way that Paris, Milan, and New York did—until the 1970s. For decades, Tokyo was considered a market in which Western corporations could invest. Helped by the booming economy in Japan in the 1980s, companies from the United States and Europe were aggressively entering Tokyo, either setting up subsidiaries or opening freestanding stores. For Western designers, the Japanese market—especially in Tokyo—provided a great commercial opportunity, but for Japanese designers, it was never a country or a city where fashion was produced. According to Akira Baba (in Lockwood 1995: 8–9), who was the president of Kashiyama (a major Japanese apparel manufacturer) at the time, there are two types of merchandise in Japan: (1) that which is produced and used for daily consumption and (2) fashion goods. For Japanese consumers, *fashion* is still a Western concept. As Koenig (1974) indicates, in democratic societies, people feel the need to be subtly different from others, and in a society like Japan, where people believe in homogeneity and conformity, fashion and clothing are the means to indicate those slight differences. Similarly, Wilson (1985) suggests that the need to distinguish oneself is perhaps strongest with regard to the group to which one has the strongest affiliation.

French luxury goods function as a status symbol, because, first and foremost, they are expensive in Japan. The image of French companies in Japan is very strong in consumer goods (Thuresson 2002), and this explains the fact that, until 2010, Japan was the largest importer of French luxury products (Lavallee 2011).[1]

THE EXOTICIZATION OF JAPANESE DESIGNERS IN PARIS SINCE 1970

Tokyo as a fashion city and Japanese designers gradually began to attract attention vicariously through the emergence of Kenzo Takada (known as Kenzo) in Paris in 1970. He was the first Japanese designer to take part in the biannual ready-to-wear Paris fashion collections. Kenzo was famous for mixing plaids, flowers, checks, and stripes—a combination that no Western designers ever imagined. The quilting technique he used was rooted in Japanese traditions, and square shapes and straight lines that derived from the kimono were also used. There was something particularly Japanese in the way he reconstructed Western clothing. Immediately after his first show in Paris in June 1970, one of his designs in *sashiko*, a traditional Japanese stitching technique, appeared on the cover of *Elle*, one of the most influential magazines in France.

Kenzo's biographer, Ginnette Sainderichinn (1989: 17), writes: "Kenzo is a magician of color. Since the mid 1960s, when he moved from his native Japan to the city of Paris, he has devoted himself to the creation of wearable, vivacious clothing: a fashion without hierarchies." Kenzo made a major contribution to the democratization of fashion. However, his identity as a Japanese designer was the focal point of his position and career in Paris, and he was constantly reminded of his ethnic background in the Western press. Kenzo's sudden appearance and his almost overnight success in Paris as a designer provoked an interest in Tokyo among the fashion professionals in the West as an exotic, mysterious city, where there could be more creative designers, like Kenzo, hidden or waiting to be discovered.

As Simmel ([1904] 1957: 545) points out, in the traditions of modern Western fashion, there "exists a wide-spread predilection for importing fashions from without, and such foreign fashions assume a greater value within the circle, simply because they did not originate there . . . the exotic origin of fashions seems strongly to favor the exclusiveness of the groups which adopt them." Fashion needs to be exotic and foreign, and Japanese designers, such as Kenzo and those who followed him, fulfilled that definition. Japanese fashion was different and completely new to the eyes of French fashion professionals.

At the beginning of the 1970s, the placement of Tokyo on the fashion map became even more pronounced when three controversial avant-garde

Japanese designers, Issey Miyake, Yohji Yamamoto, and Rei Kawakubo of Comme des Garçons, rocked the Paris fashion world by introducing clothes that were creative and unconventional to say the least—their designs were definitely not Western. Miyake had been in Paris since 1973, but when Yamamoto and Kawakubo arrived, the three together created the Japanese avant-garde fashion phenomenon, although it was never their intention to do so.[2]

The three designers destroyed and reinterpreted Western conventions of the clothing system by suggesting different ways of wearing a garment. They also redefined the nature of Western clothing itself. Western women's clothing has historically been fitted to expose the contours of the body, but these Japanese designers introduced large, loose-fitting garments. Like Kenzo, the integration of kimono elements into their designs is clearly evident, especially in their earlier works. It was the combination of Japanese and Western elements that forced the destruction of both in order to reconstruct something completely new. In this way, the designers also redefined the nature of fashion, not only clothing. The conception of fashion is synonymous with the conception of beauty. Therefore, by introducing new fashion, they simultaneously suggested a new definition of aesthetics.

Hanae Mori was the first Japanese couturier to be officially named by the Chambre Syndicale de la Couture Parisienne in 1977, and she introduced something that the other ready-to-wear Japanese designers did not.[3] Her style, methods of dressmaking, and the clients she catered to in and outside Japan distanced her from other Japanese designers. She recognized that haute couture is the product of high culture and a phenomenon of an elitist society. Thus, Mori did not challenge the Western clothing system as the others had done. Nor did she use fabrics bought at a flea market or worn by Japanese fishermen or farmers. Until her retirement from the couture organization in July 2004, she stayed within the realm of Japanese high culture and introduced the ultimate luxury and beauty of Japan to the West using Japanese cultural objects, viewed through the rules of Western aesthetics.

Jennifer Craik (1994: 41) points out that, during this period, the Japanese influence partially redrew the boundaries of fashion away from Western ideals of the body, body-space relations, and conventions of clothing. The principles of Western fashion increasingly incorporated non-European influences, traditions, and forms into mainstream practice, and Western appreciation for Japanese fashion, which many believed to have originated in Tokyo, quickly intensified. At the same time, the 1980s were the decade when Tokyo was believed to be included in the order of major fashion cities along with Paris, Milan, New York, and London. Coincidentally, it was during this time that Japan became economically powerful. Because of the strong exchange rate, Japanese tourists were flocking to expensive designer-label stores on the Champs-Elysees in Paris and were buying merchandise like never before.

THE MARGINAL STATUS OF TOKYO AS A FASHION CENTER UNTIL THE MID-1990s

The 1970s and 1980s were not the first time that clothes with Asian inspirations appeared in the West. In the late thirteenth century, Marco Polo had brought the first marvels of China to the West (Martin and Koda 1994), and in the early twentieth century, famous French designers such as Jeanne Lanvin, Paul Poiret, and Coco Chanel incorporated Asian-inspired textiles, prints, calligraphy, and pattern constructions, such as kimono sleeves, into their original designs. What was different in the late twentieth century was that the Japanese designers of the 1970s and 1980s came from the East. What made them unique was not only their clothes but their position and status as non-Western fashion outsiders. The marginality of these Japanese designers had become an asset. Before Kenzo, there were virtually no Asian designers on the Western fashion scene. Tokyo was considered an exotic city that produced talented and creative—but different—fashion designers. After the first generation of Japanese designers, such as Kenzo, Miyake, and Mori, other Japanese arrived in Paris one after another.

Tokyo became known indirectly through the marginal status of these designers. At the same time, they were brought to the center with French legitimization. But the Japanese fashion phenomenon was not enough to include Tokyo among the major fashion centers. For instance, Tokyo was not strong enough to attract Western journalists to attend and cover the Tokyo collections. As Lise Skov (1996: 148) accurately points out: "It is ironical ... that Rei Kawakubo, as one of the designers who brought 'Japanese fashion' to fame, simultaneously reinforced the interest in the Paris collections." Designers flocked to Paris because it provided (and still provides) the kind of status that no other city can, and there was no way that Tokyo could provide the same added value.

Furthermore, it was believed that the widespread popularity of Japanese fashion in the 1980s was a decisive factor in placing Tokyo on the list of international fashion capitals (Skov 1996: 134). Yet Tokyo was still far behind Paris in the production of fashion and setting of trends until the 1990s, due to the lack of an institutionalized and centralized fashion system in Japan (Kawamura 2004). Tokyo as a fashion city did not have the kind of structural strength and effectiveness that the French system took for granted. Through the exoticization of Japanese design in Paris, Tokyo did find a place on the fashion map, and many buyers and fashion insiders went to Japan but were disappointed to see Japanese consumers wearing Western brands.

According to Wilson (1985), fashion is an outstanding mark of modern civilization, and Craik (1994) questions whether fashion can be confined to the development of European fashion and argues that the term *fashion* needs revision because fashion is too often equated with modern European high fashion. It was not possible, until recently, to produce, market, and distribute fashion that was not baptized or consecrated by the West. However, this has changed over the years with the emergence of street fashion creating a separate system of fashion with a new business model. Modern fashion, which is consumer driven, comes not only from the West but also from the streets of Tokyo.

TOKYO'S EFFORTS TO CREATE A STRONGER FASHION IDENTITY

Japan's neighboring countries in the Asian region have fallen behind in building credible fashion centers because their cities have a reputation for garment manufacturing that has nothing to do with the local fashion culture. Unlike other Asian countries that are known for their cheap labor rather than for their design creativity, Japan's fashion identity had been strong among the Asian countries, while its position was weaker in the broader context of the world's fashion cities. Among Asian countries, Tokyo is the fashion capital; Japanese fashion magazines are widely read in Korea, China, and Taiwan; tourists from neighboring countries regularly visit Tokyo to purchase Japanese brands.

What fashion cities need is the symbolic production of fashion. The material production of clothing is less important. Tokyo still needs to reinforce place-based resources or images to establish fashion as a symbolic cultural product. Tokyo is becoming a true fashion city not only by consuming fashion but also by producing fashion, both of which are necessary characteristics of a fashion capital.

One way to promote a fashion center is to organize fashion shows on a regular basis. Tokyo has done this, but not successfully. When the Council for Fashion Designers (CFD) was formed in 1985 to systematize all fashion-related events and activities in Tokyo and to facilitate the relationships among designers, buyers, and the media, a French journalist wrote sarcastically:

> Is Paris going to have its Oriental rival soon? Those Japanese creators who do not look for the consecration on the Parisian podium are hoping some day to have the same power to replace Paris with Tokyo. . . . Japanese are trying to include Tokyo among the traditional route of fashion, such as Milan, New York and Paris. But isn't it ironical that many of the Japanese brands have French names, such as Coup de Piet, C'est Vrai, Etique, Madame Hani, Madame Nicole and so on. How can Tokyo replace Paris? (Piganeau 1986: 3)

The CFD is now rebuilding its internal structure and is collaborating with the Japanese government. Yet it has managed to invite only forty-seven designers and apparel companies for the Tokyo collections in October 2011, which is fewer than half of the participants in the Paris or New York collections. Thus, the structural weaknesses of fashion production in Japan forces Japanese designers to go overseas—especially to Paris, which remains supreme, at least in the minds of Japanese consumers and designers.

STREET FASHION AND SUBCULTURES: BRINGING TOKYO TO THE CENTER

Street fashion has existed in Tokyo for decades, especially in Harajuku, where between 1979 and 1981 there was a group called Takenoko-zoku (the Bamboo Tribe). A number of teenage subcultures and fashion followed, such as the New Wave, which was influenced by the British rock scene; Karasu-zoku (the Crow Tribe), who were the followers of Rei Kawakubo and Yohji Yamamoto; and Shibu-Kaji, which was a casual look worn in Shibuya, a fashion district in Tokyo. However, these subcultures were short-lived fads that did not spread far, remained within their own group, and gradually disappeared.

What is new and different about the current street fashion that emerged in the middle of the 1990s is that different institutions of fashion got together to make use of and take advantage of the marketing potential of the teenagers. There is a strong interdependence between the industries and the individuals involved. Trends that were spread by teenagers were completely independent of the Western fashion system and the mainstream fashion establishment in Japan. They have led the way in a creative mixing and matching of contrasting eclectic styles that have been extensively copied in the West (Polhemus 1996: 12). High school girls in Tokyo are the key to any trend. The popularity of a pair of white loose socks among this group was one of the first such trends to emerge.[4] Dick Hebdige, in studying subculture in 1970s and 1980s London, explained that girls have been relegated to a position of secondary interest within both sociological accounts of subculture and photographic studies of urban youth and that the masculinist bias was present in the subcultures themselves (1988: 27). But in the case of Tokyo subcultures, they are dominated by women, and by teenage girls in particular.

Fashion has always been a reflection of the current situation of the society. Ironically, Japan's economic slowdown in the first decade of the twenty-first century may have played a role in today's longer-lasting street fashion. There is a widespread feeling of disillusionment, alienation, uncertainty, and anger, which has spread throughout Japanese society. This has led to the breakdown of traditional Japanese values, such as perseverance, discipline, and belief in education—especially among children. Their norm-breaking attitude is exhibited through their appearance, which is a way to make themselves seen and heard.

Diana Crane explains that major Japanese companies' investments in the 1980s in young and exceptionally innovative Western designers suggests that the Japanese have not been able to satisfy their enormous demand for fashion talent (1993: 70). This was true until about the mid-1990s, but the new type of fashion—that is, street fashion—has a different structure. Furthermore, as Crane (2000) points out, today's fashion is consumer driven; market trends originate in many types of social groups, especially adolescent urban subcultures, and this is exactly what is happening today in Tokyo. The most recent fashion phenomenon in Tokyo originates from various subcultures. Since the mid-1990s, teenagers in Tokyo have been producing and guiding fashion trends that are unique and original, and many fashion professionals in the West are now paying attention to the latest styles in Tokyo.

This again placed Tokyo on the fashion map but in a different way. Attention has shifted from fashion designers who were professionally trained or have formal experience in the industries to the amateur, untrained teenagers on the streets who simply love directional, expressive clothing. They are the producers, marketers, and distributors of fashion. Pop culture trends, including fashion, are extremely fickle, and tastes can change overnight. But to find out what is hot and popular, the industries rely on Japanese schoolgirls.

Tokyo in the 1970s and 1980s was not the place where trends were created, but that presumption has changed. Tokyo is becoming a city that produces creative and new ideas. It is becoming a true fashion force.

SEGMENTATION AND DIFFUSION: THE CASE OF HARAJUKU IN TOKYO

Street life is made of multiple subcultures, and each has its own taste, lifestyle, attitudes, and fashion. Shibuya used to be the place where street fashion was found because of the emergence of the *Gyaru* or *Ko-gyaru* phenomenon.[5] During the weekend, these girls occupy the Shibuya 109 department store, which is the landmark of Shibuya.[6] Today, each district within the city of Tokyo is very much segmented according to different groups of teenagers. Besides Shibuya, street fashion in Tokyo is found in Harajuku, Daikanyama, Ikebukuro, and Jiyugaoka, among many others, and each district has its own distinctive look. If one is in Harajuku and dressed in a Shibuya style, one would be totally out of place. The teenagers know how they should dress depending on where they are going. The physical environment of an area helps street fashion to grow and spread, and it provides a space or a stage on which the teenagers can be fashionable. It gives them the opportunity to socialize and communicate and interact with each other—all necessary components for the formation of a subculture. Furthermore, those behaviors must be repeated for the group to continue and be maintained, and the same style and fashion need to be exposed repeatedly for the public to recognize the group as a subculture.

One of the primary reasons that the youth culture came out of Harajuku, which has become known as Tokyo's teenage town, was Hokosha-Tengoku, or Hokoten (pedestrian paradise). Between 1977 and 1998, a section of the main road in Harajuku was closed to traffic on Sundays. This place became a public sphere—a new idea in Japan—and many young people dressed in their (often handmade) creative fashion gathered there. Hokoten was terminated in 1998 (because of opposition from local residents and retailers), and Harajuku gradually returned to its original state, but the district remains a place where teenagers congregate to meet and chat with their friends who want to dress in certain styles.

Harajuku now produces distinctive subcultures. In the back streets of Harajuku, known as Ura-hara, there are many so-called select shops, small boutiques where the owners' tastes in selecting, mixing, and remixing merchandise are highly valued by customers. The stores are run and managed by semiprofessional designers, those who have just graduated from fashion schools, or artists, such as graphic and textile designers. There are a number of collaborative projects between the store owners and the artists. Those who shop in Ura-hara are the most fashion-conscious teens, and the street style in Harajuku is a hybrid of original handmade items and popular ready-made items. Many people sew their own outfits, because creating a one-of-a-kind style by combining handmade items with ready-made items is important.

Another subculture emerged from the teenagers that hang around with their friends on the Jingu Bridge near Harajuku Station. They wear clothing based on characters in anime and manga, and this trend is called costume play, abbreviated as cosplay. This phenomenon refers to dressing as a specific anime character, a waitress, or a nurse. The Gothic Lolita is one of the most popular costumes found in Harajuku since 1999. The girls are photographed by magazines and are scouted by model agencies.

No fashion is diffused locally or globally without the mass media. The production process of fashion is always strongly connected to fashion magazines (Moeran 2006). In any type of fashion, magazines are the most important medium to build the status and the reputation of a designer, to spread specific fashion trends, and to promote new merchandise. The dissemination process is a crucial stage between production and consumption. An object is first manufactured, and then it is transformed into fashion through the process of dissemination. In this respect, street fashion in Harajuku has been well documented by the monthly magazine *FRUiTS*, published since 1997 by photographer Shoichi Aoki. His goal is to report on cutting-edge street and youth fashion, and his photographs depict a revolutionary Japanese fashion movement since the mid-1990s. The focus of *FRUiTS* is not on the designers but on the consumers who have become the producers of street fashion. The diverse styles shown in *FRUiTS* are continuously evolving and often unique. Aoki (2001: 2) writes:

> Because Western clothing has a short history in Japan, there is a strong tendency for people to dress in the same style as each other. Essentially this tendency has not changed. In Japan, having a different style is a kind of risk. Even the designer brand boom of the 1980s did not change that. People only took suggestions from the designers in the same manner as everyone else. ... Therefore the fashion movement that came about in Harajuku was a revolution. This kind of fashion was not suggested by designers, but rather, the fashion of the young inspired the de- signers. On the streets of Harajuku, there was no risk in having a different style. In fact, it was considered worthwhile.

Almost all street fashion magazines published in Japan are distributed only domestically, but with the wide influence of the Internet, and through word of mouth, Japanese fashion is steadily going global. For instance, street maga- zines are found in bookstores in New York and are read by not only Japan- ese but also local teenagers and fashion students. Similarly, some of the Japanese magazines published in English, such as *International Katei Gaho*, feature Japanese fashion. What is now required to further spread Japanese fashion is a diffusion mechanism that includes internationally recognized pub- licity and promotional vehicles, such as a fashion press, major fashion shows, and events that are noticed by fashion professionals worldwide.

The Harajuku teenagers' radical fashion has become the inspiration for young street designers. Some of them—for example, Jun Takahanshi of Un- dercover or Keita Maruyama—now take part in the Paris collections, because French legitimization and recognition are the fastest way to success. Those who are not going to Paris—such as the Bathing Ape—are arriving in New York, seeking the legitimization of other fashion cities.

THE SIGNIFICANCE OF PARIS AMONG YOUNG WOMEN IN TOKYO

While Tokyo is now on the fashion map and is acknowledged and included in an urban hierarchy of fashion, Japanese consumers still have a voracious appe- tite for Western brands, and Japan has undoubtedly been playing a major role in the global surge in fashion consumption. Western designers are generally favored by Japanese consumers over their Japanese counterparts. Because the concepts of fashion and modernity are closely linked (Breward and Evans 2005; Wilson 1985), the increasing number of Western brands in Tokyo can be in- terpreted as a sign of modernization, Westernization, and that Tokyo has been transforming into a major metropolitan city. Despite more than a decade of economic downturn, consumers are still purchasing European luxury goods. No matter how bad the Japanese economy gets, there are those who are willing to pay hundreds of thousands of dollars for big names like Chanel and Dior.

Paris is the imperial fashion city. It has become the symbol of fashion that adds value to designers' names because of the efforts taken by the Paris fashion establishment to maintain and reproduce that ideology. Paris as a fashion city has held an exclusive place in the minds of modern Japanese consumers ever since Pierre Cardin visited Tokyo and introduced his brand in the 1950s. Paris carries far more weight than London, New York, or Milan. Even for Kenzo, the Japanese market was secondary to his business, and his core customer base was in France. His French customers' acceptance and legitimization guaranteed Kenzo's worldwide fame and reputation, which were followed by financial rewards. One of the Japanese magazine editors in my study said: "Every time we do a feature story on Paris or French fashion, the circulation figures go way up for that particular month. It may seem redundant sometimes, but we do that a few times a year for that reason. Milan and New York come next. London is so-so."

In contrast to street fashion, which is a teenage phenomenon, among women in Tokyo who are in their twenties, 94 percent own something made by Louis Vuitton, 92 percent own Gucci, almost 58 percent own Prada, and almost 52 percent own Chanel, according to the Saison Research Institute (Prasso and Brady 2003). The country has developed a leisure class, known as "parasite singles," who still live at home with their parents, giving them plenty of disposable income. The most popular brand among this group is undoubtedly Louis Vuitton, and the company has been actively investing in the Japanese market by increasing the number of stores throughout Japan, especially in Tokyo. When the world's largest Louis Vuitton store opened in September 2003 in the Omotesando district, which is near Harajuku, it set a single-day sales record for the company, selling merchandise worth 125 million yen, or about $1.05 million, and more than a thousand people waited in line for the grand opening (Prasso and Brady 2003). Other luxury retailers, such as Salvatore Ferragamo, Cartier, Christian Dior, and Gucci, have also opened new stores or are planning to do so soon. French companies have been very successful in entering the Japanese market. Despite Japan's weak economy, consumers remain passionate about imported brand-name goods.

CONCLUSION

Japanese street fashion used to be explained by the existence of one or two conspicuous subcultures in the mid-1990s, but today the subcultures have multiplied in different directions and fragmented into smaller groups, and, thus, the phenomenon appears to have slowed down. Nonetheless, much of Japan's cultural output that traveled mostly to other parts of Asia is now transcending cultural boundaries and is spreading worldwide. Likewise, Japan's street fashion influence on popular and youth cultures is spreading globally. Paris as a fashion capital has been successful because its institutions have accepted the fusion of the local and the distant, and there has been an international exchange of clothes, design, and designers between Paris and other cities. The Japanese designers who became successful in Paris took advantage of the system in Paris, while Japanese teenagers created their own fashion with their own force, making a major contribution to Tokyo as a fashion center. Fashion's world cities are determined by the flows of goods, ideas, and people. This is what Tokyo needed for a long time, and it is finally happening.

–3–

Japanese Youth in a Changing Society

This chapter outlines the social, economic, and cultural factors in Japan today, since a theoretical framework that examines subcultures needs to consider the complex and inseparable relationships between a subculture and the larger society in which it exists. Subcultures have always been about youth, times of economic uncertainty, and employment pressures, and they are reliant on class distinction (Van Krieken et al. 2006: 517–18). Therefore, any changes in the structure of the family, the development of the media, and the organization of school and work affect the makeup of subcultures. Youth subcultures can be related to wider structural problems in society, and the emergence and the continuous presence of subcultures and their empirical data can be used as a tool to analyze Japanese society as a whole.

On March 11, 2011, the northeastern part of Japan was hit by a 9.0 magnitude earthquake followed by a massive tsunami that violently ripped into the entire region. Then the nuclear power plants in Fukushima were damaged. According to Japan's National Police Agency, 15,391 people are confirmed dead, and 8,171 are still missing, as of June 8, 2011. Japan's economic power had already been undermined by a long recession since the beginning of the 1990s, and now the Japanese government is desperately trying to restore the country whose economy is pessimistically predicted to continue its downward spiral.

Since beginning my research in 2004, I have noticed the many issues that Japanese youth face. Initially, they told me about their favorite brands, music, and stores, but after a while, they began to express the boredom and frustration they feel at work and in school, their insecurity about the future, the desperate desire to find people that they can trust, and the intense urge to find a place or a group to belong to. Performing a semiotic analysis of each item or the details of clothing is merely the first small step in understanding and interpreting the deeper and latent meaning of a subculture.

Fashion reflects the current social, economic, and cultural conditions. That is why, before I introduce my empirical findings on Japanese youth subcultures, I will briefly explain what has been happening in Japanese society. How has Japanese society changed in the past twenty or thirty years? According to Inui (2003), since the mid-1990s the transition from school to work for youth in Japan has been changing radically, and youth unemployment and the number of part-time employees are increasing rapidly. The transition process has been prolonged, and the pattern has become diverse and complicated; it appears that youth is being restructured profoundly. Young people in Japan have every reason to feel frustrated, angry, and socially alienated.

This chapter looks at the current employment system, marriage rates, fertility rates, divorce rates, and suicide rates in an effort to understand what youth are experiencing in today's Japan. I refer to various official statistical data released by Japanese government agencies and organizations to get a broad view of Japanese society and to determine which direction it is heading.

JAPAN IN THE 1980s AS AN ECONOMIC GIANT

Japan in the 1980s was a seemingly invincible economic superpower. Parents of today's teens are in their forties and fifties, and experienced the country's unprecedented economic growth and success of the 1980s. Both corporations and individual consumers were wealthy, and major Japanese corporations had the ambition to conquer the world. In 1986 Mitsui and Company, a Japanese conglomerate, bought the Exxon Building, part of the Rockefeller Center in New York City (Scardino 1986). In 1989 Mitsubishi Estate Company, a Japanese real estate developer of the Mitsubishi Group, bought control of the Rockefeller Group, and the Sony Corporation bought Columbia Pictures (Cole 1989). On the last day of 1989, the Nikkei 225 stock average closed at an all-time high of 38,916.[1] Japanese banks were lending money freely, and property prices rose so high that it was said that the Imperial Palace in central Tokyo was worth more than all the real estate in California (Cole 1989). The world looked toward Japan to learn from the country and understand why and how Japan rebuilt itself to such great heights after losing World War II. Americans and Europeans began studying Japanese so they could read *Nikkei*, Japan's leading financial daily, and do business with the Japanese. At the same time, Japanese consumers went on a spending frenzy and were buying expensive European brand items, such as Chanel, Dior, and Armani. Parents sent their children overseas to study English and other foreign languages. The Equal Employment Opportunity Law was implemented in 1986, which prohibited gender discrimination with respect to vocation training, fringe benefits, job assignment, promotion, retirement, and dismissal. It appeared that there were opportunities everywhere for everyone. Japan and the Japanese people were in a state of euphoria, which everyone now realizes was not permanent.

JAPAN'S ECONOMIC DOWNTURN AND THE COLLAPSE OF THE LIFETIME EMPLOYMENT SYSTEM

After the economic prosperity of the 1980s, economic bubbles burst after real estate and stock prices peaked in 1992, followed by a stock market crash. This led to a massive national debt and the start of Japan's economic nightmare. The country has since been in the worst and longest economic recession in its history. In 1997 one of the major securities firms in Japan, Yamaichi Securities, announced bankruptcy, which shocked the entire country. The experiences of today's youth are completely different from those of their parents. Today's teens and those in their early twenties have never experienced Japan's economic prosperity.

Japanese society is famously cohesive and conformist, but as Nathan (2004) explains, this cultural trait may be fracturing under the strain of economic stagnation, and it is splitting along lines of ethnic, racial, and gender differences (Ishida and Slater 2010b: 1). Japan is no longer a unified and homogeneous society, and the overall societal values have changed. Working for a major corporation used to guarantee a permanent job and thus lifetime stability; a strong belief among the Japanese, which is now a myth.

As Ishida and Slater (2010b: 1) explain, the discourses that promoted the image of monolithic Japan come under critical scrutiny from many quarters, and they sum up the problems that Japan faced in the 1990s.

> Japan went into recession as land stock market prices collapsed by the early 1990s. Banks were overextended and could not extend on outstanding debt, curtailing further loans and slowing any rebound in expansion. Employment opportunities shrank rapidly, bringing a record high unemployment rate, and with it, reduced consumer spending. As absolute growth slowed, the differences in relative class position became more obvious and the promise of middle class membership began to hollow out. Many of the most significant changes are occurring in the labor market: massive restructuring of the economy; increased unemployment rates; shift in the structure of the labor market away from lifetime employment and into part-time and short-term work. Just as important, the confidence that society had in the strength of the economy and in the state to be able to manage prosperity was shaken. Maybe most fundamentally, the stability of the firm as a marker of the social identity for individuals has receded as the institutional commitment from the firm has been withdrawn. (Ishida and Slater 2010b: 7)

Japan's lifetime employment system was central to the people's beliefs, values, norms, and ideologies. Japanese culture is said to be more rigid than Western cultures, and people often abide by their cultural norms that dictate at what age to enter college, when to graduate, when to look for a job, at what age it is appropriate to get married and have children, and so on. Once a person strays away from these norms, it is very difficult to get back on track and lead a financially stable lifestyle. Lifetime employment obviously provided men and women with security and stability both financially and psychologically. This system allowed workers to stay within their company until retirement. Changing jobs for better pay was not part of the Japanese tradition. That was considered "Americanized," which had a hint of negative implications. Workers were rarely fired for incompetency or lack of skills. Financially stable men tended to get married younger, and when couples had children the mothers stayed at home as full-time homemakers and took care of all household chores while the fathers worked to feed the family. The public and social space was the father's responsibility, and the private and domestic space was the mother's. With secure jobs, it was easier to get loans and take out a mortgage to buy a house or an apartment. People could enjoy their vacations, send their children to good schools, and plan their comfortable retirement. This scenario is what those who are now in their forties and fifties experienced and believed in during their young adult lives; a lifestyle that was shattered in the 1990s.

The downturn of the Japanese economy led to the collapse of the lifetime employment system and had countless repercussions on society. This is the root of the transformations that had ripple effects throughout Japanese society. Men who never dreamed that the lifetime employment system would ever disappear are getting laid off for the first time in their lives. Losing a job is an earth-shattering experience for many, and, expectedly, the suicide rate among middle-aged men has increased. As Emile Durkheim explains in his famous study *Suicide* ([1897] 1951), men are more likely to commit suicide because they are more independent and are less socially integrated than women. Furthermore, many men define themselves by their occupation, so that once they lose their job, they lose their social identity altogether. Mothers who used to be full-time homemakers now have to look for part-time jobs to supplement their household income. Women are forced to become independent financially and psychologically, although the labor market conditions are not favorable for women workers.

Japan's unstable political system is another detrimental factor that is creating insecurity and concern. Before and after Junichiro Koizumi, who served as Japan's prime minister between 2001 and 2006, no one has lasted for more than a year or two in that same role (see Table 3.1 in the Appendix). Japan does not have a leader who can pull the country out of its economic malaise.

INCREASE IN UNEMPLOYMENT AND PART-TIME EMPLOYMENT

While Japan's unemployment rate is relatively lower than that in the United States and Europe,[2] those who were unemployed for more than a year in Japan in 2010 reached 1,210,000, up 260,000 from 2009, according to data released by the Ministry of Internal Affairs and Communications of Japan.[3] Those who were unemployed between the ages of 25 and 34 reached 320,000, up 60,000 from 2009, and those unemployed above the age of 55 reached 300,000, up 70,000 from 2009.

The deterioration of the traditional lifetime employment system led to an increase in temporary or part-time employment (see Table 3.2 in the Appendix). Full-time employment rose until 1997, but after 1998 it declined, and since 2007 it has almost leveled out. Additionally, part-time employment increased until 2009. The percentage of part-time employment increased from 20 percent in 1990 to 35.4 percent in 2011. This means that one out of three employees is a part-timer. In 2011, of the 17.17 million who are employed part-time, 11.75 million are women and 5.42 million are men, revealing a large discrepancy between the sexes.

A woman with a master's degree told me:

I have been in contract employment for several years. You register at a job bank, and they send you to a company where you work for three to six months or sometimes a year. Then after the contract is over, they send you to a different company. When you are hired as a part-timer or a contract employee, you will never ever be hired as a full-timer. It's like an iron-clad rule. It's a dead-end job. We are not protected by labor laws. There are no promotions or future opportunities. I work from Monday to Friday just for money. I feel that I need to look for a future husband to secure my life, but the guys I meet have no confidence and are all unreliable. I am not sure if there is a guy who can support me.

It has become difficult for both men and women to get a full-time job with reasonable benefits, even for those with a bachelor's or a master's degree. Parents used to tell their children to study hard so that they could get into a good college, which would allow them to get work in a major corporation and guarantee stable and secure employment. One of the strengths of Japanese companies was the devotion and loyalty employees had toward their employers. This loyalty was a pillar of the Japanese economy. That has disappeared and has become a myth. The Ministry of Health, Labour and Welfare recently announced that, in March 2011, the number of men and women who are now on welfare has exceeded two million for the first time in fifty-nine years.

GROWING SUICIDES AMONG MIDDLE-AGED MEN

The changes in the structure of the labor market have clearly taken a toll on middle-aged Japanese men who support families. Although the total number of suicides in 2010 declined by 3.5 percent from 2009, the number has exceeded 30,000 for thirteen years (see Table 3.3 in the Appendix).[4] Seventy percent of all suicides in Japan are committed by men. In 2010 the highest suicide rate was among men in their fifties (18.8 percent), followed by those in their sixties (18.6 percent) and those in their forties (16.3 percent). Together, more than half of suicides among men occur between the ages of forty and sixty-nine, those who in the previous economy might be working as managers and executives. The reasons for suicide, based on 23,572 people who left notes before committing suicide, were health reasons (15,802 people), economic/financial reasons (7,438 people), family/personal reasons (4,497 people), work-related issues (2,590 people), and relationship issues (1,103 people). Men's high suicide rates undoubtedly have much to do with their employment situations. Men often define themselves by their work and occupation—a crucial part of their identity construction. Men are also expected to be good breadwinners. With a recession and declining economy, many Japanese men are no longer able to provide for their families sufficiently. A poor economy has led to the collapse of patriarchy as well.

DECLINING MARRIAGE AND FERTILITY RATES

During the 1980s the goal of a young girl was to find a man who was high in income, height, and educational background: She wanted someone in "three-highs." But since the collapse of the lifetime employment system, for girls, marriage is no longer a guaranteed "permanent job." Women never know when their husbands might be fired or get depressed and collapse at work and can no longer work. The most popular and desirable occupation for a future wife was and still is a nurse. A single man in his twenties told me: "Men like nurses. We want to marry a nurse. It used to be because they are kind and take good care of their husbands. But the reasons have changed these days. A nurse has special skills and it is a very stable job. Even if we get fired, we have a wife who still has a job and can support her family."

According to Shirahase's study (2010: 60–61) based on data released by the Ministry of Internal Affairs and Communications Statistics Bureau in 2007, from the 1970s onward, more than half of all men were still unmarried in their late twenties. By 2005 the nonmarriage rate for men in their late twenties had reached 70 percent. Even for men in their late thirties, some 30 percent remained unmarried. As for women, in recent years, the nonmarriage rate for those in their early twenties has approached 90 percent, leaving almost everyone in this age bracket single. During the 1990s the nonmarriage rates also rose for women in their thirties, exceeding 30 percent by 2005. In fact, the total number of marriages is estimated to reach only 670,000 couples in

2011. Since 2005 the number has fluctuated, but in 2011 the second biggest decline from the previous year is expected. Experts predict that the population of marriageable age is on the decline, so the decline in marriage rates is likely to continue.

Both men and women are delaying marriage (see Table 3.4 in the Appendix). Economic factors affect one's decision to get married. According to a study conducted by the Ministry of Internal Affairs and Communications in 2007 (Shirahase 2010), of the men in their twenties and thirties who got married in the past five years, 24 percent were employed full-time and 12.1 percent were employed part-time. In 2007 the marriage rate among full-time workers was 2.4 times that of part-time or contract workers. Men whose income is below four million yen (approximately US$50,000) are less likely to marry.

Furthermore, the rise in the nonmarriage rate for men with low education levels in recent years is related to the rate of youth unemployment and the steady rise in nonstandard forms of employment. For young men who are expected to support a family, the inability to find stable employment is a major obstacle to marriage. We may assume that the prolonged post-bubble recession was a particularly severe blow for men with low levels of education, already in a weak position in the labor market.

Japan's total fertility rate stood at 1.32 in 2005, well below the 2.08 required to maintain the population at a steady level (see Table 3.5 in the Appendix). In 1989 the fertility rate fell to 1.57, below the figure recorded in 1966. The realization that a fertility rate that looked like a drastic but temporary decline twenty years ago was now the norm provoked a wave of panic (Shirahase 2010: 57). Shirahase (2010: 60) explains that the declining number of children in the population has two main underlying factors: the increasing number of unmarried people and a decline in fertility among those who are married. It is still relatively rare for children to be born out of wedlock; marriage and childbirth are closely related issues, and the decision of each individual about whether to marry can have a direct impact on the fertility rate.

GROWING DIVORCE RATES AND SINGLE-MOTHER HOUSEHOLDS

In 1993 the number of divorces in Japan reached an all-time high, and the number has almost doubled since 1990 (see Table 3.6 in the Appendix). One in every four marriages ends up in divorce. In 2002 the divorce rate was the highest since World War II, reaching 289,836. It has declined slightly since 2002, and in 2008 it was 251,136 couples—or 1.88 per 1,000 people. In 2010 the number of divorces declined slightly to 251,000 from 253,353 in 2009.

Divorce results in single-parent—primarily single-mother—families. In 2003 Japan's single-mother households numbered 1,223,400, while single-father households numbered 173,800. Of all households, single mothers head 2.7 percent and single fathers head 0.4 percent. In the past, child custody was mostly granted to fathers, but by 1996, 78 percent was granted to mothers. That leads to difficult financial consequences for single-mother families (see Table 3.7 in the Appendix). The full-time employment status of single mothers is 50.7 percent, while it is 75.3 percent for single fathers. The average annual income of full-time single-mother households is 2.29 million yen (approximately US$28,265), while that of single-father households is 4.22 million yen (US$52,750). The overall average single-mother household annual income is 1.6 million yen (US$20,000), and that of single-father households is 3.1 million yen (US$38,750), both of which are lower than the two-parent household average income of five million yen (US$62,500). It is statistically apparent that children who are raised by their mothers are in financially tight environments, which could affect their choices in life regarding school and career. Thus, the increase in divorce rates requires more government assistance for single-parent households.

DRASTIC VALUE TRANSFORMATION

Teens and young adolescents have very little hope for their future in Japan, and a widespread feeling of disillusionment, alienation, uncertainty, and anger has permeated the society among both adults and children. Sometimes, youth discontent is expressed through explicit outbursts and aggression or, sometimes, is communicated quietly through social isolation. There is clearly a breakdown of traditional family, social, and economic systems.

HIKI-KOMORI: A PHENOMENON OF SEVERE SOCIAL WITHDRAWAL

Hiki-komori is a Japanese term that refers to those who are reclusive and voluntarily withdraw and isolate themselves from society. In addition to a plummeting birth rate and a sagging economy, the country is struggling with a youth crisis. The Japanese Ministry of Health, Labour, and Welfare defines *hiki-komori* as people who refuse to leave their homes and who isolate themselves from society and stay in their homes for a period exceeding six months. The number of *hiki-komori* has been estimated at one million in Japan and 25,000–27,000 in Tokyo. The problem is becoming more widespread and results in a new underclass of young men who cannot or will not join the full-time working world. They carry an enormous sense of failure and of not being able to get back on track.

Many of those in their twenties, thirties, and forties (and even older) have failed at something and have lost the opportunity to be an active member of society. It has been a major social problem. Japanese society is a rigid one that does not encourage young people to stray from the mainstream or to violate cultural norms. Japanese youth apply to college at the age of eighteen. If they fail the college entrance exam once, they can try a second time the following year—but not a third time. If they start college late, they will graduate late, which affects their eligibility to apply for a good job.

A man in his mid-thirties, whom I met when I was doing fieldwork in Akihabara, said to me:

> I have been a *hiki-komori* for about eight years. It used to be bad. I used to be in my room all day long watching anime videos and reading manga. I would sleep during the day when everyone else is up and get up when everyone is sleeping. I would go out in the middle of the night to get something to eat. Therapists and counselors didn't work for me. I now belong to an organization for *hiki-komori*, and I have been getting a lot better since then. Instead of just talking to counselors, they have clubs which are like extracurricular school clubs. And I enjoy them. I feel that I'm experiencing a school life again. I didn't have much of that because I used to get bullied in school all the time.

It is difficult to find out in ethnography or in an interview setting whether an individual comes from a single-parent family, or whether the father is employed, because the information is too personal and private. But it is crucial for a researcher to take a macro perspective of a society to understand what kind of social and economic environment youth are placed in and what opportunities they might find in the future. Every social and economic phenomenon has a chain effect and reaction. The deterioration of the old system affects society as a whole on a macro level and on each individual's life on a micro level.

A GROWING SUBCULTURAL PHENOMENON DURING AN ECONOMIC SLUMP

Subcultures do not emerge from nowhere. They do not appear for no reason. Economic, social, and political factors have major impacts on the growing number of subcultures in Japan. The entire society's—and especially teens'—value system is changing. The previous generation's traditional Japanese beliefs, such as selfless devotion to employers, respect for seniors, and perseverance, are collapsing. An intentional shift from an old ideology and way of life is evident in today's Japan. Teens today see the assertion of individual identity as more important and meaningful than that of family or company identity, which used to be the key concept in Japanese culture. Such attitudes are reflected in their norm-breaking and outrageous, yet commercially successful, styles that attract attention. Hebdige (1988: 35) accurately pointed out that subculture forms in the space between surveillance and the evasion of surveillance; it translates the fact of being under scrutiny into the pleasure of being watched.

Therefore, although it may seem ironic, it is under these social and economic conditions that Japanese street fashion became increasingly creative and innovative, as if the teens wanted to challenge and redefine the existing notion of what is fashionable and aesthetic. They went against the grain of the normative standard of fashion. They are in search of their identity and a community where they feel accepted.

CONCLUSION

Because fashion and society are interdependent, interconnected, and inseparable, I look at the economic, social, cultural, and political factors that may have attributed to today's growing subcultural phenomena in Japan. The collapse of the lifetime employment system resulted in numerous consequences and repercussions in Japanese society in social, cultural, political, and economic spheres. The structure of the labor market is undergoing a major transition. The gap between the rich and the poor is growing, and the number of people applying for government subsidies is at an all-time high. When the traditional values and ideologies no longer work for a society to properly function, it is only natural that individuals, especially the youth, begin to question the status quo and search for something else.

II: GEOGRAPHICALLY AND STYLISTICALLY DEFINED JAPANESE SUBCULTURES

Subculturalization is the result of urbanism (Fischer 1975), and there is a link between the growing number of subcultural groups and urbanization (Fischer 1972). The concentration in urban areas of large heterogeneous groups of people weakens interpersonal ties, primary social structures, and normative standards. Dynamic population density leads to a complex, structural differentiation with consequences of alienation, social disorganization, deviant behavior, and anomie. The more urban the setting, the more the variety of subculturalization (Fischer 1972, 1975). This is precisely the phenomenon found in Tokyo, one of the most densely populated cities in the world, with a population of approximately thirteen million as of April 2010, according to the Tokyo Metropolitan Government. The majority of those who live and work in Tokyo come from elsewhere. As a result, the society is shifting increasingly from gemeinschaft relationships to gesellschaft relationships, in which appearance becomes crucial due to the prevalence of generally shallow, businesslike social interactions.[1]

Today's Japanese youth subcultures are geographically and stylistically defined, and the different fashion landmarks in various districts are not only geographic but also biographical and personal. The construction or securing of space can reinforce identity, which can be empowering for some. We need to think about all the factors that come into play in the process of making those spatial divisions for youth to develop their identities. "Who am I?" and "Where do I belong?" are questions that define one's identity. These places where subcultures emerge and remain have been invested with a great deal of different meanings. They play a crucial role in the process of identity formation. Spaces are divided and reveal how structures of power are at work within those groups and speak to how the culture of those youth works. Different geographies have different norms, and thus the roles that youth play vary according to their geographical placements in the social order. A particular subculture with a specific look or style exists only in a specific geographical territory. For example, if you are a member of Lolita, you hang out in Harajuku and not in Shibuya. If you consider yourself Gyaru-o, you are in Shibuya and nowhere else.

As explained in chapter 2, "Placing Tokyo on the Fashion Map," Japanese fashion has been an inspiration for many fashion professionals in the West, starting with Kenzo Takada's appearance in Paris in 1970, followed by Issey Miyake in 1973, Hanae Mori in 1977, and Yohji Yamamoto and Rei Kawakubo of Comme des Garçons in 1981.[2] Japan is becoming a country that is a genuine fashion force. Today's Japanese fashion contributes to the aesthetic aspect of fashion as well as the business model. The stereotypical Western view of Japanese style, such as boringly suited salarymen and their demurely dressed wives, is knocked upside down when we see the range of styles worn by the young people on the streets of Tokyo (Polhemus 1996: 12).

Japanese street fashion does not come from the professional world-famous Japanese designers; rather, it is led primarily by high school girls who have become extremely influential in controlling fashion trends. A different type of fashion is being dictated directly and indirectly by these fashion-conscious or fashion-obsessed youngsters. It is not an exaggeration to say that they are the agents of fashion who take part in the production and dissemination of fashion. Japanese street fashion emerges out of the social networks among different institutions of fashion as well as various street subcultures, each of which is identified with a unique and original look. These teens rely on a distinctive appearance to proclaim their symbolic, subcultural identity, which, they claim, is not political or ideological.

While many fashionable Japanese consumers simply imitate Western styles in a straightforward way, teens have led the way in a creative mixing and matching of contrasting eclectic styles that has been extensively copied in the West (Polhemus 1996: 12). Similarly, many apparel manufacturers and retailers from neighboring Asian countries, such as Korea and Taiwan, visit Tokyo in search of new ideas, and knockoffs are found throughout Asia. A buyer from Hong Kong explained to me:

> Telling a teen customer that an item is popular in Japan is a big selling point in Hong Kong. Girls in Hong Kong can identify with girls in Japan because both have black hair and black eyes. If something looks cute on a girl in Tokyo, they think it will look good on a girl in Hong Kong as well. That's why it's important for us to know what is going on in Tokyo. I'm here every three months to catch up with the latest trends. Tokyo is definitely the fashion capital of Asia.

The most recent fashion phenomenon in Japan goes beyond the conventional model of fashion business. Since the mid-1990s a separate system of fashion with a new business model has been created in Japan in order to commercialize street fashion and boost the market. In this new model occupational categories within various institutions of fashion are blurry, and the model supports the trickle-up/bubble-up or trickle-across theory of fashion that Blumer (1969a) proposed.

To understand Japanese youth and their subcultures, I use Diana Crane's theoretical and analytical framework of the postmodern culture of fashion, in which the emphasis is placed on consumer fashion rather than class fashion postulated by earlier theorists such as Georg Simmel ([1904] 1957), Herbert Spencer ([1896] 1966), and Thornstein Veblen ([1899] 1957). According to Crane (2000), the consumption of cultural goods, such as fashionable clothing, performs an increasingly important role in the construction of personal identity, and the variety of lifestyles available today liberates individuals—especially youngsters—from tradition and enables them to make choices that create a meaningful self-identity. Like Crane, Davis (1992) also points out the ambivalent nature of identity and fashion. Simply put, fashion in postmodern times is all about finding and defining one's identity.

It is evident on the streets of Tokyo that Japan is becoming a country that can produce unique styles. What is particularly eye-catching is the distinctive appearance of the teens and young adolescents that belong to subcultural groups that are often female-dominated. Japanese street fashion emerges out of the social networks among different institutions of fashion as well as various street subcultures, each of which is identified with a creative and original look.

My empirical study is a macrosociological analysis of the social organization of Japanese street fashion and a microinteractionist analysis of teen consumers who form various subcultures to which they can belong and who directly and indirectly dictate fashion trends. It attempts to show the interdependence in the production process of fashion between various institutions of fashion within the fashion-related industries and the Japanese teens. Street fashion in the fashionable districts of Tokyo, such as Harajuku and Shibuya, is independent of and separate from any mainstream fashion system and differs from the conventional model of fashion business with different marketing strategies and occupational categories.

The diffusion process of subcultural fashion is the best example of a trickle-up theory of fashion. In order for fashion trends or phenomena to be successful, there needs to be institutional involvement in maintaining and expanding the subcultures. In subsequent chapters, I explore the expansion of subcultural groups, some of which were supported by an entire district, with retailers and the media collaborating to sustain the subcultural phenomenon because it helps their businesses. The subcultures that remain small and marginal are the ones that have started and collected some followers but are not spreading because there is little institutional input. For instance, Shibuya and Harajuku are the major fashion districts for the youth because there are strong institutional as well as individual networks, while Nakano, Tachikawa, Saitama (outside Tokyo), and Kouenji as subcultural fashion districts are still marginal and completely out of the mainstream.

In chapters 4 through 8 I examine the characteristics of subcultural groups in different districts of Tokyo based on my empirical findings between 2004 and 2010. Subcultures have the power to institutionally create a fashion district that caters to the followers of the subcultures. The trends start from the bottom—that is, with the subcultural members themselves. The diffusion process is the complete opposite of that for high fashion, which begins at the upper social stratum. The youth are often poor and cannot afford to buy anything expensive, but the collective power to initiate a fashion trend is stronger than anything else.

Chapter 4 discusses the girls (*Gyaru*) and boys (*Gyaru-o*) in Shibuya. Since the mid-1990s this subcultural phenomenon revolves around a landmark called Shibuya 109, an eight-floor shopping center with stores that sell Shibuya-style clothes. One of the first Japanese fashion subcultures was known as *Ganguro* (face black) and was characterized by artificially tanned faces and heavy makeup. Ganguro wore bright colors and short skirts with high platform shoes or boots with no socks or stockings. Ganguro led to *Yamamba* (mountain witch) and more recently to *Mamba* and *Bamba*. These groups are subdivided into smaller groups, such as *Celemba* and *Cocomba*, depending on which brand one prefers to wear. The Gyaru and Gyaru-o wear blonde or brunette shaggy hair and very tight jeans. Gyaru and Gyaru-o share many of the components found in Western subcultural groups because the majority of them belong to a youth gang in Shibuya. Thus, making themselves look intimidating is an important element of their style, and the keywords for Shibuya fashion are *ero-kawaii* (erotic and cute) and *kowa-kawaii* (scary and cute).

The Lolita subculture of Harajku is described in chapter 5. Lolita is one of the most popular Japanese fashion subcultures overseas. Harajuku, which is only a couple of train stops from Shibuya, has completely different fashion subcultures. Harajuku is known as the mecca for those who belong to the Lolita subculture, which appeared in the late 1990s in opposition to Shibuya subcultures, and members congregate on a small bridge near Harajuku Station. Lolita girls portray the image of a Victorian doll, wearing dresses with frills and lace trimmings, bonnets, and sometimes blonde wigs, cute handbags, and umbrellas. The keywords are *girlie* and *princesslike*. Lolitas are subdivided into different subgroups, such as Gothic Lolita, Sweet Lolita, Punk Lolita, and Wa-Lolita, and each group has its own stylistic characteristics. Chapter 5 examines the origin of the Lolita look and how various institutions of fashion are making an effort to spread it further.

Akihabara and Ikebukuro, discussed in chapter 6, are the mecca for anime and manga fans who make up a distinct subcultural community. Akihabara used to be known as a shopping area for electronics, but in 2000 the anime trend emerged out of computer games and Akihabara began to attract *Otaku* (nerds), who are mostly boys obsessed with anime, manga, and video games, and they together create a huge subcultural community in Akihabara. At the same time, maid cafés began to flourish in this district, where waitresses are dressed as characters in anime and manga and welcome male customers by saying, "Welcome home, Master!" Providing a space for the Otaku community creates a sort of stability and security for those who are often considered nerdy, introverted, and deviant. On the other hand, in Ikebukuro, there is a butler café for women, where male waiters are dressed as butlers and greet female customers by saying, "Welcome home, Princess!" There are also stores that sell costumes for cosplayers who dress themselves in their favorite anime and manga characters. Cosplayers dress as a fictional character and put on a different identity for entertainment.

Chapter 7 is about Shinjuku and *Age-jo*. It is fairly common for women college students in Japan to work as part-time bar hostesses to earn extra money, and many students work at bars and pubs in Shinjuku. A monthly magazine titled *Koakuma-Ageha* (Small Devilish Butterflies) was launched in 2006 with these part-time hostesses as the target readers. The magazine became extremely successful while solidifying and expanding the subculture. There are some similarities between Shibuya's Gyaru and Age-jo, because many Gyaru work as bar hostesses. But Age-jo treat their outward appearance extremely seriously since it is their weapon.

Chapter 8 discusses an emerging subculture in Kouenji called Mori Girl (Forest Girl), which is still marginal and less known. There are many vintage and secondhand clothing stores in this district, and each store has its own expertise, features, and characteristics. Mori Girls wear layers of secondhand clothes. They are supposed to portray an image of a girl in a forest. The keyword for them is *girlie*, but their style is different from Harajuku Lolita's girlie image, and they have their own version and definition of the term. The scale of diffusion of this subculture is limited due to a lack of structural support and industry involvement. This grassroots movement is not popular enough to spread widely, although some youth are attracted to the subculture because of its marginality.

Chapter 9, the final chapter in Part II, investigates and analyzes the similarities and differences among the subcultures discussed in chapters 4 through 8 and explains why some subcultures spread farther than others. I also look at how the youth of these various subcultures are connected. I attempt to understand what they are thinking and what it means to them to belong to these groups. This chapter also discusses how individuals and institutions are connected within a subcultural system. Unlike high fashion, which places much emphasis on biannual fashion collections in major fashion cities, Japanese subcultural fashion has other diffusion mechanisms within their own social networks.

My intention is not simply to introduce different fashion styles in different districts of Tokyo but to understand why the youth in these subcultures dress in a way that is out of the norm and what the phenomenon says about Japanese society as a whole. Subcultures are situated within a culture; cultures are situated within a society. Although there is much insightful research on subcultures, no study deeply investigates Japan's contemporary youth subcultures and theoretically analyses the individuals and institutions involved in producing and reproducing the subcultures.

As indicated in chapter 1, "Understanding Subcultural Studies," an ethnographical method allows a researcher to get close to the empirical social world and dig deeply into it through face-to-face communication and interaction with research subjects. This is the method that many symbolic interactionists adopt, and it cannot be achieved through quantitative methods with statistics.[3] This approach helps us understand the communication process among teens because it is committed to an inductive approach to the understanding of human behavior in which explanations are induced from data. Social theorists tend to ignore and dismiss human emotions as irrelevant in order to explain the social world, while symbolic interactionists focus on subjective meanings and value human emotions, which can only be studied through direct human contact.

Furthermore, a macrolevel sociological theory directs attention to the informal nature of youth institutions and reveals their distinguishing characteristics found in the structural-functional approach. This type of analysis may be a promising method for the interpretation of sociological data for youth subcultures. According to the structural-functional approach, every society has a socially approved institutional structure composed of interdependent institutions that facilitate or impede the fulfillment of essential social functions. Where structural obstacles appear, alternative institutions emerge to carry out the obstructed functions (Merton 1946: 18, 52–53, 72). Applying this insight to the study of youth subculture, we find precisely in its informal institutions an outlet for the functions that are not fulfilled by the formal adult socializing institutions. Interrelated social institutions work toward the maintenance of relatively stable social conditions, and where a formal institution is ineffectual, informal institutions arise to contribute to the stability of the society. In an analysis of youth subcultures, we see the series of interrelated institutions bound together by the activities of their members.

An important contribution of the functional approach is that it limits analysis to the sociological level of observable, objective consequences of institutional behavior and excludes the subjective, psychological level, which can be compensated for with symbolic interactionist perspectives. The objective consequences may be revealed either as positive functions, which make for the adaptation of a given institution or the adjustment of given individuals, or as dysfunctions, which lessen such adaptation or adjustment. It is at the points of the dysfunctions of formal social structure that this theory focuses on youth subculture, for such dysfunctions implicitly give clues to discontinuities in the formal structure that are bridged over by the emerging youth institutions.

The distinction between manifest and latent functions directs analysis to the informal youth subculture. Manifest functions are the socially approved and intended structural patterns basic to formal institutions. The latent functions appear in the informal institutions, where the behavior patterns are unanticipated and often not socially approved (Merton 1949: 26, 50, 72). It is this basic shift of attention from the manifest functions of formal institutions to the latent functions of informal institutions that has resulted in a significant increase in sociological knowledge.

Another significant contribution made by the structural-functional approach in its application to youth subculture is that it directs specific attention to the functions within the given institutions of youth subculture. Fundamentally, the functions are found in the contributions that a given institution makes to the maintenance of youth subculture itself. On the other hand, when the functions of one institution are projected into a subsequent institution, the effect is called a dysfunction. Since youth communities are subcultures, their requirements must be satisfied through the latent functions of the structural substitutes.

However, we need to be aware that no theoretical models are set in stone, and they are as tied to their own times as the people that produce them. The idea of subculture-as-negation grew up alongside punk, remained inextricably linked to it, and died when punk died (Hebdige 1988: 8).

My research data come primarily from an ethnographical study in Tokyo for two months during the summer and three weeks during the winter every year between 2004 and 2009, and from January to August 2010. I combined direct observation, both participant and nonparticipant, with structured and semistructured in-depth interviews to attain a close and full familiarity with the world I was examining. I relied on each person I met and interviewed to refer me to their friends and colleagues. I interviewed eighty-two individuals— subcultural members, manufacturers, retailers, designers, and salesgirls— who are involved in starting, spreading, commercializing, marketing, and distributing Japanese subcultural fashion. I met individuals in various sectors of the fashion industry to get a macro perspective of the subcultural fashion phenomenon. I visited various department stores, large and small stores, and events, and visited a maid café and a butler café. I also reviewed Japanese fashion periodicals, such as *Koakuma-Ageha*, *Popteen*, and *Kera!* to perform a textual analysis of the magazines, since these publications are very popular among the subcultural members.

—4—

Shibuya: The Youth
in Outspoken Rebellion

I begin this part with a chapter on Shibuya because this is where one of the first distinct subcultural phenomena in Japan appeared in the 1990s, and it shares similar components and traits with subcultural groups in the United Kingdom and the United States, such as deviance, delinquency, aggression, rebellion, and antisocial behavior. I explore the emergence of the *Gyaru/Ko-gyaru* and *Gyaru-o* phenomenon that started in Shibuya and show how the institutions of fashion—such as fashion retailers and the mass media—have contributed to the spread, maintenance, and reproduction of the subcultures. The members of the subcultures and the industries rely on each other and are interdependent and interrelated.

Subcultures in Shibuya can be used as a typical case study to define what a subculture is. Many of the youth in Shibuya belong to gangs, which are almost always deviant in nature. They set themselves apart from mainstream society, creating their own values and norms that intentionally go against the normative standards. The way they speak, the way they dress, and the places where they hang out all symbolize their membership to the group and to this district. The existence of these subcultures makes the district lively, exciting, and attractive to youth from all over Japan. I explore the relationship between the Shibuya 109 shopping center and various subcultures in the area. The retailers and brands sold in the famous Shibuya 109 provide styles that are considered cool and fashionable to members of the youth subculture while making a major contribution to sustaining the fashion-related businesses in Shibuya.[1]

THE SHIBUYA 109 SHOPPING CENTER:
FASHION LANDMARK

Subcultures in Shibuya cannot be explained without mentioning a landmark known as Shibuya 109, which is a major shopping center with eight upper-level floors and two basement floors. It has been operated by Tokyu Malls Development (TMD) since 1979. The stores in the building until 1995 sold conventional women's wear, but in 1996 the entire building changed its customer target to the younger market. As of June 2011 there were 116 tenants/stores in the building, all of which target young girls and women in their teens and early twenties. According to Kunio Soma, managing director of TMD, "For the past thirteen years, Shibuya 109 has been growing its annual sales every year. This upward trend in sales was definitely due to the Gyaru or Ko-gyaru phenomenon, which began to creep up in Shibuya in the mid-1990s, and multiple youth subcultures that came out of it."[2] On weekends, every floor is filled with teen girls while music blasts in the background like a disco. It has become a sign of status for the teens who come from outside Tokyo to shop in Shibuya 109. One girl shopping there told me:

> It is cool to buy clothes in 109 even if you can buy them online. 109 sells the latest and the coolest clothes, accessories, and jewelry. They are not expensive so I can buy them with my pocket money. You can meet so many fashionable girls in Shibuya. They are inspirational. It's fun just to watch them. I learn a lot from their fashion.

This building is central to Shibuya fashion and subcultures. It has become a sacred place for those who adore and worship Shibuya fashion.

BEGINNING OF THE GYARU AND KO-GYARU PHENOMENON

Shibuya's distinctive street fashion was started by young teenage girls known as Gyaru or Ko-gyaru. Gyaru wear popular brands sold in Shibuya 109, such as Cecil McBee, Egoist, and Alba Rosa, which are known as cute and erotic. The girls dye their hair and wear heavy makeup. Ko-gyaru are known for wearing short plaid skirts that look like a school uniform and loose knee-high white socks. Like Gyaru, their hair is often dyed blonde and brown. Initially, both Gyaru and Ko-gyaru were generally associated with a minority of social dropouts and deviants, but their effects and influence extended far beyond the confines of a particular subculture. This phenomenon consequently redefined Japan's sartorial and sexual norms.

The term *Gyaru* comes from the English word *gal*. Basically, Gyaru is a college student, and Ko-gyaru (a child of Gyaru) is a high school girl who is a Gyaru wannabe. Lately, there is *Mago-gyaru* (a grandchild of Gyaru), which is a middle school student. If Gyaru is considered a professional major league player, Ko-gyaru is a semiprofessional, minor league player. After Gyaru, one becomes *Onee-gyaru* (a sister of Gyaru). Those who used to be Gyaru and are now mothers are known as *Gyaru Mama*, and *Chibi Gyaru* is a child of Gyaru Mama. More recently, there are *Kuro-Gyaru* (black Gyaru) and *Shiro-Gyaru* (white Gyaru), depending on whether they tan their faces. But the distinctions are not clearly marked, and they are all known as Gyaru or former Gyaru.

Slang

In addition to distinct fashion and makeup, Gyaru have their own slang and idioms that are quite unlike conventional Japanese language and that ordinary Japanese people cannot understand. Gyaru often abbreviate and combine English and Japanese words, such as *cho-mira-supa-beri-ba*, which means extra, miraculously, super, very bad, or *cho-mira-supa-beri-goo*, which means extra, miraculous, super, very good. *No-pro* means no problem; *one-pi* means a one-piece dress; *pa-Gyaru* means only partially Gyaru—that is, not real or authentic.

GANGURO AND YAMAMBA

One of the first and most prominent fashion subcultures that evolved from the Gyaru phenomenon in the mid-1990s is known as *Ganguro* (face black).[3] Ganguro girls artificially tanned their faces and bodies, dyed their hair, and wore very heavy makeup. They wore bright colors and short skirts with dangerously high platform shoes or boots with no socks or stockings. This trend was enhanced by a young Japanese singer, Namie Amuro. For most teens, their life revolved around Shibuya station, and they subconsciously and unintentionally created a subculture.

A designer who used to be Ganguro said:

> I was a hardcore Ganguro when I was in high school. I had to be. Otherwise, I wouldn't be accepted by other kids. I would be totally out of place if I looked normal. We all want to fit in when we are teenagers. We all shopped in 109. We went there almost every weekend because every time we go, the stores have new stuff, and we could not resist buying them.

Toward the end of the 1990s and in the early twenty-first century, a fashion trend and subculture called *Yamamba* (mountain witch) appeared to replace the Ganguro look. Yamamba was more extreme than Ganguro in terms of makeup and fashion, but, according to an industry professional I spoke with, "Yamamba was probably too extreme that it did not last long."

MAMBA, BAMBA, AND OTHER SHIBUYA SUBCULTURES

More recently, Yamamba evolved into *Mamba* and *Bamba*, which no longer have any literal meaning in Japanese. There are multiple interactions occurring simultaneously on the streets of Shibuya, and the subculture groups with specific appearances have spread to so many different sub-subcultures that it is almost impossible to keep track of all the groups. Each subculture in Shibuya is also tied to a particular brand in Shibuya 109. There is a Shibuya subculture group called *Lomamba*—that is, Mamba with a Lolita touch—and the label they wear must be LizLisa, which is sold at Shibuya 109. Similarly, *Cocomba* is Mamba who wears the brand Cocolulu, also sold at Shibuya 109.

I approached one of the girls in Shibuya and asked her if she was a Mamba. She replied, "No, I'm a *Celemba*." She then explained the difference between a Mamba and a Celemba. Celemba is a combination of a celebrity look and a Mamba. The Celemba tend to wear expensive brands, while the Mamba do not. Mamba use white eye shadow around the eyes, but the Celemba use silver. As for fashion, the Celemba look more mature and sophisticated and always have a scarf or a shawl around their neck. A self-claimed authentic Mamba said, "There are so many girls who are only partially Mamba, and they are not authentic Mamba. Authentic Mamba is not tied to one brand." Authenticity appears to be important, and only the insiders can detect the subtle differences and details between what is real and what is not.

GYARU-O: THE MALE COUNTERPART OF GYARU

While the majority of Japanese subcultures are initiated by girls and are still female-dominant, Shibuya is an exception, where there is a male counterpart for Gyaru known as Gyaru-o. Just like Gyaru, Gyaru-o have tanned skin, brightly colored hair, and flamboyant outfits. They want to express overtly that they are not normal people, and that is an important part of their identity. They need to look and act cool, and they have their own definition of what is and is not cool.

In 2005 TMD opened Shibuya 109-2 across the street from Shibuya 109. The top four floors are dedicated to Gyaru-o brands such as Vanquish, Jack Rose, Varosh, Cocolulu Men's, Diavlo, Roi Franc, and Gennaro. In March 2011 the name of the building was changed to 109 Men's, and it was announced that by 2012 all the floors in the building will be occupied by tenants that sell Gyaru-o fashion, expanding and promoting the Gyaru-o subculture even more widely. The rising popularity of Gyaru-o fashion has led to openings of other Shibuya 109-2 shopping centers in districts such as Fukuoka, Machida, Shizuoka, and Nagoya. The Gyaru and Gyaru-o subcultural phenomenon is not confined to Shibuya; it is spreading throughout Japan and raising the authority of the status of authentic Shibuya fashion in Shibuya 109.

TEENS' ROLES AS PRODUCERS OF FASHION IN SHIBUYA

One of the first trends that Japanese teens started was the white loose socks that became the rage among high school girls in 1993. They are long, loose, white baggy knee socks that were deliberately pushed down on the shin like leg warmers. Many teens have their own style of wearing the loose socks. They know how high the top part of the socks should be to achieve the right amount of wrinkles on the legs. Some like the socks to be as long as one yard. By 1996 there were as many as thirty-five different types of loose socks sold in stores. A girl who used to wear the socks in high school said, "These loose socks look stylish. They make your legs look longer. If you didn't have them, it was really embarrassing. My school had a strict dress code, so I would carry one pair in my school bag, and I would put it on on the way home after school."

The loose socks have been a necessary item for junior high and high school girls. The trend is not as strong as it once was in Tokyo, but it is still popular in the suburbs and smaller towns. The product was not marketed by fashion professionals but by the teens themselves. This is when the fashion industry began to notice the marketing potential of teens. The trend that the girls promote to their friends is independent of and goes against the grain of the mainstream fashion system.

POPULAR SALESGIRLS AS DESIGNERS, MARKETERS, AND MERCHANDISERS

Since fashionable clothing—especially in women's wear and even more so in street fashion—depends on rapid changes in style, calculations as to what to buy are fraught with risk (Entwistle 2006: 1). Speed is another important characteristic of Japanese street fashion, especially in Shibuya 109, where merchandise changes quickly. Moreover, teens' tastes are very fickle. No one can accurately predict how long the trends will last. Tokyo girls are soon copied by those in the countryside, and then the girls start looking for a newer and more *kawaii* (cute) look. A store owner explained, "Some brands in 109 retain high sales even after their popularity declines in Tokyo. This is because girls from outside Tokyo come to Shibuya and buy up all the brands that have already lost popularity among Tokyo girls."

Unlike the mainstream fashion industry, the retailers in Shibuya 109 provide new products every two or three weeks so that the teens find something new every time they shop. The clothes are set at a reasonable price; each item is roughly within the price range of thirty to fifty dollars, inexpensive enough for the girls to buy with their own pocket money that they earn by working part-time jobs. Newness has always been the essence of fashion, and shopping is a major form of entertainment among teens.

The market is extremely competitive, and companies cannot afford to lose any profit. Hiring teens as salesgirls, stylists, designers, and marketers is one of the surest ways to boost profits. For instance, such employees know the exact shade of pink that the teens like, the exact length of a T-shirt that is in trend, or how low the teens like to wear their jeans.

Teen-targeted labels also recruit designers from a pool of famous and popular salesgirls working in Shibuya 109. A former salesgirl said, "I used to work there, and once the magazine people took my picture, and I appeared in the magazine, and then I was approached by a fashion company to work as a designer for them." According to her, the company's sales increased by 180 percent after she was hired as a designer. Most of the salespeople are not formally trained in fashion design, but that is not a required qualification to know intuitively which items are *kawaii* and what will sell. They have the ability to pick the right items. Being young and understanding the meaning of *kawaii* gives them an edge over others. The salesgirl explained, "I sometimes go to thrift shops in New York or Los Angeles and buy things that are *kawaii* as samples and bring them back. I might change the color, size, or minor details so that they would meet the taste of the Japanese teens."

Traditionally, fashion designers sketch, make presentation boards, choose fabrics, make samples, and instruct the production process. But this procedure no longer works or is effective. The companies need the teens' ideas for their businesses to survive. A manager at the most popular shoe store explained, "I listen to what my salesgirls and customers say and take their advice seriously. I would change the designs or even the merchandise display according to their taste. Whatever they say usually works."

Shibuya 109 is where the most fashionable salesgirls work. Working in sales in a boutique is not a high-paying job, and many are hired as part-time workers. Their position in the occupational ranking is rather low because the job requires no licenses or special qualifications. In the past a salesperson was often seen as a cashier who put merchandise in a shopping bag. She was usually not that well educated and did not come from a wealthy family. However, this notion is completely reversed in today's Japan, especially among teens. One of the girls who was shopping in Shibuya said:

> It's really difficult to work in Shibuya 109 as a salesgirl, you know. It's competitive to get that position. You should go to the store every Saturday and Sunday and become friends with the salesgirls. Then when there is a position available, they might call you if you have the right look. But the waiting list is really long. If you work at 109, you get a lot of respect from your friends. They envy you.

In many of the stores in Shibuya 109, the salesgirls are so influential in setting the new trends that the teens will buy the exact same outfits that the salesgirls are wearing. The salesgirls are no longer merely selling clothes but buying merchandise and designing for the store labels. They know firsthand what kind of tastes the teen consumers have and what type of merchandise they are looking for because of their direct day-to-day contact with them. The salesgirls become icons, known as *karisuma tenin* (charismatic salespeople). They create their own Web sites and give advice to their followers about how to coordinate the latest items. A salesgirl who once worked in a 109 store said, "In our store, there was a monthly theme, and we salesgirls would dress according to the theme. Many customers would purchase the items that I used to wear. They believed that I was the fashion leader; so as long as they dressed like me, they would be considered fashionable. That makes me feel really good."

The media no longer pay attention to the charismatic salesgirls, and the trend has spread outside Tokyo. One high school girl in Gyaru fashion said:

I go to Nagoya every now and then because my favorite brand has a main store in Nagoya, and I love one of the salesgirls there. I can buy their stuff online, but I still like to go to their store. I like her as a person. I like her style and fashion. I like how she coordinates the items. She is my role model. I want to be like her. I want to work as a salesgirl after I finish high school.

Popteen, one of the major Japanese street fashion magazines, surveyed five hundred teens in Shibuya in 1999 and asked who their role models for fashion were. No celebrities ranked in the top five. The list included amateur high school models who appeared in street fashion magazines and salesgirls in Shibuya 109 who became famous. There is a consensus among the teens that, to find out what is in trend, they need to go to Shibuya 109, which itself has become a brand, and talk to the salesgirls who work there.

SOPHISTICATED CONSUMERS AS PRODUCERS OF FASHION

Those who come to shop at Shibuya 109 also play a crucial role in the production of fashion trends. One of the salesgirls explained why becoming friends with her teen customers is important:

I can get a lot of information through a chit-chat with these girls. I learn what kind of color combination they like or they don't like. They tell me if the skirt is too short or too long. The pant legs are too wide or too narrow. If they say something is *kawaii*, that usually sells. It's very difficult to describe the real meaning of *kawaii*.

The teens' opinions and voices are reflected directly in their merchandise selection.

Many young designers who started their own teen-targeted labels used to be followers of street fashion. They represent the young teenagers and attract a cultlike following. For instance, a designer who was not trained in fashion but who is one of the most popular street designers said, "Making clothes is not enough. You need to imagine who will be wearing your clothes and how they will be worn. We, designers, need to create a lifestyle that comes with the label. We make clothes to communicate with our consumers." The late 1990s was the time when many teens thought that anyone could become a designer without training, and many without any formal fashion degrees did become commercially successful. The definition of a designer as an occupation has changed. This topic will be elaborated further in chapter 10, "The Deprofessionalization of Fashion."

KAWAII AS AN INDUSTRY

As I roam around inside Shibuya 109, on every floor I hear teens screaming "*kawaii!*" at the top of their lungs. *Kawaii* is often translated as *cute* in English, but the term is more than just an adjective. If retailers and manufacturers can materialize *kawaii* into fashion items, their brand will be successful. *Kawaii* is a marketing concept, and the street fashion business in Japan boils down to this one word; it is repeated like a mantra. The concepts *ero-kawaii* (erotic and cute) and *kowa-kawaii* (scary and cute) represent various Shibuya subcultures. More recently, there are *gro-kawa* (grotesque and cute) and *kimo-kawa* (creepy and cute).

According to Sharon Kinsella (1995), young women were the main generators of and actors in cute culture in Japan, and from the consumption of cute goods and services and the wearing of cute clothes to the faking of childish behavior and innocent looks, young women were far more actively involved in cute culture than men. Cute culture permeates among Japanese teens, and it started as youth culture among teenagers, especially young women. It was not founded by business (Kinsella 1995), but the fashion industries took advantage of and made good use of girls' fondness for cute products as a marketing strategy. *Kawaii* is an industry.

According to a survey conducted by Kinsella in 1992, 71 percent of young people between eighteen and thirty years of age either liked or loved *kawaii*-looking people, and almost 56 percent either liked or loved *kawaii* attitudes and behavior (Kinsella 1995).

One of the girls shopping with her friends in Shibuya explained, "*Kawaii* is a state of mind and a lifestyle. My whole life is about being *kawaii*. I'm always thinking about how I can make myself even more *kawaii*."

Japan's teen fashion industry revolves entirely around what girls in Tokyo say is *kawaii*, for this determines what is hot and cool and therefore must be the basis of any fashionable products. What is or is not *kawaii* can only be determined by the teens themselves. A middle-aged man who owns and runs an apparel company or a store has no idea what *kawaii* means to the youth and what will be commercially successful. What is defined as *kawaii* is a mystery to many. One of the store owners said, "Even the teens probably cannot define what is *kawaii*. It's a feeling. When they see something that is *kawaii*, there is an immediate reaction. They intuitively know that it's *kawaii*. That's why we need to have their input as a designer or as a salesperson."

TOKYO GIRLS COLLECTION

The Tokyo Girls Collection (TGC) started in 2005, targeting a niche market of young girls in Shibuya fashion, mostly sold in Shibuya 109. This fashion organization is separate from the semiannual fashion show organized by the Japan Fashion Week in Tokyo. The TGC has created a new mechanism of fashion diffusion and has been far more successful and popular than the Japan Fashion Week, which promotes Japanese high-fashion designer labels. The TGC event showcases youth fashion made by domestic Japanese brands, and the models who appear in the TGC are famous *doku-mo* (reader models, explained in chapter 10, "The Deprofessionalization of Fashion") from various street fashion magazines. The event is open not only to buyers and journalists but also to the general public. The admission is about 5,000 yen (approximately US$63), and the tickets sell very quickly. The event lasts for seven to eight hours. The audience can choose the brands and models they wish to see, and the clothes on the catwalk can be purchased immediately via smartphones. This event has become phenomenally successful, and it is held in Tokyo, Kobe, and other places in Japan, and in Beijing, China.

BLEA: SCHOOL IN SHIBUYA FOR GYARU

The Business Life Education Academy (BLEA) is an all-girls private educational institution that was established in 2000. It offers courses in fashion, nail services, and makeup. In 2001 a high school division was established, and in 2005 a four-year college was in place. United Business Institute, which is affiliated with BLEA, is a similar co-ed institution. It runs high school programs and two- and four-year colleges. It accepts about 250 students per year, and the instructors are all industry professionals.

Both schools provide courses that train students to sharpen their artistic abilities and creative skills. BLEA was initially set up to train salesgirls to work at Shibuya 109. Although unaccredited as a school and completely unknown outside Shibuya and the Gyaru and Gyaru-o communities, it is considered a very hip vocational school among those communities because it is located in the center of Shibuya and has connections with the fashion industries. Tuition is just as expensive as at any other college or university. The schools are not widely exposed and advertise only in pertinent publications. A professor who teaches at BLEA explained to me that "the school is worried about its image since Gyaru does not have a positive image in mainstream Japanese society."

GYARU AND GYARU-O IN SHIBUYA YOUTH GANGS

Two types of social clubs or communities in Shibuya organize huge parties and events for youth. Members in one group are hardly noticeable because they dress in normal clothes. The other group, however, is a youth gang, and they stand out because they are Gyaru and Gyaru-o. They are flamboyant and intimidating in appearance, and that is their definition of aesthetic beauty, according to a Gyaru-o.

While not all Gyaru and Gyaru-o are gang members, youth who belong to a gang in Shibuya are almost always either Gyaru or Gyaru-o. Their gang life starts early, in middle school or high school, which is a prerequisite to becoming a member of a Shibuya gang. One of the members said, "When I was a teenager, I was in a gang in my hometown, in the suburb of Tokyo. But no one hears about you even if you are a gang leader there. But if you are number one in a gang in Shibuya, it means you are number one in Japan!"

The term gang typically refers to small groups that are bound by a common sense of loyalty and territory and that are hierarchically structured around a gang leader. Although the term occurs in a variety of contexts, it is most commonly employed in the sociology of deviance to refer to groups of male adolescents engaged in various deviant activities. According to Frederick Thrasher (1927) and William Foote Whyte (1943), the existence of delinquent gangs was seen to be the product of the urban disorganization of working-class communities providing young men with a sense of identity and excitement. Thrasher demonstrated that gangs were not loosely organized collections of individuals, but rather were integrated groups, bound together by conflict with the wider community and by a strong sense of loyalty and commitment. Albert Cohen (1955) treated working-class gangs as subcultures that rejected middle-class values. He argued that the gang values were nonutilitarian, negative, and delinquent. Richard Cloward and Lloyd Ohlin (1961) explained that delinquent gangs were caught between opportunity structures of the working and middle classes, and this gave rise to different types of subcultures. Subcultures were seen as defensive reactions to limited social opportunities by young, predominantly male, adolescents. The gangs in Shibuya are tightly organized, primary groups for a certain period of time and are impermanent.

Events and parties that the gangs organize act as rituals for the members. The members spend a great deal of time and money preparing for the parties, which occur once or twice a year. Rituals are important for creating feelings of group membership and moral obligations. But any ritual involves some physical activities, which are given a new meaning as ceremonial actions. Some rituals are explicitly ceremonial, while others are natural rituals that are not recognized as such; either way, rituals are a way to bind individual members together.

THE STRUCTURE OF THE SHIBUYA GANG CIRCLE

The number of gangs in Shibuya reached its peak in 2000 (Arai 2009), when the mass media began to pick up Ganguro and Yamamba fashion along with Shibuya 109. Gyaru who used to be in the same group as Gyaru-o began to create their own groups in 2001. By 2008 there were similar circles for Gyaru and Gyaru-o throughout Japan. In Shibuya alone, there were an estimated two hundred gang circles (Arai 2009). There are college divisions as well as high school divisions. For those in the college division of the gang, one can remain a member until the end of the third year in college. They then "retire" or "graduate."

The organization is hierarchical, and one's position depends on when he or she became a member. There is a leader; a deputy leader, who is second in rank; and sometimes a third in rank, who oversees the finance. These three are the ones who have the decision-making power. A leader is chosen by vote as well as discussions by the outgoing/retiring members, especially by the leader and the deputy leader. Evaluations are based on contributions they have made to the group up to that point, their ability to handle girls and flirt, and whether they are intimidating enough in behavior and appearance.

Since Japanese language has formal and informal ways of speech, one can easily tell by listening to people's conversations which speaker is higher in social status or whether the speakers are of the same social standing. No matter how antisocial and deviant they may be, this is something that gang members maintain strictly. Courtesy, politeness, and good manners are intact among the members' ways of communication.

UNOFFICIAL ADMISSION CRITERIA

For any organization to survive, it must recruit new members, and the gangs in Shibuya are no exception. But not everyone is welcome. There are some hidden, but not absolute, requirements that need to be met in order for one to become a member, such as promiscuity or out-of-the-norm behavior. A former member said:

> Those who came to Shibuya from the suburbs or the countryside, the stories they tell tend to be more outrageous than those who are from Tokyo. You can brag and exaggerate about your past because there are no ways to prove or disprove it.

Ninety percent of the admission decision is determined by one's appearance. Potential members are judged by their clothes, makeup, skin color, and hair color. A former gang leader explained:

> You need to look cool if you want to be a member of our gang circle. The basic criteria that we look for are the teenagers who have tanned skin and dyed hair. Boys must look like Gyaru-o. Tanned skin is important. I used to go to a tanning salon two, three times a week so that I look strong and intimidating. Girls are Gyaru or Caba-kura-kei [bar hostesses]. We don't recruit studious, hardworking types wearing boring clothes and a thick pair of glasses. These kids who look normal are not for us. They are totally uncool. They are not welcome to our gang.

Those who are at the top of the hierarchy in the gang are not trend followers but, rather, trendsetters. Trends truly come from the streets. Once the styles are in stores or magazines, they are already uncool among those who initiated them. Once everyone starts to wear a style, it is no longer new and it does not stand out. Gyaru or Gyaru-o fashion is exhibitionistic in nature. Their outward appearance, behavior, speech, and lifestyle should not be normal. If their values follow the mainstream society, they will not be conspicuous. In order for them to receive attention, they need to be different—outrageously different.

DEVIANCE AS VIRTUE

Anything that is unconventional, abnormal, and deviant is a virtue and is considered cool because it stands out from the crowd and attracts social attention. To members, Gyaru and Gyaru-o is an extremely cool gang, and they do not wish to associate with those who are uncool. One needs to be cool to be in the gang.

Sexual norms are extremely liberal among Gyaru and Gyaru-o. According to Yusuke Arai, the members of the gangs value deviance in every sense: sexually, morally, and socially. He writes about an anecdote that a gang member told him:

> One of the members in my gang talked about his experience with a girl who belongs to a different gang. After they had sex, that girl said "Yeah! Now I have 7.5 points this month!" ... Apparently, the girls in that gang compete with the number of guys they sleep with every month. They can't sleep with the same guy twice to get a point. It has to be a different guy each time. Sex without a condom earns them 1.0 point; with a condom, it's 0.5 point; only 0.2 point for oral sex. (2009: 156)

According to gang members' sexual values and norms, the more promiscuous one is at a younger age, the more settled one becomes as an adult. Therefore, promiscuity is very much encouraged for both boys and girls when they enter the gang. New members are often asked about their past sexual experiences. However, this does not apply to the leader or the top executives in the gang because, as Arai (2009: 158), a former gang member, explains, "Our views on sex and relationships are slightly different ... because whatever we do reflects our organization so we tend to maintain abstinence. ... If you are having sex just for the sake of having sex, that could lower the status and the reputation of the gang."

Antisocial behavior, such as jumping into a lake in the middle of the cold winter, drinking your own urine, or setting pubic hair on fire, is viewed as positive behavior. Staying out all night, drinking and dancing, and never going back to your own house but staying at your boyfriend's or girlfriend's house are part of a lifestyle that is encouraged and respected as socially deviant.

One thing that gangs avoid is legal deviance. Some members are involved in jobs that are directly and indirectly tied to professional gangs. Any trouble or conflict, whether legal or illegal, should be resolved within the gang and should never become public. They should never be reported to the authorities. "If you are arrested by the police, that's totally uncool! It means that you did not have the ability to resolve it within your own circle," according to a former gang member. Gang members walk a fine line between the legal and the illegal. Hurting your reputation and having a criminal past on your record is something no one wants after they retire from the gang. But these days gangs are becoming less violent. There may be a situation where the members from different gangs clash and appear to get into fights, but they actually never do.

LIFE AFTER GYARU AND GYARU-O

Unlike many other subcultural groups in the West or in Japan, Gyaru and Gyaru-o retire from the group at a certain age. While they create their own values, beliefs, and norms within the confined district of Shibuya, some of which may be incomprehensible to others, they do not remain deviant for the rest of their lives. The boys in particular know that there is a point at which they need to get out of the group.

When I met a former leader of the gang, he had just retired from his group and had his hair dyed black, getting ready to look for a full-time job after graduating from college. He said, "Because I was so involved in the group, and I was a leader, I now feel so empty." Shibuya subcultures are the only ones that require the members to graduate and retire at a certain age. They throw huge parties for the "retirees," and the members bring flowers and gifts. They need to remain on the stage until everyone finishes giving the gifts. Those who remain on the stage the longest receiving gifts are the ones who are the most popular.

Even today, Arai sends flowers to those who are retiring, and he is a regular customer at one of the flower shops in Shibuya. As he was showing me around Shibuya, a salesperson at the flower shop recognized him immediately. He explained, "This is the shop I always order the flowers at and send them to the members of the gang I used to belong when they retire."

Gyaru become *Onee-Gyaru* (like a sister to Gyaru). Many work in bars and as hostesses, and some stay connected to the gang and help organize events and sell tickets. Gyaru who become mothers are known as *Gyaru Mama*. A magazine called *I Love Mama* was launched in March 2009 targeting mothers who used to be Gyaru, and an association called Gal Mama Association (galmama.jp) has been established. Many Gyaru are rather conservative and marry young compared to Japan's average marriage age. They also have children at a rather young age. Since the Gyaru phenomenon has lasted for almost twenty years, those who used to be Gyaru are already in their thirties, and the Gyaru community is expanding to cater to those who used to be Gyaru.

These boys and girls are not as radical as one may think. Many of the girls have a very conservative outlook on life. One Gyaru I met said, "I now work as a bar hostess, but after I have enough money, I want to go back to school. Eventually, I want a stable job like a social worker. Now, I am just trying to save money." When asked what their future goal is, many answer "to have a nice family."

While they do not remain permanent members, the networks of Gyaru and Gayru-o continue throughout their lives. They play the role of a deviant in a marginal subcultural group but are well aware of what is expected for a normal individual.

CONCLUSION

In an age when anything can be purchased online, teen girls still make the trip to Shibuya because it is sacred territory for Gyaru and Gyaru-o. Shibuya 109 and 109-2 are not merely shopping centers but are major landmarks of Shibuya and pilgrimages for boys and girls. Multiple subcultures emerge from this district, and they are promoted and diffused by different institutions of fashion. Teen boys and girls are the producers of fashion, and the industries move quickly to commercialize the trend before the teens come up with a new one. This is how Shibuya as a fashion-producing district and Gyaru and Gyaru-o subcultures have remained.

–5–

Harajuku: The Youth in Silent Rebellion

Harajuku is only a couple of train stops from Shibuya (see chapter 4) and is also a very popular fashion district among youth. In the early 1980s a subculture called the Bamboo Tribe appeared in Harajuku on weekends, and the members danced to music in Yoyogi Park wearing bright-colored silky costumes. But, unlike the current subcultures that have been in existence for more than a decade, the Bamboo Tribe did not last long and faded away after a couple of years. Broadly speaking, there are two genres of fashion in Harajuku today (Kawamura 2006a): Lolita subcultural fashion and *Ura-Hara* (back streets of Harajuku) fashion.[1] The focus of this chapter is the Lolita subculture that emerged in the late 1990s. I explore the origin of the Lolita look, variations of Lolita fashion, what these particular stylistic expressions mean to the members, and how this subculture has spread within Japan and overseas.

HARAJUKU AS A SACRED TERRITORY FOR LOLITA

Jingu Bridge is sometimes called Harajuku Bridge because it is next to Harajuku station. When I began my fieldwork in Tokyo in 2004, the place was full of Japanese teens dressed in different costumes. Some were dressed in very feminine dress with lots of lace trimmings and frills around the skirt hem and the edge of the sleeves; a style known as the Lolita look. Harajuku is a mecca for the Lolita subculture, just as Shibuya is a mecca for Gyaru and Gyaru-o. Lolita style can be seen as a counter-reaction to Gyaru style in Shibuya and others that evolved out of it. Lolita girls portray the image of a Victorian doll, with fair skin and wearing a dress with ruffles, a bonnet and ribbons, flat shoes, and sometimes a blonde wig, a feminine handbag, and a small umbrella. The keywords for this look are *girlie* and *princesslike*. Like many other subcultures in Japan, Lolita is dominated by girls. The followers create and use their own language and abbreviations that outsiders cannot comprehend, such as *Loli-bra*, which means a Lolita brand, or a *cardi,* which means a cardigan. The followers of this style are bound together by their stylistic expressions, and many have created online communities and are constantly communicating online or via text-messaging.

Lolita is one of the most popular subcultural styles found in the Harajuku area. One of the girls I interviewed said, "I love Harajuku. I go there almost every day. I like to watch people walking down the streets of Harajuku. I love the atmosphere of Harajuku. I like the smell of Harajuku. It's a sacred place for us."

Local landmarks of Harajuku are Takeshita Street, with small stores selling Lolita brands, and La Foret, a department store. Similar to Shibuya 109, the streets around Harajuku station on weekends are so packed that pedestrians hardly have space to walk.

The population of Lolita on the Harajuku Bridge started to decline in the past few years, and some claim that this is a sign that the subculture is dying out. On the contrary, Harajuku remains exclusive and sacred for Lolita. A Lolita girl says:

> I've been there only a few times. The Lolita girls you see on that bridge are simply cosplaying and are not real Lolita. We, the real ones, never go there. Those who used to hang out there were the fans of the Visual-kei musicians with heavy makeup and flashy outfits, and they are not real Lolita. The real ones are well and alive, and we are here to stay.

Lolita fashion was once a fad, but as a fad it has died out because Harajuku subcultures are very much tied to Visual-kei rock bands, which emphasize their costume and makeup, and the popularity of such bands is on the decline. Those who are left are the authentic Lolita members who are here to stay. The authentic ones enjoy being marginal. Unlike the Gyaru and Gyaru-o subcultures found in the Shibuya district, which require members to leave the group when they reach a certain age, Lolita have no graduation or retirement age. They can, according to one of the Lolita girls I interviewed, "remain a Lolita as long as you look young and don't have wrinkles around your eyes."

LOLITA AS AN IDENTITY AND A LIFESTYLE

Westerners may mistakenly associate the Lolita subculture with the novel *Lolita*, written by Vladimir Nabokov in 1955. The book is internationally famous for its controversial plot in which Humbert, a middle-aged man, becomes obsessed with a twelve-year-old girl named Dolores Haze, also called Dolly, Lolita, Lola, Lo, and L. Similarly, in Japan, the term *Lolita complex*, often shortened to *Loli-con*, refers to a man's perverse sexual preference for young girls. Therefore, the term *Lolita* carries a negative sexual connotation. However, the Japanese Lolita subculture that emerged in Harajuku has nothing to do with such references. Many Lolita members know nothing about the Nabokov novel. According to Momo Matsuura, author of *The World, Myself and*

Lolita Fashion (2007) and herself a Lolita, the term first appeared in the September 1987 issue of a Japanese fashion magazine called *Ryukou Tsushin*; Lolita as a category of fashion appeared in the early 1990s.

THE ORIGIN OF LOLITA STYLE

Following the historical evolution and development of Japanese fashion, it is evident that today's Lolita style is nothing new. Some of the main characteristics of a Lolita look have been present for many years.

The brands Milk (established in 1970 by Hitomi Okawa) and Pink House (started in 1973 by Isao Kaneko) were the forerunners of this fashion genre. Both brands became extremely popular among teens in the 1970s and 1980s. Milk still has a store in the middle of Harajuku and holds a very high status among Lolita followers. Kaneko sold Pink House and remained a head designer for a number of years, but eventually left the company in 1994. These brands often appeared in *Olive* magazine, which created a trend called Olive Girls. Milk and Pink House clothes had all the characteristics found in Lolita fashion, such as frills, lace trimmings, ribbons, sheer fabrics such as chiffon, and layers of petticoats, projecting a childlike, innocent, girlie image.

The designers who used to work for Milk later created their own labels with a similar taste and image. Rei Yanagikawa began a children's wear label called Shirley Temple in 1974; Megumi Murano started a brand called Jane Marple in 1985. Atuski Onishi's brand that began in 1984 had a girlie image, and Akinori Isobe, who used to work for Onishi, started a brand called Baby, the Stars Shine Bright in 1988. More and more brands with a Lolita touch followed: Metamorphose in 1993, Marble in 1998, Victorian Maiden in 1998, Mary Magdalene in 2003, and Innocent World in 2009, among many others. Among the foreign brands, Vivienne Westwood, which began in 1971, is a symbol of Lolita fashion. Her first store in Japan opened in La Foret in 1978, and it has been popular among Japanese Lolita.

One of the Lolita girls said:

> From the outsider's viewpoint, our dresses seem all the same. They may look like a uniform. That is a false conception. New styles and new collections come out every season from Lolita brands. Lolita styles do change. They are not static. So we always try to catch with the latest trend in Lolita fashion. Some are manufactured only in limited numbers and that's how the prices go and its status goes up. Sometimes, you have to place an order at the beginning of the season. They don't sell it in the store.

While Gyaru and Gyaru-o fashion bought at Shibuya 109 is rather inexpensive, Lolita dresses can be expensive, so many followers buy them at secondhand stores in Harajuku. Some stores sell only secondhand Lolita brands, such as Maiden Clothing in Osaka and Closet Child, which has stores in Harajuku, Shinjuku, Ikebukuro, Yokohama, and Sagamihara. Subcultural members create their own values and norms, and purchasing exclusive Lolita items gives members status and respect among followers.

FROM COLLECTIVE TO INDIVIDUALISTIC IDENTIFICATION WITHIN THE LOLITA SUBCULTURE

While Western youth subcultures, such as British punk or U.S. inner-city hip-hop, often convey a strong political or ideological statement, the Lolita girls claim that they have no message and say that their distinctive styles are purely for enjoyment. Fashion and how they dress are of utmost importance, because they want to stand out and be noticed; they have no intention of rebelling against the formal and traditional ways. None of them consider their community as a counterculture. They enjoy hanging out in small or large groups around train stations, going to events together, and taking pictures of each other. Those who belong to the subcultures are connected by a strong bond and spend time with friends who dress in similar fashion. One's choice of dress and fashion is a representation of one's inner self as well as one's group membership. Having no message to express does, however, convey a message; it may be a hidden one of helplessness and hopelessness. Thus, group members do have a message—silent rebellion.

Muggleton (2000), who is in support of postmodern theory, explains that subcultures today exist in postmodern form. His idea of postmodern subculture involves a combination of hybridity, diversity, and fluidity. According to Muggleton (2000: 15), traditional points of collective identification, such as class, gender, race, and place, are gradually replaced by elective, build-your-own, consumer identities, and the members of subcultures are postmodern in that they demonstrate a fragmented, individualistic, and stylistic identification. This is a sensibility that manifests itself as an expression of freedom from structure, control, and restraint, ensuring that stasis is rejected in favor of movement and fluidity (Muggleton 2000: 158).

Style differentiation no longer defines different social classes. There is a great deal of interclass and intraclass mobility. Social identity that used to be based on the economic and political sphere is now based on something outside of these spheres. The consumption of cultural goods, such as fashionable clothing, performs an increasingly important role in the construction of personal identity, while the satisfaction of material needs and the emulation of superior classes are secondary (Crane 2000). There is a shift from class fashion to consumer fashion. In postmodern cultures, consumption is conceptualized as a form of role playing, as consumers seek to project conceptions of identity that are continually evolving. Social class is less evident and less important in constructing one's self-image and identity in contemporary society.

MASKING ONESELF WITH A LOLITA IDENTITY AND ACHIEVING A SENSE OF SELF-LIBERATION

We are what we wear. Many of the Lolita girls I talked to said that when they dress Lolita, whether it is Punk or Sweet or another variation, their personality changes. They feel more confident and strong. It is empowering. One girl said, "My life revolves around Lolita. I am constantly thinking about Lolita. I went to a fashion school because Lolita brands are so expensive and I cannot afford them. Now that I have acquired the sewing skill, I can design and make my own Lolita dress. I even created my own brand online." Another high school girl dressed in Punk Lolita said: "I couldn't talk to you if I were not dressed like this. When I am at school, I am usually quiet and shy. I am an introvert. But I can change when I dress Lolita. I feel powerful." The Lolita girls are playing the role of a princess. An Italian Lolita girl said:

> I like the feeling when I look at myself at the mirror with Lolita clothes. I may be naive, but I really feel like a princess. I love it. I like the Lolita culture too, but probably because it suits my usual way to act and think. And if I'm dressed like a princess, I act even more properly like a lady.

A Japanese Lolita girl who wears the style on weekends goes to a butler café (see chapter 6), where waiters are dressed as English butlers and treat female customers like princesses. She continued:

> When I dress Lolita, it changes my demeanor. The way I talk. The way I walk. Everything about me changes. I feel like a princess. I love coming to this café, because I am treated like a true lady. This is real me. When I am not dressed Lolita, that's not me. Lolita is real me. When I put on a Lolita dress, I am thinking to myself "which look do I want today?" After deciding that I want to go Ama-Loli,[2] then I put all the accessories together to make that look. That thinking process itself and turning into a princess are great fun.

Another Lolita told me:

> I became interested when I was sixteen to seventeen years old. I first saw *Kera!* [magazine]. Then my mother bought me a dress at Marui One that costs about 30,000 yen [about US$370]. I like the attention I get. I get a sense of superiority

when people look at me. I change from a style to style. One time I liked *Hime-kei* for six months and wore LizLisa. It just happened that the type of dress I like is Lolita.[3]

Lolita followers are aware that their style is often perceived as strange, and people turn their heads to look at them when they walk on the streets. The Japanese Lolita said, "If my boyfriend doesn't like me in Lolita, I would rather break up with him than change my style." Lolita is self-expression and self-satisfaction. Just by looking Lolita, girls may appear as if they are subservient and dressing in a way to get male attention. On the contrary, these girls do it for themselves or for other girls. If they care at all about what people think of them, it is the opinion of other Lolita girls. They compete among themselves and criticize each other. A Lolita follower said: "When I pass another Lolita girl on the street, I cannot help but check her out. Just look at her in the corner of my eyes to see how she put her Lolita outfit together from head to toe. If she looks great, there is a slight sense of jealousy, I admit." Adornment and self-display are always social. The girls never simply wear Lolita dress and stay at home. They dress Lolita when they go outside to meet their Lolita friends. For some it is an authentic identity; for others, it is a temporary identity with a mask. One thing that is certain is that dressing Lolita takes them to a different world psychologically and emotionally, and that in turn affects and changes their personae for that moment.

A Lolita who goes by the name Alice said:

I got interested in Lolita in my second year in high school after I saw a magazine *Alice*. My family did not like it first. But I used to go to secondhand stores such as Bodyline and Closet Child and bought them. I took a night class at Bunka so I can now make Lolita-style dresses. My boyfriend doesn't like me in Lolita, but I don't care. I feel happy when I am wearing Lolita. I enjoy people's attention. It is the image of Marie Antoinette. I basically dress Classic Lolita. My favorite brand is Innocent World. . . . Lolita is my life itself. My life is all about Lolita. I am always thinking about Lolita.

Recently, some fashion schools have launched classes that teach Lolita fashion. Ueda Yasuko Fashion School in Osaka created a major in Gothic and Lolita fashion, in which students learn to design, drape, create patterns, and sew Gothic and Lolita-inspired dress. Vantan Design Institute, a fashion school in Tokyo, also has a major in Goth and Lolita fashion that trains students to become brand designers or costume designers.

All the Lolita girls I met dressed Lolita only on weekends or during their free time, and never to their jobs. The majority of them change into a Lolita identity on a weekly basis. During my research in Tokyo, I met only one student who said she always wore Lolita wherever she went. She was studying to be an accountant, so once she passed the exam to work as an apprentice accountant she felt that she would have to give up Lolita.

A separate identity is assumed when girls dress Lolita. One Lolita girl I interviewed said:

> From Monday to Friday, I work as an administrative assistant. I wear a uniform. I feel so oppressed on weekdays. But on weekends, I dress Lolita and go out shopping or to events. I feel so free. It is another identity. It is a totally different identity from the one that I have on weekdays. In fact, my real identity is the one I have on weekends. My Lolita identity is real me. This is *real me*.

Humans need to define their identity in one way or another whether it is based on gender, sexuality, occupation, income level, or race/ethnicity. Being a Lolita is an identity that gives the followers of this subculture a solid sense of belonging. Through dress, they assure themselves that they are part of the group.

Lolita followers have created numerous online communities around the world. There are rules as to what kind of topics can be posted on the Internet so that the subcultural identity of each site can be maintained. There are discussions on Lolita brands, instructions about how to put together a Lolita look, and how to make handmade Lolita items. Members share images from different Lolita brands and auction, sell, and buy Lolita-related items. The Lolita members are bound together by their stylistic expressions and have created a global subcultural network. They communicate both face-to-face and online. They organize meetings and tea parties and get together on weekends to take pictures of each other to post online.

There are no official organizations, clubs, or gangs that Lolita belong to. They tend to organize groups of their own and engage in Lolita-related activities together.

A girl who likes Sweet Lolita said:

> I organized a Christmas party last year. I posted it on Mixi. Only two girls showed up, but that's okay. It was fun. We went to a restaurant that Lolita girls often go to. Even if we don't know each other and we have never met before, we can connect right away because we all love Lolita. We are connected by Lolita. We end up talking about it for hours.

Like many other Lolitas I have met, this girl's work is unrelated to fashion or Lolita; she works at a fast-food restaurant so she cannot dress Lolita when she is working. But otherwise, she is almost always Lolita. She said: "Lolita is central to my everyday life. I cannot imagine a life without Lolita."

VARIATIONS OF LOLITA STYLE

Lolita girls put much effort into getting the right look from head to toe. A Lolita girl explains: "It is difficult to coordinate a Lolita style, so many of us end up buying the entire outfit with accessories and shoes from one brand. That's why it gets expensive." Variations to a Lolita look include:

- *Ama-Loli* (Sweet Lolita): the typical Lolita style with lots of lace, ruffles, and frills; mostly white and pastel colors such as blue and pink.
- *Classical/Elegant Lolita*: similar to *Ama-Loli* but with fewer ruffles and frills.
- *Ero-Loli* (Erotic Lolita): a controversial style because, in principle, Lolita has no erotic elements, and too much skin should not be exposed.
- *Futago-Loli* (Twin Lolita): two girls dress in the same Lolita outfit.
- *Gosu-Loli* (Gothic and Lolita): the combination of Gothic and Lolita elements; monochromatic palette, often black and white.
- *Guro-Loli* (Gore Lolita): using bandages or blood splatters or anything that looks gory.
- *Hime-Loli* (Princess Lolita): similar to Classical Lolita, with pastel colors; princess-looking, often with a tiara.
- *Kuro-Loli* (Black Lolita): black from head to toe.
- *Ouji* (Prince for Lolita): the male version who would accompany a Lolita, or a Lolita girl who does not want to wear a skirt.
- *Pinku-Loli* (Pink Lolita): pink from head to toe.
- *Punk Loli* (Punk Lolita): a combination of Lolita and Punk elements, such as leather, zippers, safety pins, and chains.
- *Qi-Loli* (Chinese Lolita): Lolita combined with traditional Chinese elements.
- *Sailor-Loli* (Sailor Lolita): nautical style inspired by Japanese school uniforms.
- *Wa-Loli* (Japanese Lolita): Lolita combined with traditional Japanese elements, such as kimono and obi. (Lolitafashion.org n.d.)

New variations or combinations of existing ones—such as Light Gothic Lolita, Candy Lolita—or those that merge with other subcultures—such as *Loli-Gyaru* or *Gyaru-Loli*—are appearing. According to a magazine editor I spoke with, these new groups occur naturally, and one cannot tell exactly who or how it started.

Each Lolita variation has its own distinctive style and rules that the followers adhere to. The Lolita subcultural lifestyle has spread worldwide among teens in the United States, Europe, and Asia. While some belong to a specific Lolita category, others enjoy choosing a style depending on different occasions. Some Lolita impose strict rules as to what is considered authentic Lolita, and heated discussions take place on Internet message boards.

Whichever Lolita look one dresses in, it is difficult to tell whether one is a real Lolita or a cosplayer. When I started my research on Lolita subculture in 2004, I thought Lolita was part of cosplay, and I could not tell the difference between a maid costume worn by a waitress at Maid Café in Akihabara and Lolita fashion.

Even industry professionals are confused about the differences. A fashion marketer I interviewed in Tokyo explained, "This is a style that has been developing out of the cosplay phenomenon in the streets of Japan since the mid-1990s. The look has evolved and is slowly beginning to take roots in other countries around the world." Lolita girls are often mistaken as cosplayers who dress like their favorite characters in Japanese anime and manga, but they insist that they are not.

An American Lolita girl told me, "When people see us on the streets or coffee shops, they think we are in a play. They think this is our theatrical costume. That's why a lot of people think this is part of Japanese cosplay, and we are cosplayers. But we are *not!*" I heard similar comments from Japanese Lolita and European Lolita over and over again. For the authentic Lolita followers, it is highly offensive for them to be called cosplayers. Lolita is an important part of their life; sometimes, it consumes their entire life. Reflecting many Lolita followers, one Lolita girl said:

> I am constantly thinking about Lolita. It is my whole life and identity. Cosplay is not a reflection of your inner self. It is just an entertainment. It's their hobby. You are playing a character in anime for a couple of hours. We are not like that at all. We live Lolita. We breathe Lolita. Lolita is our authentic self.

MASS MEDIA EXPOSURE TO SPREAD LOLITA SUBCULTURE

To sustain a subculture—and keep it from simply being a group of friends who share the same values, norms, and beliefs that may go against the mainstream—it needs to spread to the masses first through word of mouth and then through the media. Yusuke Tajima, editor-in-chief of *Kera!* magazine said:

> We need to make more occasions and places where the girls can go to wearing Lolita dress because Lolita styles are very distinct. The majority of them don't wear it every day. They wear it for special occasions when they meet other Lolita. Otherwise, the Lolita market will shrink, and Lolita-related businesses will shrink.

An owner of a well-known Lolita brand says:

> When we started the brand, I told my girls to always dress in Lolita. If we had a new bag designed, I gave it to all my workers and told them to carry it every day, every where they go. They were like walking advertisers. Then people would ask them, "Oh, that's cute. Where did you get it?" Luckily, people and the media began to notice our brand slowly. Our two designers started to appear on TV and in fashion magazines.

Fashion as a genre or a category spreads quickly through the media and via the Internet. There needs to be a network of industries and institutions to help spread the subcultural fashion phenomenon.

Kera! is the magazine that Lolita followers read. (It was launched in 1998 with the title *Kerouac*.) *Kera!*'s editorial team arranges a photo shoot every month at the Marui One department store in Shinjuku (not Harajuku) so that anyone who wants to show off her style can line up and get her picture taken by a professional photographer.[4] The best ensembles appear in the magazine. Readers' comments in *Kera!* show that the girls eagerly await the chance to appear in the magazine:

> Hi, everyone; I have been influenced so much by Kera! that I am now going through a make over. ... I will definitely be on the magazine someday! (January 2010: 118)

> Some day, I will be cute enough to appear in Kera! (April 2010: 110)

> I didn't buy Kera for two months because I wanted to be an ordinary girl. But I saw the January issue and felt an intense urge to buy it. I am now convinced that it is a source of my life. I don't care if people around me don't understand me. ... What's best for me is not normal for others or how people look at me strange as long as I am happy, I can bear it. ... I am back to Kera-kko. (March 2010: 108)

> Kera! is my textbook. (July 2010: 104)

> Just started highschool! Gonna walk around Harajuku and dress up so that I'd get my picture taken! (July 2010: 105)

> I want to be Kera's model. (November 2010: 61)

Regarding Marui One, one of the girls I interviewed said, "I come here almost every month. It is a great feeling to get your picture taken. It is a thrill to check in the magazine whether I am in it or not every month."

Besides *Kera!* there is *Gothic & Lolita Bible*, a quarterly magazine that began publication in Japan in 2001 and has been published in English since 2008.

A novel titled *Shimotsuma Monogatari* (Kamikaze Girls), written by Nobara Takemoto, was published in 2002 and became a movie in 2004. A character in the novel, Momoko, wears the brand, Baby, the Stars Shine Bright. She commutes two and a half hours by train from Ibaragi to Tokyo to buy the Lolita outfits. Momoko is obsessed with Lolita fashion. "If you claim that you are a real Lolita, you have seen the movie and must have read all the novels by Nobara Takemoto. We look up to him," according to a Lolita girl.

Mana-sama of Malice Mizer, a Visual-kei band, is another figure who is worshipped within the Lolita communities. He is the most extreme in terms of outfits and makeup. He is known to have started a genre called Gothic Lolita, based on the separate genres of Goth and Lolita. He started a label called Moi-Même-Moitié, and his fans dress Gothic Lolita to attend his concerts. He is androgynous in appearance and wears men's as well as women's clothes, just like Nobara Takemoto. Over time, celebrities eventually lead the subculture and become the followers' role models.

Various organizations host events and parties for Lolita, and many Lolita organize meetings and arrange tea parties (they do not drink coffee or alcoholic beverages) themselves. Lolita brands, such as Angelic Pretty and Triple Fortune, organize tea parties on a regular basis for their customers and show their new collections. There is also a trade fair twice a year for Lolita fashion called A La Mode Market. To further promote Lolita fashion subcultures, major events are organized such as La Foret x Kera x Rock Collections in 2009, Harajuku Style Collection, Butoukai Cool Japan Style 2010, and Hyper Japan 2010 in London. These are the events that mobilize Lolita followers, and they confirm the girls' camaraderie and sense of belonging.

CONCLUSION

Harajuku is a sacred place for Lolita followers. Although those who used to hang out on the bridge next to the station are, for unknown reasons, no longer there, the Lolita subculture is still intact. The fad has diminished, but hard-core Lolita fans persist on the streets of Harajuku. Their territory may be expanding to the neighboring district, Shinjuku. Lolita is probably the most popular subcultural fashion overseas, with Lolita followers in Europe, the United States, South America, and Asia. With the Internet, subcultures are becoming borderless and are spreading to every corner of the world. The exclusive Lolita look in any country functions as a visible group identity for the teens, creates a bond, and becomes a shared sign of membership affiliation. It is also used to communicate their ideas, intentions, purposes, and thoughts. These styles are functional and purposeful only within the specific symbolic territory among particular groups of people. The Lolita girls rely on a distinctive appearance to proclaim their subcultural identity by which they define themselves. It is the ultimate self-expression for them that asserts their social self.

Akihabara and Ikebukuro: Playing with Costume as Entertainment

Akihabara and Ikebukuro are districts in Tokyo where anime and manga fans, many of whom are cosplayers, visit. This chapter will describe some of the differences and similarities between the cosplay subculture and the other Japanese youth subcultures discussed in this book. In Akihabara and Ikebukuro, there are anime- and manga-related stores throughout the districts in addition to coffee shops, where waiters and waitresses dress in costume. One of the most popular types of places are maid cafés, where the waitresses dress in a traditional maid look with a black dress, a white apron, and a white headband or cap. Unlike Gyaru and Gyaru-o in Shibuya, Lolita in Harajuku, or *Age-jo* in Shjinjuku (see chapter 7), anime and manga fans are not immediately recognizable, but they represent a large subcultural group in Akihabara, and they are bound together by their interest in costume entertainment. Ikebukuro is primarily a district for female anime and manga fans.

OTAKU SUBCULTURE IN AKIHABARA

After the start of radio broadcasting and the invention of television, Akihabara became, in the early 1950s, Japan's largest electronics district; it was *the* place to purchase electronics. As consumption increased among the Japanese population, so did the popularity of Akihabara in Japan and even overseas. Foreigners and tourists visited Akihabara to purchase Japanese electronics, such as refrigerators, ovens, Walkmans, rice cookers, and DVD players, at reasonable prices.

In 2000 the anime trend emerged out of computer games, and Akihabara began to attract *Otaku* (nerds), who are mostly boys obsessed with anime, manga, and video games. The Otaku created a huge subcultural community in Akihabara. The manga and anime industries are central to the Akihabara subculture, and there are related auxiliary industries, such as video games, anime songs, anime and manga figurines, maid cafés, cosplay restaurants, and cosplay costumes.

OTAKU

According to the *Otaku Encyclopedia* (Galbraith and Schodt 2009), the term *Otaku* originates from a formal second-person pronoun meaning "your home" or "your house" in Japanese. Since the 1980s the term has been used to refer to people who are heavily interested in Japanese pop culture, such as anime, manga, and video games. A whole generation that was previously marginalized with such negative labels as *geek* and *nerd* are now the mainstream. The Otaku subculture has achieved international recognition, and Otaku is a term used even in English-speaking countries. Recently, besides anime Otaku and manga Otaku, the term has been used to refer to anyone with obsessive interests, such as Train Otaku, Doll Otaku, PC Otaku, and Movie Otaku; they are fanatics and collectors who are experts in one area. It is more than just a hobby because they invest a great deal of time, money, and energy in the related activities. They are hard-core fans and are self-claimed information fetishists of manga. An Otaku explained: "We are fanatics, so once we find a person who is also Otaku, we go on and on talking about our favorite anime and manga for hours, sometimes for ten hours or so. People probably think we are crazy."

The implication of the term Otaku used to be somewhat negative and derogatory. Tustomu Miyazaki, a serial killer, kidnapped and murdered four girls in Tokyo and Saitama between 1988 and 1989. When he was arrested, the police found a huge collection of anime and manga in his apartment. The media labeled him the Otaku Murderer, which brought the term to the attention of the general public, who was not familiar with it prior to this incident. Since then, Otaku has been associated with the negative image of an antisocial, deviant individual, and has resulted in a moral panic in mainstream society, which has led to prejudice against the Otaku community.

Furthermore, individuals with an obsessive interest in anime and manga may spend a lot of time alone in their room, not interacting or communicating with others. While there is no scientific correlation between Otaku and *hiki-komori* (those who are severely withdrawn from society; explained in chapter 3, "Japanese Youth in a Changing Society"), Otaku can be isolated, having cut off all social contacts with their peers and with family members in some cases. *Hiki-komori* can weaken and lessen the degree of social integration, which is a key to well-being. A recovering *hiki-komori* boy I interviewed said, "I've spent five to six years as a *hiki-komori* and hardly ever went out of my room. I was playing with the video game or watching anime in the middle of the night on TV or on DVD or surfing on the Internet. I am also Otaku, maybe a *hiki-komori* Otaku."

Providing a space for the Otaku community creates a sort of stability and security for those whose obsessive interests are not validated. Subcultural membership gives the sense of belonging and the affirmation that there are others who share the same interests and the same values.

COSPLAY: PERFORMING A TRANSIENT IDENTITY AS ENTERTAINMENT

Anime and manga fans share common interests and hobbies, one of which is called cosplay, a portmanteau of the words *costume* and *play*. Cosplay is a trend sweeping through the anime and manga subcultures not only in Japan but also the world. People dress themselves as characters from Japanese anime and manga. The purpose of cosplay is fun and entertainment by dressing up as favorite characters. Although cosplay is transient and temporary, its adherents enjoy playing the role of a character and emulating the character from head to toe. Although not all anime and manga fans are cosplayers, cosplayers are almost always anime and manga fans.

Many stores in Akihabara and Ikebukuro sell ready-made costumes for cosplay. Younger children who have no sewing skills buy them so they can attend cosplay events that take place almost every weekend throughout Japan. But the cosplayers who earn the most respect from their peers are those who make their own costumes. One of the long-time cosplayers I interviewed explained:

> The fundamental rule among the cosplayers is that they must make and sew their own costume. The closer to the character in anime or manga you get, the higher the respect and status you earn as a cosplayer. Once I know which character I am playing, I watch the DVD hundreds of times and draw sketches to check all the details. To make a two-dimensional character three-dimensional is the biggest challenge, but it's also great fun.

A group of cosplayers decides on a particular anime or manga, they negotiate who will play each character, and they set a date to complete their costume. Once everyone finishes sewing their own costume, they attend an event, rent a photo studio, or choose an appropriate scene and take pictures.

Two major magazines target cosplayers in their teens and early twenties. *Dengeki Layers* was launched in 2003 with a circulation of 80,000, and *CosMode*, which started in 2008 and has been published in Thailand since December 2009, has a circulation of 100,000. Both provide detailed instructions on how to create a particular character and make it as authentic as possible. The magazines provide life-size paper patterns that readers can use to make the costumes.

In addition to the magazines, numerous books explain what type of makeup to use, what color contacts are needed to create a specific face, and how to make a wig with the right color, length, and texture. There are also books on how to make a Japanese kimono–inspired costume, because doing so requires specialized dressmaking skills that are different from Western dressmaking techniques.

In cosplay the youth play a role and become actors simply by changing their outfits, which in turn changes their identity temporarily. Cosplayers feel an enormous sense of satisfaction from the experience. They continue to attend various events to show off their handmade costumes, and sometimes they take part in cosplay contests. They post their pictures on blogs, Facebook, or Myspace and ask others to look at them and comment.

A cosplayer told me:

> You become someone else at that moment when you are cosplaying. The process of making a costume is fun, and wearing it and getting people's attention is also fun. Then you display it to everyone.

She likes to cosplay a male character. Her favorite manga is about a Ninja named Nintama Rantaro and his friends and peers at a Ninja school. She said she loves the characters in this manga, so her cosplay is always one of the Ninja characters. She told me, "The purpose of cosplay is in its interpretation of particular manga or anime. You try to become a character just as an actor or an actress in the movie tries to play a role. You study the character's mannerisms or body language."

COMIC MARKET: A PERFORMANCE STAGE FOR COSPLAYERS

The largest and the most important event for anime and manga fans as well as cosplayers is the Comic Market, known as Comi-ke, which takes place in Tokyo twice a year in August and December.[1] It runs for three days and attracts more than 500,000 people from all over the world. This convention—where anime and manga fans get together and their works can be bought, sold, displayed, or exchanged—and other comic book conventions give fans the opportunity to cosplay. Elizabeth Licata, a U.S. cosplay champion in 2009, explains how she started cosplaying:

> I'd been going to comic book conventions since middle school, and it just seemed to make sense that I would dress up. Everything about it keeps me interested. A new series that I get really excited about will make me want to dress up, or I might see a design I want to try, or maybe I'll read about a sewing technique and I'll want to give it a try so I'll look for a way to include that. Sometimes, I just see a wig that is so gorgeous I have to have it, and then I'll buy it and figure out ways to wear it. (quoted in Fasano 2009: 14)

Comi-ke organizers provide locker rooms in which cosplayers can change their outfits and designate a space outside the halls for registered groups of cosplayers. Some cosplayers are regulars and attract many photographers.

Comi-ke hosts the Doujin-shi Market, which is an exhibition for self-published manga or novels by unknown amateur artists and writers. Exhibitors rent a space or a desk within the huge exhibit halls and sell their work. *Doujin* means folks who share the same taste, and *shi* means magazine. Since 1975 anime and manga fans at Comi-ke can distribute or sell self-published magazines to specific groups and communities.

The popularity of Japanese manga, both in Japan and abroad, has created not only a lucrative commercial industry but also a huge amateur comics scene, and there are countless groups of amateur artists who create and publish their own works (Schodt 1996).

One of the popular genres in fanzines is a kind of erotic manga that features homosexual relationships between male lovers. It is called *Yaoi* or BL, an acronym of boys' love. This genre is particularly popular among female anime and manga fans, who call themselves *Fujoshi*, literally translated as Rotten Girls, and are the female counterpart of Otaku, who are mainly boys.

COSTUME/COSPLAY CAFÉS

In 1999 a manufacturer and retailer of video games, anime, and manga called Broccoli opened a cosplay restaurant on a trial basis. Waitresses dressed in high school uniforms. It received positive responses from customers, so the company set up a coffee shop in one of its other stores in 2000 and had the waitresses dress in different anime and manga characters. A year later, in 2001, it changed the waitress outfits to traditional maid costumes and renamed the place Cure Maid Café, which is still in existence in Akihabara.

What is distinct about these coffee shops or restaurants is not only the way the waitresses dress but also how the customers (mostly men) are treated— as masters coming home, not as guests entering a coffee shop. As they enter the shop, the girls say, "Welcome home, Master!" The waitresses play games with the customers, chat with them, and make them feel at home. These cafés aim to create an atmosphere that is soothing and comforting. I asked a man in his mid-twenties who told me that he frequents a maid café why he goes there. He said:

I enjoy going there a couple of times a week. On Friday nights, I am always there. It's a great feeling when a girl says, "Welcome home, Sir!" You feel so welcomed.

My grandmother was married and divorced three times, and my mother was married and divorced twice. I never knew where I belonged while growing up. Now I live by myself. I don't have a girlfriend. When I go home, there is no one who says to me "welcome home." I guess I don't have the warmth of a family. So it's really comforting in a sense when I go there and meet all these maid girls, and they say to me "welcome home!" the moment I walk in.

Another anime fan told me why he thinks maid cafés are so popular:

These days, girls are getting really independent, tough, and strong. It seems that they no longer need us men. But if you go to these cafés, the girls are cute, innocent, and sweet. When a guy meets a girl who looks so vulnerable, it makes you want to protect her. It, in a way, satisfies our ego, and it is also a relief to know that these submissive girls still exist today.

Similar to amateur models or salesgirls who become popular and turn into celebrities, some maid café waitresses have become popular singers and dancers. Thus, many of the girls working in Akihabara are treated as potential celebrities. Customers are not allowed to take pictures without permission. When they are allowed to take pictures, they are often charged for them.

I visited a cosplay restaurant with my photographer. When we went there, the waitress was wearing a high school uniform. The interior of the restaurant looked like a classroom with desks, chairs, and a blackboard. We found out that each day of the week is a different cosplay theme. Monday is school uniforms, Tuesday is nurses' uniforms, Wednesday is something else, and so on. We took pictures of the waitress for ten minutes, and we paid 1,000 yen (about US$12.50).

Cosplay cafés, especially maid cafés, are extremely popular, and thus they are becoming very competitive. It has been ten years since the first maid café appeared in Akihabara, and the phenomenon peaked in 2006. The popular ones are Cafe Mai:lish, Cos-cha and Pinafore, Jam Akihabara, and @home café.

Maids are now appearing in different fields—such as a maid hair salon where a hairdresser is dressed as maid, or a maid pub where a bartender is dressed as a maid. Sometimes, instead of maids, waitresses are dressed as nurses, train conductors, and so on. This phenomenon has spread to other parts of the world, such as Hong Kong, Taiwan, the Philippines, Singapore, Canada, and Mexico.

FUJOSHI (ROTTEN GIRLS) IN A BUTLER CAFÉ IN IKEBUKURO

Ikebukuro is a smaller district than Akihabara and is known as the female counterpart of Akihabara that caters to *Fujoshi* (Rotten Girls), the female equivalent of Otaku. All the anime- and manga-related stores are on Otome (Princess) Road in East Ikebukuro.

There is a butler café for girls and women where waiters are dressed as English butlers and greet female customers by saying, "Welcome home, Princess!" The café opened in 2006 as a female version of a maid café and it provides psychological comfort to young girls. The customers are treated as princesses. If you want something, you ring a bell on the table, and a butler comes running to fulfill your request. If you need to go the ladies' room, the butler will carry your bag, take you to the bathroom, and wait for you outside the bathroom. Unlike maid cafés, which are abundant, the butler café in Ikebukuro is exclusive, and reservations are required.

Fujoshi are obsessive about *Doujin-shi*—self-published manga or novels by amateur artists and writers—and the most popular type of story among Fujoshi is a love story between two good-looking boys. A self-claimed Fujoshi said:

> This genre is very popular because it's an unrealistic world. In real life, you can't have two really good looking boys falling in love with each other. It's not real, and that's why it is portrayed so beautifully. No guy is that good looking in real life. It's so truly beautiful and romantic, and it's not sleazy at all.

THE GLOBALIZATION OF COSPLAY

Cosplay is a global phenomenon sustained by the huge anime and manga industries. Between June and November 2011, sixty-eight anime- and manga-related conventions and events took place in Europe and the United States (see Table 6.1 in the Appendix). The largest event for cosplayers outside of Asia is the annual San Diego Comic-Con, held in California at the end of July.

The annual Cosplay Summit takes place every summer in Nagoya, Japan, and it includes a cosplay competition. The cosplayer champions from different countries come to Japan for the grand championship. Since 2005 champions have been from Italy (2005 and 2010), Japan (2009), Brazil (2006 and 2009), and France (2007).

Elizabeth Licata, the U.S. cosplay champion, explains her approach to creating a costume:

> A lot of people are crazy for accuracy, but it's not that interesting to me. Sometimes I'll try to stay 100 percent true to the source material, but a lot of the time I want to change things. If a design is amazing on its own and the construction is challenging or unfamiliar enough to absorb all my attention, I generally won't embellish it at all. But if the construction is simple and something I've done a hundred times, it probably won't keep my attention, so I might do things to it to make it more interesting to me. (quoted in Fasano 2009: 10)

NAKANO, TACHIKAWA, AND SAITAMA
FOR THE MARGINAL HARD-CORE OTAKU

Just as Ikebukuro targets a particular segment of anime and manga fans, Nakano and Tachikawa are also marginal but well known among enthusiasts. For those who value the sense of marginality and privacy, Akihabara is becoming too popular and too big.

Inside a shopping arcade called Nakano Broadway near the train station, a number of small stores sell secondhand manga and anime DVDs, figurines, and cosplay costumes. According to an Otaku, "you find rare items in Nakano. Hardcore anime and manga fans go there. Akihabara is becoming too mainstream. Some say that Nakano is actually the true birthplace of Otaku subculture."

Mandarake, a store that buys and sells anime, manga, toys, and related collectibles, had its first store in Nakano Broadway in 1987. The salespeople who worked there cosplayed in different outfits, and the customers could vote on them. There are now several stores spread out over three floors inside Nakano Broadway in addition to other stores in Shibuya, Ikebukuro, Osaka, and Fukuoka.

Although the anime and manga subculture is huge, like other youth subcultures, it is not a highly respected community. A journalist at a fashion trade paper told me, "When a fashion school in Nakano was asked to design a uniform for the staff who work at Mandrake, they flatly turned it down. I supposed they do not want anything to do with the anime and manga subculture."

However, the anime and manga subcultures are expanding their territory as far as Tachikawa in the western part of Tokyo. Tachikawa may be the next Akihabara. Several scenes in anime were inspired by Tachikawa, and the Tachikawa Chamber of Commerce and the Tachikawa Tourist Bureau are using them to promote the district to welcome more tourists and visitors to revitalize the district. Some anime fans consider the place as a holy land and make pilgrimages to Tachikawa and take pictures to reproduce ones that appeared in manga.

The Washinomiya Shrine in Saitama Prefecture outside of Tokyo is another popular place for anime fans to visit, because the shrine appears in a popular anime. A magazine called *Newtype*, which covers the anime and manga industries, published an article in August 2007 about the places and scenes that appear in major anime and manga and gave directions to these locations. One of them was this shrine. Groups of anime and manga fans came to see the shrine to take photographs. Before this, hardly anyone ever came to visit the place.

CONCLUSION

Similar to the other subcultures examined in this book, anime and manga fans assume the identities of fictional characters. They invest an enormous amount of time, money, and effort to make a costume to achieve and play the role of the perfect character. Their identity performance is not their entire life, but it consumes them for several hours a week on a somewhat regular basis. The cosplay phenomenon is globally popular and is expanding every day. It provides evidence that other Japanese youth subcultures with distinct stylistic expressions may have a positive impact on the youth around the world.

Shinjuku: Girls of the Nightlife Using Beauty and Youth as Weapons

Shinjuku is a district famous for its nightlife, especially for its red-light section, Kabuki-cho. There are hostess bars known as *caba-kura*, night clubs, restaurants, motels, small inns, massage salons, and pubs. This is where Japan's sex and sex-related industries prosper. Like red-light districts in any part of the world, the visitors and those who work there are often anonymous or use aliases. Shinjuku is a place for those who consider themselves marginal, dismissed, neglected, or deviant. It is always assumed that if one is working in Kabuki-cho, he or she is doing it unwillingly, simply for money; this is not the type of occupation that one would be proud of. But if we define a subculture as a group who shares the same values and norms that go against the mainstream, then a group of women who work in Shinjuku can be considered an emerging subculture. These women are part of a subculture that is occasionally treated as an extension of the Gyaru subculture in Shibuya, since many of the Gyaru work in Shinjuku as bar hostesses because it is the easiest way for them to earn money. Bar hostess is a popular occupation to which Japanese teen girls aspire (Miura and Yanauchi 2008). Bar hostesses, who used to be hidden and anonymous, have mobilized and created an occupational subculture that is gaining social recognition and popularity. The emergence of this subculture is evidence that ideologies and values can change dramatically with institutional legitimization.

KOAKUMA AGEHA MAGAZINE: LEGITIMATING A DEVIANT/ UNDERGROUND OCCUPATION AS A SUBCULTURE

A magazine called *Nuts* targets Gyaru in Shibuya, and in October 2005 it published a special edition called *Koakuma and Nuts: Volume 1,* which was so popular that the publisher decided to increase its circulation after just three days. In April 2006 *Koakuma and Nuts: Volume 2* was published. In June 2006 the special edition was renamed *Koakuma Ageha*, and since October 2006 the magazine has been published monthly. The word *Nuts* was deleted from the title because it carried an image of tanning and implicitly targeted the Gyaru, whose skin is always tanned. To expand its readership, it became *Koakuma Ageha* (Small Devilish Butterfly). The target readers are young women who work as bar hostesses, known as *Age-jo* (*Age* is taken from *Ageha* [butterfly] and *jo* [lady]). When it was launched in 2006 the magazine had a circulation of 50,000. By October 2010 its circulation had increased to 400,000. The editorial staff has grown from two to ten. In this economic slump, when many Japanese fashion magazines, such as *High Fashion* and the Japanese edition of *Harper's Bazaar*, have closed down, *Koakuma Ageha*'s success is impressive.

Although it is aimed at young bar hostesses, the magazine is supported by a wider audience, ranging from schoolteachers to office workers. The magazine is packed with photos and articles about fashion, hairstyles, shoes, and accessories for Age-jo, some of whom work as models for the magazine. The pages are filled with practical information about makeup and hairstyles. One article, for example, explains in detail the way a popular model for the magazine applies eyeliner, with a picture of magnified eyes.

In a rare interview with a journalist at *Gigazine*, Hisako Nakajo, editor-in-chief of the magazine, explains the concept of the magazine:

> Before our magazine, there were magazines that talked about "how do men choose places to go to at night." But I wanted to make a magazine that the girls throughout Japan who are working at night can refer to about make-up, hairstyle and fashion. They work in those places for various reasons, and since they are not exposed to the sunlight and keep drinking, and many of them get exhausted and get depressed. The only fun they have is to have a big hair or wear pretty dresses. That's why I wanted to create a magazine that these girls can refer to when they do their hair and choose their dress before going to work.[1]

Nakajo explains that a magazine needs to be written to cater to its readers, otherwise it may appear to condescend to them. She says:

> People in publishing houses are too intelligent. We are not well-brought up so we understand what people with a similar background feel, but not those intelligent people. Perhaps the readers feel the same as well. When you read a magazine that was made by intelligent people, it is too difficult and seems to be looking down on us. Even if you write, "this will be in trend," they can't buy it. My readers live in a different world. My readers are different from a small segment of population that is intelligent or wealthy. . . . I want to be on the same level as my readers and create the magazine with them.

Nakajo understands how the women live, think, dress, eat, and feel.[2] She says:

> I myself was working as a hostess when I was in college. I always wondered why there was no magazine for us who work at caba-kura . . . the magazine is created

from the eyes of the reader. ... I don't want to play golf. If I do, it means that I am no longer reading this magazine. I need to remain poor just like these girls.

Stories and feature articles in the magazine are told from the readers' perspectives. The editor knows what kind of information readers are looking for and will be useful to them. Conventional fashion magazines tend to feature products that are not reachable by the middle class. They create an image that is portrayed as ideal but is unrealistic for many. Nakajo's magazine is the opposite of a conventional fashion magazine; the items and products featured in *Koakuma Ageha*'s articles and ads are reasonably priced and accessible to readers.

AGE-JO AND CABA-JO: THE MAGAZINE'S TARGET READERS

The launch of *Koakuma Ageha* gave the women of Shinjuku a place to belong to and a name to identify themselves with. The readers are Age-jo or Caba-jo. The magazine is for young women who want to be prettier, richer, and happier. It is cool to be an Age-jo or Caba-jo; marginal or underground girls who never had a place in mainstream fashion magazines are appearing as models.

Caba-kura is an abbreviation of the combination of a cabaret and a club. The first *caba-kura* opened on May 25, 1984. It was called Shinjuku Cats and was in Kabuki-cho, the red-light section of Shinjuku. The club hired as bar hostesses young women and college students between the ages of eighteen and twenty-two who were completely untrained and inexperienced. It built a reputation for allowing men who went there three times to ask the girls to go on dates with them in their private time (Miura and Yanauchi 2008). Following the success of Shinjuku Cats, similar *caba-kura* were set up one after another, and by 1986 there were 1,000 of them. The women who work there are also known as Caba-jo. In principle, there is no sex involved. A *caba-kura* is not a prostitution house, and Age-jo and Caba-jo are not prostitutes. However, Akemi Tsukino (2009: 49), a Caba-jo who published an autobiography, writes: "Yes, in fact, many of us do sleep with our customers."

Koakuma-Ageha was the first magazine that featured bar hostesses as models, and it attracted much attention from readers and other hostesses. Some of the women were part-time models for the magazine, and some full-time hostesses became full-time models. Nakajo explains the selection process of the models as follows:

We conduct a questionnaire about who is more popular among the models, and the most popular ones often become full-time models for the magazine. Our editorial staff as well as the models read these questionnaire postcards and find out who is popular. In a way, giving some sort of status to the popular ones is very similar to the system in caba-kura.

Those who work as a Caba-jo also read the magazine and some dream of appearing in it as a model. A twenty-year-old full-time Caba-jo who was interviewed in a study (quoted in Miura and Yanauchi 2008: 153–54) said:

> After graduating from high school, I needed the money to get a driving license, so I started working at a caba-kura in my hometown. I also wanted to pay back my mother, who borrowed money to send me to a private high school. ... When I was twenty, I came out to Tokyo without any purpose. I started working in Tokyo and expanded my network and even appeared in *Ageha*. ... our occupation is being socially acknowledged because of *Ageha* so I want to appear more in the magazine and try new things. It's a great feeling to get people's attention.

BEAUTY AS A WEAPON: OBSESSION WITH APPEARANCE

According to Nakajo, there are two types of girls: pretty and not pretty. Her magazine gives readers detailed instructions on how to look beautiful, because for the readers who work as bar hostesses, beauty is their weapon used to conquer men, and their earning power depends on how they look.

I conducted a textual analysis of the back issues of *Koakuma Ageha*, because textual studies of the mass media are one way to understand how hegemony and ideologies are produced and operated. The media play a crucial role in reproducing ideologies. They produce definitions of reality. Drawing on Gramsci ([1929–1933] 1992) and Althusser ([1968] 1988), Stuart Hall (1980a) claims that ideological messages in the media work predominantly by creating a false image of reality. Although Gramsci provided the basis for thinking about the social implications of the mass media, theories from semiotics proposed by de Saussure ([1916] 1986), Barthes (1967), and Lévi-Strauss (1955) provided the concrete tools for dissecting particular items of data by reading messages and images. We can pull apart media texts and uncover the hidden ways in which they worked. However, as Hall (1980a) argues, not everyone understands the texts in the same way. In textual studies, attention is given to the work of media producers and consumers in creating and reading messages.

Koakuma-Ageha is not exactly a fashion magazine but, rather, could be called a makeup and hairstyle magazine. Makeup and hairstyles are two components that are seen as extremely important to creating a pretty face. The magazine gives detailed instructions about how to make eyes "super huge" and eyelashes "super long."

Putting the hair up as high as possible is one of the trademarks of Age-jo or Caba-jo, and it is a style that can also be seen among Gyaru in Shibuya since many Gyaru work in Shinjuku. It is believed that a tall hairstyle makes one's face look smaller, which is one definition of physical beauty. The cover of the August 2009 issue says, "The reason why we put our hair up so high is not just to make our faces look prettier but because it is a weapon that protects ourselves from external enemies. … we also need an armor around our heart."

The magazine is a trendsetter for the community. *Koakuma-Ageha* is oblivious to fashion trends that are featured in mainstream fashion magazines; it creates its own trends. There are different hairstyle trends in different districts where *caba-kura* are found: braided with highlights in Kabuki-cho and straight hair in Roppongi (*Koakuma-Ageha*, September 2009: 66). There are two types of loose curls: loose curls that start beside the cheeks and loose curls that are not curled beside the cheeks (*Koakuma-Ageha*, October 2009: 75–81). A feature story in the November 2009 (50–64) issue states: "The reason why my face is the prettiest is because of my big hair!" The year 2007 was when big hair became the norm; the bigger, the better. Highlights were in trend especially in the first half of 2008. The girls sometimes need to go to a special hairdresser to get their hair done, and their hair is almost always dyed light brown or blonde.

The instructions for makeup are so detailed and professional that those who master the techniques have skills similar to professional makeup artists. The main idea of the makeup instructions in *Koakuma-Ageha* is how to make one's eyes look bigger. This is a theme that has appeared in every issue of the magazine since its launch. The bigger the eyes, the better you look. Eyeliner and mascara are indispensable items, and details on application are exacting. In the December 2009 issue, the so-called Ageha Eyeliner Research Institute explains how to make the eyes look big, and says that the average width of an eyeliner is 1.7 millimeters. The cover of the February 2010 issue says: "There are numerous/countless schools that train you to get into college, to become a doctor, but the one that teaches you how to make your eyes look big is this one [magazine] only!" Inside the issue there are pages on an intensive training seminar called "Gigantic Eyes at Ageha School" that illustrates how to apply eyeliner to upper lash lines and lower lash lines (*Koakuma-Ageha*, February 2010: 2–19). A very thin strip of tape is used to raise the eyelids so the eyes look bigger.

Other cover stories include a "Gigantic Eyes Exercise Book," which states: "If you shift your fake eyelash 1 millimeter toward the tip of your eye, or if you make the width of your eyeliner 0.1 millimeter thinner, we may be a little prettier," and "Changing the width of your eyeliner and fake eyelashes may lead you to happiness or unhappiness" (*Koakuma-Ageha*, August 2010). Achieving beauty is the obsession, and the beauty advice seems to be empowering to some. "We may be born as ugly ducklings, but once we go on a make-up pilgrimage, now we know we can be close to a swan!" (*Koakuma-Ageha*, November 2010: 4–5).

Every issue implies that if a Japanese woman wants to be pretty, she needs to make her face appear as close to a Westerner's face as possible. Almost all Age-jo or Caba-jo dye their natural black hair brown or blonde. They expend arduous effort to make their eyes look more like Western eyes. "If you want to make yourself look half/biracial" (*Koakuma-Ageha*, August 2010: 68); "even if we can't be a foreigner, we have the make-up technique to make our face three dimensional" (*Koakuma-Ageha*, September 2010: 65).

In addition to beauty tips, the magazine offers advice on customer service at *caba-kura* (*Koakuma-Ageha*, August 2009: 50–63), such as "pretend you are drunk," "start being friendly on their third visit," and "with quiet customers, just keep talking."

FROM DARK UNDERGROUND TO POSITIVE SOCIAL RECOGNITION

A major transition in social values and sexual norms becomes evident in studying those who work in bars and pubs. *Koakuma-Ageha* helped solidify and expand this occupation as a distinct subculture.

According to Miura and Yanauchi (2008: 49), Japan's old ideology that women get married and become full-time homemakers has collapsed in today's society, which is less strict regarding gender roles. Although many Caba-jo and Age-jo dream about getting married and depend on men emotionally and financially, men are becoming less reliable and not all can handle the responsibility of being a full-time breadwinner. If a young woman comes from a poor family, does not like school, and drops out of high school or college, the only way she can support herself and become self-sufficient is to work as a bar hostess.

In a survey conducted by Miura in 2007 of 1,935 young women between the ages of fifteen and twenty-two, *caba-kura* hostess ranked as the ninth most popular or desired occupation among the twenty-nine occupations listed (see Table 7.1 in the Appendix). This study is somewhat biased, because among the twenty-nine occupations listed there are no high-status occupations such as lawyers, doctors, or politicians. In a similar study conducted by Miura in 2008, fifty-nine more occupations were listed and the age range of respondents expanded up to thirty-two. In this study Caba-jo ranked twelfth (see Table 7.2 in the Appendix).

According to Miura and Yanauchi (2008), the average annual income in 2008 for women who work full-time was approximately three million yen before taxes (US$33,000). Some Caba-jo earn up to fourteen million yen (US$175,000), which is higher than the average full-time income for a man. The average monthly income of Cabo-jo who work full-time is about 450,000 yen

(US$5,625); for those who work part-time, the average monthly income is 291,000 yen (US$3,638) (see Table 7.3 in the Appendix). The average age of Caba-jo is 21.1 years, and their income is higher than that of most middle-aged men in Japan.

YOUTH AS EARNING POWER

In addition to physical beauty, the Age-jo and Caba-jo use their youth as a weapon to conquer a man's heart. Humans use different resources to attain particular goals. Women have used beauty and youth to attract a potential mate so that they can settle down and have a family, adding stability to their life. Age-jo and Caba-jo use both beauty and youth to increase their earning power. Former Caba-jo Akemi Tsukino writes (2009):

> There was a customer who only likes young girls sitting next him. So every time a new girl sits next to him, his first question was "how old are you?" I said, "I'm twenty-three." Then he goes, "Twenty-three? Too old! Get out, get out. I don't need you." ... The next time he came to our bar, I thought it was useless for me to go and sit next to him, but then I realized he probably doesn't remember me. ... He asked me, "how old are you?" so I replied "twenty-one." ... Then he goes, "Okay, okay. You can order whatever drink you want."

It is common knowledge in this occupational subculture that the women lie about their age by two or three years, sometimes even by five years. Youth is power in an occupation that lasts only for a number of years. The slogan is "earn as much as you can while you can."

The clubs can hire women as young as eighteen, and the women are usually between the ages of eighteen and twenty-seven. Some bars have age limits. The girls are beautiful, and they need to be: That is what they are selling. They put an incredible amount of effort into maintaining their beauty: they get their nails done at least once a week and go to aesthetic salons once a month. Their hair and makeup must be perfect every time they go to work. At work, they perform like stage actresses; that is the whole idea of Age-jo and Caba-jo.

DIVERGENCE OF SUBCULTURAL TERRITORIES: LOLITA IN SHINJUKU

A recent phenomenon shows a divergence of subcultural territories. Shinjuku is no longer just for Age-jo and Caba-jo. Lolita girls are entering the territory because of the Marui One department store, which was launched in 2000 exclusively to sell Lolita-related labels, such Angelic Pretty, Peach Boys, and

Baby, the Stars Shine Bright. Because of this landmark store, Lolita who never had a reason to come to Shinjuku are now coming there to shop. One Lolita girl said, "I go to Shinjuku just to visit Marui One. A lot of Lolita girls are now shopping at Marui One."

In 1998 Marui rented a temporary space for Metamorphose Temps de Fille, a well-known Lolita brand, and made a sales profit of 2.5 million yen (approximately US$31,250) in two weeks. The company continued to operate the space for another three months and during that time made five million yen (approximately US$62,500), according to a buyer at Marui One. A Lolita subculture had taken hold in Shinjuku with the help of the media, including television, magazines, and Web sites.

While the socioeconomic status of those who follow subcultural fashion is extremely difficult to find in ethnography, Marui One conducted a focus group and found that most of its customers are from wealthy families, and the girls spend about 50,000–60,000 yen (approximately US$625–759) per visit. Many of them attend private schools and take lessons in violin and piano. The customers range in age from fourteen to twenty-five. Marui One is attempting to make Shinjuku the second mecca for Lolita followers after Harajuku. There are also popular tea houses for Lolita followers in Shinjuku. What used to be geographically and stylistically defined subcultures are becoming increasingly democratic, and some are merging with other subcultures to create new ones.

CONCLUSION

Age-jo or Caba-jo is an occupational subculture whose members have distinct hairstyles and makeup. This case study shows how a magazine almost single-handedly legitimized an occupation that used to be underground and transformed it into an attractive occupation. This case study also illustrates a major value transition among the Japanese youth. Whether the subculture is giving girls and women greater ability to earn money and, thus, more financial independence during the economic slump is debatable, but the obsession with appearance empowers some as beauty seems to directly impact their earning power. Subcultural districts are no longer as territorial as they used to be, and they are beginning to diverge to create new subcultures.

Kouenji and Other Fashion Dist. From Secondhand Clothes Lovers to i Fashion Followers

This chapter explores a marginal subculture known as Mori Girl (Forest Girl), which emerged in Kouenji.[1] This subcultural group is slowly gaining popularity, but it is relatively small. There are no major fashion landmarks in the district such as Shibuya 109, which contributes to promoting the Gyaru and Gyaru-o subcultures, or La Foret and Takeshita streets, which support the Lolita subculture. The Mori Girl subculture is not as tied to a particular district as are other subcultures discussed in this book. But Kouenji is famous for small secondhand clothing retailers, and one of the characteristics of Mori Girls is their passion for secondhand clothing. The style and the philosophy very much coincide with the current trends in the fashion industry of sustainability and social networking. Followers of the Mori Girl subculture value nature and ecology, and the subculture emerged online. While slow in its progression, it is diversifying into other communities. This chapter also examines other fashion districts, such as Shimokitazawa and Kichijouji, which are similar to Kouenji, and Ginza, where fast fashion retailers compete to attract young Japanese consumers.

MORI GIRL AND KOUENJI

Mori means forest in Japanese, so Mori Girl is a type of girl found in the forest. A friend said to Choco-san, a typical Japanese girl, "you look like a girl who belongs to a forest." Then Choco-san decided to create a community site on August 24, 2006, on Mixi, one of the most popular social networking services in Japan.[2] Five years later, the Mori Girl community has 36,000 members. Rather than congregating in Kouenji, Kichijouji, or Shimokitazawa, which are famous for secondhand and vintage retailers, Mori Girls socialize and communicate online because one of the main characteristics of a Mori Girl is that she enjoys loneliness and doing things alone rather than moving around in groups, like in other subcultures. Rather, Mori Girls are connected in virtual space. If you search for "Mori-Girl" in Mixi, you will get sixty community sites

ited to the subculture. Out of the sixty, if you narrow your search down to
fashion category, there are twenty-seven communities (see Table 8.1 in the
Appendix).

The image of a subculture in Western societies is aggressive, rough, loud,
and violent, but Mori Girl as a subculture does not fit these images. Its followers prefer a slow-paced, relaxed lifestyle. Mori Girls enjoy being nonmain-
stream and marginal while keeping a low profile. They enjoy sharing their
values with their peers.

MORI GIRL STYLISTIC EXPRESSIONS

The image that Mori Girl tries to adhere to is that of Northern European and
Scandinavian cultures. Subcultural fashion is often tied to particular brands
that serve the members of the subcultures and later spread as a mass fashion. For Mori Girl stylistic expressions, there are no specific brands, but one
brand that may represent the subculture is Sirop, which was established in
2002 long before Choco-san started her community site on Mixi. Sirop has
many of the elements mentioned in the following list. It tries to create a certain image or an atmosphere through its clothing, which is often found in
secondhand stores. Followers of Mori Girl mix and match brands, and if they
cannot find something in stores, then they make it. Mori Girls like handmade
crafts.

Major characteristics for Mori Girl stylistic expressions were listed in special
editions of *Spoon* magazine (March 2009 and September 2009) as follows:

- A-line dress
- Fairy tale books
- Flat and round-toed shoes
- Fluffy hats made out of wool, fur, or other natural fibers
- Handmade jewelry rather than expensive brands
- Layers of clothes
- Like to stroll with a camera in hand (they are also *Sha-Girl*, a subculture of
  girls who like taking pictures)
- Natural fabrics
- Neutral, earthy colors
- Nothing too sweet or girlie
- Ponchos, vests, shawls, and big scarves for layering
- Puffy, childlike sleeves
- Retro flower prints, lace, plaids, and polka dots
- Vintage, antique, and secondhand
- Weak perm and straight-cut bangs for a childlike look

A Mori Girl who was formerly a Lolita explains some of the differences in dress: "Lolita styles are difficult to put together, and they tend to buy all items from head to toe from one brand, but Mori Girl's style is more economical and inexpensive to put together, because as long as you have the major components in your style, you can easily create a Mori Girl style."

A new subculture called *Dolly-kei* began to appear in 2007, immediately after the emergence of the Mori Girl subculture. Dolly-kei is a combination of Mori Girl and Lolita and uses a lot of vintage skirts, dresses, jewelry, and accessories imported from Europe. Like Mori Girl, Dolly fashion fans cherish one-of-a-kind antique items. Their vintage clothing and accessories are seen as their assets and treasures, and therefore are extremely precious and valuable. They like items and accessories that are retro and handmade. Despite the many similarities, followers say "there are differences between Mori Girl and Dolly-kei fashion." A genre called *Cult-Party kei* emerged for those who bought vintage clothes at a store called Cult Party in Kouenji. The store closed in 2010 and reopened in Shibuya with a new name, The Virgin Mary. The store is popular among Dolly-kei fans.

However, one or two stores are not enough to make a group of fans or followers an established subculture, although they may call themselves a subculture. But since those who prefer to be part of the subcultures are often not in favor of mainstream tastes, beliefs, or lifestyles, the keyword in some cases is *marginality*. These subcultures enjoy the process of searching and looking for a one-of-a kind item that no one else has or is wearing.

LIMITED DIFFUSION AND RECOGNITION: A LACK OF INSTITUTIONAL INVOLVEMENT

The Otaku subculture is widely promoted in Japan and overseas through the Akihabara district, which is home to mega stores that sell anime, manga, and other related items. *Koakuma Ageha* magazine was so powerful that it gave social recognition to an underground occupation and made it into a subculture of Age-jo and Caba-jo. Shibuya is famously tied to the Gyaru and Gyaru-o subcultures, while Harajuku is central to the Lolita subcultures. Mori Girl, which is not yet a full-fledged subculture, has not expanded as widely as the subcultures described in previous chapters because of the lack of institutional involvement. There is no one landmark in Kouenji that attracts vintage lovers to the area. There are small, scattered retail stores. There are no monthly magazines that feature vintage lovers and collectors. The industries do not pay much attention to the Mori Girl subculture.

In order for a subculture to have a strong presence, it needs to be widely diffused through the media, retailers, and celebrities. In 2009 actress Yu

Kurai appeared on the cover of *Spoon* magazine wearing a Mori Girl–looking dress. Some celebrities favor the style, but it is not enough to make the subculture into something bigger and famous. Mori Girl does not have a strong identity.

If a subculture does happen to emerge in a small district like Kouenji, popular stores will relocate to Shibuya and Harajuku. Thus, subcultures are becoming less geographically specific. New subcultures do not grow or expand commercially unless there are institutional supports to respond to consumer demands. Unlike high fashion, which places a lot of emphasis on semi-annual fashion shows, subcultural fashion labels do not require fashion shows to spread. However, they still need mega stores to sell clothing and fashion items that project a certain image of a particular group.

Few magazines target the Mori Girl fashion phenomenon. *Spoon* is probably the most well known, but it is published only six times a year. Mori Girl can be passed as an ordinary fashion that prefers A-line dresses in subdued, earthy colors. The clothes are not as intense as Gyaru or as extreme as Lolita. Whether it is high fashion or subcultural fashion, fashion needs an institutionalized system. For example, in France an entire network of institutions works together to spread French and foreign brands.

THE DEMOCRATIZATION OF GINZA

A fashion district is a site where so-called legitimate taste is produced and reproduced. As explained in the chapter 9, "Individual and Institutional Networks within a Subcultural System," what is happening in today's Japan is a struggle in taste between high fashion and youth fashion.

The two most expensive upscale fashion districts in Tokyo are Ginza and Omotesando. In Omotesando, which is only a ten-minute walk from Harajuku, there is a shopping area built in 2006 called Omotesando Hills, which carries upscale European and U.S. brands. Along the streets of Omotesando there are freestanding stores of Ralph Lauren, Chanel, Gucci, Prada, and others. The stores are not doing well, but Omotesando still manages to maintain its place in high fashion with an upscale fashion arcade. In contrast, the façade of Ginza is slowing transforming into a new expression. A monthly magazine, *AERA*, wrote: "Is Ginza Becoming Ame-yoko [*sic*]?" (February 15, 2010). Ameyoko is a working-class neighborhood where there are inexpensive grocery stores. The title refers to the fact that fast-fashion, casual-wear retailers are now encroaching on Ginza, which used to be a district with the most expensive stores and upscale departments stores, such as Matsuya, Mitsukoshi, Matsuzakaya, Seibu, and Hankyu. The department stores that used to be popular and successful are barely hanging on. Many have started to close their branches throughout Japan. Foreign and Japanese retailers that sell casual wear are now present in Ginza, such as Zara from Spain, Forever 21 from the United States, H&M from Sweden, and Uniqlo of Japan. Because of these new stores, Ginza is now attracting younger customers.

Although we still do not see any new youth subcultures emerging out of Ginza, the district is becoming a site where high fashion and street fashion meet, and there is a clear struggle in taste. Japanese teens are sophisticated and creative consumers, and they may soon dominate Ginza and create a new subculture. In this case, department stores will be likely to contribute to the expansion of the new subcultures.

THE FAILURE OF UPSCALE JAPANESE DEPARTMENT STORES IN THE TWENTY-FIRST CENTURY

Japan was one of the first Asian countries to set up department stores similar to the ones in Europe and the United States. The department store concept played an important role in creating a new consumer culture and made a substantial contribution to Japan's economic development in the face of Western capitalism. The Japanese learned sales techniques from Europe and the United States, drastically changed their traditional retailing methods, adopted a Western-style accounting system and a new system of personnel management, and employed personnel with good educational qualifications. Advertising and other public relations activities were pursued as a means of creating a fashionable shopping experience. Families and women with children began to spend their days in the city's new shopping areas.

Mitsukoshi department store, which started in 1893 as Mitsui Gofuku Store, was a leader in this new retailing system. It survived mass production and also played an important role in the development of department stores in Japan, which entered an era of modernity through consumption. Mitsukoshi's success had an immediate effect on other drapery and dry goods stores. Matsuya followed suit and installed display cases in 1901, followed by shop windows in 1904. Shirokiya followed in 1903. Unlike other, more traditional department stores in Tokyo, such as Takashiyama, Isetan, and Matsuzakaya, which became incorporated as department stores in the 1920s, Seibu, which was established in 1949, was located in Ikebukuro and not in the prestigious Ginza shopping district. Seibu embarked on a comprehensive image strategy in the 1980s and became very successful. Isetan, which in the twenty-first century has nine branches in Japan and nine branches overseas, later followed Seibu, revamped its image, and became known among youth as a popular fashion-oriented department store that carries the latest styles.

Despite their earlier success, with a few exceptions, department stores in Japan are barely surviving. A journalist who has been covering the industry for many years told me:

> The department stores in Japan have very long and tight connections with some manufacturers that they refuse to get rid of the old ones that are not selling well and replace them with newer brands. They are not adventurous and do not welcome new designers or new labels. Consumer demands and tastes are changing, but these department stores did not bother to catch up with them. That's why they are now paying the price for it. It's about time that they realize what they were doing wrong, and are now desperate to change their image and attract a new set of customers. This is a matter of a life-and-death situation for them.

Ginza, which used to be firmly established as the wealthiest district in Tokyo, has become a site where aesthetic taste is contested. Stores that sell casual-wear labels are successfully invading Ginza, and they are getting closer to Omotesando as well.

CONCLUSION

While the Mori Girl subculture is slowing gaining followers online, it is not as large as the other subcultures discussed in this book due to a lack of institutional involvement. But it may be precisely its marginality that contributes to its popularity. More and more districts in Tokyo are turning into fashion districts, but at the same time, some are changing their images from luxury brands and high fashion to places where fast-fashion followers shop. The old legitimate taste and the new taste are competing with one another.

Individual and Institutional Networks within a Subcultural System: Efforts to Validate and Valorize New Tastes in Fashion

I have categorized various Japanese youth subcultures into different districts in Tokyo for the purpose of our discussion regarding the subculture and fashion that each district has produced. But some of these geographical subcultural boundaries are beginning to diverge and expand. Youth are beginning to transcend the geographical boundaries to create and re-create new subcultures. For instance, we now hear of *Mori-Gyaru*, which is a combination of Mori Girl in Kouenji and Gyaru in Shibuya; *Loli-Gyaru*, which is Lolita of Harajuku with a touch of Shibuya's Gyaru fashion; and *Caba-Gyaru*, which describes someone who is Gyaru but likes a bar hostess look. Shibuya is expanding to Shinjuku, and Lolita is now shifting to Shinjuku, Akihabara, and Ikebukuro.

As Hebdige explains (1979: 23): "Each subculture provides its members with style, an imaginary coherence, a clear-cut ready-made identity which coalesces around certain chosen objects (a safety pin, a pair of winkle-pickers, a two-tone mohair suit). Together, these chosen objects form a whole—a recognizable aesthetic which in turn stands for a whole set of values and attitudes."

The number of youth subcultures is growing in Japan. The members are building friendships with those who have similar stylistic expressions and similar tastes in fashion, and their external appearance nonverbally communicates their dilemmas and contradictions. Their interpersonal networks help sustain, reproduce, and perpetuate the subcultures because, without the members, the subcultural groups would not survive and a fashion district would disappear. In this chapter, I examine and analyze the fashion subcultures discussed in Part II.

Fashion is all about aesthetic taste, but it is not about an individual aesthetic taste. Rather, it is concerned with collective aesthetic taste that is constructed by different institutions in the fashion system (Blumer 1969a; Kawamura 2004). In my previous research on Japanese designers in the French fashion system (Kawamura 2004), I examined the structural mechanism of French fashion and the role the system plays in legitimating designers and spreading French fashion culture worldwide. One of my intentions in this current work on subcultural youth fashion is to explore how the structural mechanism of subcultural fashion, using Japan as an example, differs or overlaps with that of high fashion.

I argue that the creative and unique subcultural fashion emerging from Tokyo is the product of Japan's unstable social, economic, and cultural situations. The youth express themselves via material objects, such as clothing and makeup, that represent their inner feelings.

There is a taste struggle manifested through people's preferences in fashion. Aesthetic taste in the styles of Gyaru, Gyaru-o, Lolita, and Age-jo are looked down on and devalued by mainstream fashion professionals in Japan. This chapter discusses how individuals and institutions are connected within a subcultural system to validate and valorize new aesthetic tastes in fashion. Unlike high fashion, which places much emphasis on semiannual fashion shows in major fashion cities, youth subcultural fashion has other diffusion mechanisms within their own social networks. They do not read mainstream fashion magazines and are not interested in mainstream fashion labels. Overt stylistic expressions represent protest—outspoken or silent—on the part of the youth who feel oppressed and suppressed by the mainstream dominant ideology. As the popularity of high fashion begins to decline in Japan, it appears that the youth's taste is winning this taste battle.

JAPANESE YOUTH LIVING IN DILEMMAS AND CONTRADICTIONS

Hebdige explained in his study of punk subculture (1979: 23): "Amongst kids, this desire for coherence is particularly acute. Subculture provides a way of handling the experience of ambiguity and contradictions, the painful questions of identity." Likewise, Japanese youth who belong to subcultures carry a great deal of insecurities, dilemmas, and contradictions, which are reflections of the society's uncertain future. An interplay of ideological, economic, and cultural factors bear on subcultures. Under their rebellious and deviant behaviors, complex and complicated emotions run deep. According to Phil Cohen (1972), the "latent function" of subculture was to express and resolve the contradictions that remain hidden or unresolved in the parent culture.

The youth live in a dilemma, shifting from one ideology to the next, from one value to the next, trying to find out what is most comfortable, which ideology or beliefs to agree with, who to get advice from, and which norms to abide by. As the sense of insecurity and anxiety permeates society, the youth are trying to hang on to something concrete. They never knew the good times of Japan in the 1980s. They are the children of men and women who experienced Japan's economic euphoria and the drastic economic downturn after that. Adults themselves feel helpless and hopeless and do not have the means to protect the youth in dire economic situations.

DESIRE TO BE CLOSE AND PERSONAL VERSUS
DESIRE TO KEEP DISTANCE AND BE IMPERSONAL

As Emile Durkheim ([1897] 1951) indicated in his famous sociological investigation, *Suicide*, the degree of social integration is the key to a person's sense of well-being and happiness. In a Japanese society where conformity was valued and strongly emphasized in schools and workplaces, social integration was not even questioned because it was obvious that men would automatically earn a sense of belonging, especially in a company where lifetime employment was guaranteed. Men worked together, went out drinking together after work, and organized company events on weekends. No one ever imagined how it might feel to not belong. Durkheim explained that when the sense of belonging disappears, people feel an enormous sense of emptiness and loneliness that, in extreme cases, can lead to suicide. Thus, according to Durkheim, suicide is affected by social and environmental factors. This is already evident in the increasing suicide rates in Japan, as explained in chapter 3. Even toward the end of the nineteenth century in Europe, Durkheim's study found higher rates of suicide among men than among women.

Many young individuals that I interviewed said that they are bored in school or at work. They go to school or go to work just for the sake of going and have no interest in whatever they are studying and doing at work. One of the Lolita girls explained:

> Since I got involved into the Lolita subculture, I made more new friends who are into Lolita just like me. That is a rewarding experience, and something I did not expect before I became so obsessive about it. My Lolita friends are very important to me because at work I am just a contract worker so I change the company I work for when the contract is over. Then I go to another company for six months or ten months. There is no excitement at work. There is no way I can meet good friends at work. My Lolita friends are now my best friends.

But the group identities among today's youth are not as solid as the family and company identities of the previous generation, because subcultural membership is voluntary and can be transient, and anyone is free to enter or leave at any time they wish.[1] Members are confined by subcultural norms and rules as long as they are within the subculture, but once they leave, they do not need to abide by them and thus experience a decline in social integration.

Subcultural members are aware that their friendships and relationships may end in the near future, so they keep a certain amount of distance with their friends. They enjoy meeting members of the same subculture at events or parties, but their relationships with their peers are not as deep as one might imagine. One girl explained:

> We never use our real names.[2] I call myself Sara. I took it from my favorite anime. My real name is totally different. I go by Sara when I meet friends outside of my school. We never ask each other's real name. We never ask where we live, about our families, or the name of the school we go to. We never talk about our friends at school. We go to different schools so I don't know their friends, and they don't know my friends either. It's boring when you hear about someone you don't know … I can vaguely tell which direction my friends live by the train or the subway they take when they go home. But we never ask the exact address. These things are not important to us. We talk about our favorite music, our favorite fashion labels, and so on. We communicate by e-mails and text-messages. We go to concerts and events together.

Youth meet new friends on Mixi, one of the most popular Japanese social networking sites, similar to Facebook. They share their hobbies and the brands they wear, exchange text messages constantly, and sometimes they meet and attend events together. Since they do not have each other's personal information, it is easy to end relationships abruptly. The girl continues: "Sometimes, a friend suddenly stops e-mailing and becomes unreachable. That happens. I have no idea why people do that sometimes. Well, but that's life. Then I look for other friends on Mixi. That's okay."

REVELATION OF AUTHENTIC SELF VERSUS IDENTITY PERFORMANCE

When the youth put on a unique outfit or costume, they are playing a role of someone who they are not. Humans play multiple roles in different social functions, and the roles are always connected to identities, whether individual or collective. We all put on an act depending on which role we are playing or which mask we are putting on. Today's Japanese youth use their everyday lives as a stage and perform an act with appropriate costumes. In that way, their authentic selves do not have to face what is in front of them in real life and who they really are. The way we dress can express our identity—our internal thoughts, beliefs, and values. Thus, by manipulating and controlling our external appearance, we can, to an extent, manage the impressions and the image we project to society. Japanese youth drastically transform themselves by putting on a completely different sense of self. Whether subcultural fashion is the revelation of authentic self or the masking of it to create a new self depends on the person's awareness and consciousness. For some of them, the transformation of their identity by wearing subcultural fashion is their authentic self.

Erving Goffman's dramaturgical ideas in *The Presentation of Self in Everyday Life* (1959) help us examine ourselves from multiple viewpoints to create the best possible impressions of ourselves. Goffman takes the familiar sociological concept of *role* and puts it back on stage by placing the analysis of human behavior in a theatrical setting. He applies the theatrical representation of actors and actresses on stage to the everyday lives of ordinary men and women who are acting out their roles in the real world. His analytical focus is on impression management, the ways in which the individual guides and controls the impressions others form of him or her. Goffman offers two additional dramaturgical concepts: the front stage and the back stage. The front stage is "that part of the individual's performance which regularly functions in a general and fixed fashion to define the situation for those who observe the performance" (Goffman 1959: 22). The front stage includes items of "expressive equipment," such as clothing, rank, sex, age, size, posture, speech patterns, facial expressions, and body gestures (Goffman 1959: 24).

The youth use all aspects of their personal front—such as clothing, posture, facial expressions, and body gestures—to present themselves in the best light. The front includes anything observed by the audience while the actor is on stage that makes for a successful performance. It is the place where the actor is seriously laying out the script of impression management. It is taken for granted that there will be an audience and that the actors will be getting attention.

The back stage is the place closed to and hidden from the audience, where the techniques of impression management are practiced. Many forms of assistance to the actors are given in the back stage region—for example, adjustment of costumes and prompting. "He can drop his front, forego speaking his lines, and step out of character" (Goffman 1959: 11). The back stage is where the actors do not need to engage in impression management; they can be themselves.

Thus, we can use Goffman's dramaturgical concepts to analyze subcultural phenomena in which youth place an emphasis on their appearance. The subcultural members' encounters with other members are the front stage, while encounters with nonmembers and being alone are the back stage. The public space is the front stage for many people, but for the subcultural members, it is still the back stage; thus, many youth can be seen putting on makeup while riding public transportation on their way to one of the fashion districts.

A girl dressed in Punk Lolita said to me:

My personality changes when I dress like this. If I were wearing normal clothes, I don't think I can even talk to you so openly. I am more confident, talkative, and articulate when I am dressed in Punk Lolita. I feel powerful but also cute. That is why I like Punk Lolita. If it's just Punk, it's too strong, but if I add a Lolita touch, there is a sweet element as well.

SEXUAL OBJECTIFICATION VERSUS FEMALE EMPOWERMENT

The female-dominated Japanese subcultures express an exaggerated femininity, cuteness, and sexiness, and one may wonder whether this is a symbol of submission and sexual objectification. As indicated in the previous chapters, Gyaru in Shibuya is erotic and cute, Lolita in Shinjuku is excessively feminine and girlie, a waitress at a maid café is cute and obedient, Age-jo is sexy and erotic, and Mori Girl in Kouenji is innocently childlike. Veblen once said that women are the vehicles of vicarious display after men had to denounce adornment and fashion as the male values changed during the Industrial Revolution. However, none of the girls and women who I interviewed agreed that they dress up for men, except for Age-jo in Shinjuku, who dress sexily for men and their money since it is their occupation.

One Lolita said, "My ex-boyfriend never liked me in Lolita. In fact, he hated it. But I tried to convince him and make him understand why this was so important to me. It's my life. Lolita is my life. If he doesn't like Lolita, it means he doesn't like me. Then why bother?" Similarly, an American Loltia said, "Lolita girls are in fact feminists. We feel so strong when we dress Lolita. This is our armor. We don't do this to make boys happy. We couldn't care less if they didn't like us in Lolita."

Although Lolita girls are very much into self-display, they are not controlled by men or men's desires. They themselves are in control of their look. As Wilson, a postmodern feminist, explained (1994), while modern feminists have taken issue with women's concerns over appearance and their interests in fashion, postmodern feminists find no problem with such interests as long as they are controlled by women themselves. During my study, I did not meet any girls whose boyfriends or fathers buy Lolita outfits. They all work part-time at restaurants as conventional waitresses or in small firms as secretaries, and spend their earned income on their subcultural fashion. A girl dressed in Gothic Lolita said:

My mother never buys me any clothes. It's not that she doesn't allow me to wear it. I'm really picky about fashion. I work part-time at different places after school, and then save money to buy my favorite brands. That's why when I can afford something that I wanted for a long time, it is rewarding. It's so precious.

Another girl said: "Lolita fashion is empowering. When people look at us, we feel very strong outside and inside. It feels good."

MATURITY VERSUS INFANTALIZATION

If the young women have feminist viewpoints, they would be expected to want to mature and grow up to be independent. However, like many other contradictions they experience, they prefer not to grow up. They want to remain a child.

One of the Lolita girls I interviewed said:

> When I dress Lolita, it means to intentionally cut off all ties with the rest of the world and enter the world that is uniquely mine, and that is the world that is not mundane. Lolitas wear a girl's Victorian dress, and a girl is not a woman; she is a child, and a child is free of any responsibility, and she can do whatever she wants to. She can play and have fun. Many of us are confined by daily social rules and regulations in schools and offices, and on weekends we dress Lolita and there is a sense of freedom of being a child. Lolita is a child's festival, a festival that can be enjoyed by that child alone.

A female cosplayer described a certain clinging to childhood:

> It may sound evasive and irresponsible, but there is a sense of not wanting to grow up, because adults are mean, cruel, and unkind. We want to play, have fun, and remain childish. We dress in an anime character and cosplay because in that way we can just keep playing and remain a child. We have the tendency to not want to grow up. We just want to have fun. But isn't it contradictory that Fujoshi like to read sexually explicit BL [Boys' Love] manga, which is not exactly for children?

For Gyaru and Gyaru-o in Shibuya, once members retire from their gangs their youth days are over, and they have to become law-abiding citizens. Many leave the group reluctantly, feeling a great deal of emptiness and a sense of loss, not knowing what to do in the next stage of their life. Unlike many teens during the 1980s—when Japan's economy was at its peak—who had grand social ambitions, today's youth are enjoying life in their own way while they can.

WESTERN IMITATION VERSUS
QUINTESSENTIAL JAPANESENESS

The subcultural groups discussed in chapters 4 through 8 are not the only subcultures that exist in Tokyo. There are hip-hop, punk, and rap subcultures that are the Japanese versions of Western subcultures. But my selection of subcultures was geared toward those that are quintessentially Japanese and that emerged in a Japanese context.

However, from the Western perspective, many of the youth appear to be simply imitating whites, since most of the girls dye their black hair blonde or brown or wear blonde wigs, and they wear Western-style dresses. A Lolita girl explained: "Lolita dresses do not go along with black hair. Black hair and Lolita fashion do not match at all. We need to coordinate the entire look literally from head to toe." On the other hand, Age-jo bar hostesses do attempt to make-up their faces to more closely resemble white women, with higher cheekbones, thicker eyelashes, and bigger and rounder eyes. However, when these characteristics are combined with other subcultural elements and packaged as a subculture, the Japanese subcultures are found nowhere else and are genuinely and authentically Japanese.

Japanese subcultural fashion is an example of the cultural authentication process, which is the process of selectively borrowing a cultural object, such as an item of dress, and making it a part of the receiving culture. The transformation occurs at four levels. First, the object is selected and used. Second, it is given a name different from its original name to make it distinctive. Third, the object is incorporated into the social life of the people in a way that gives the object significance. Finally, the object is transformed by applied design into an object truly unique from the original object (Eicher, Evenson, and Lutz 2008: 247–48). Therefore, Japanese subcultural fashion has roots in the West but has added uniquely Japanese components to create a new genre of fashion.

JAPANESE SUBCULTURAL FASHION AS A NONELITE PHENOMENON

As I began my fieldwork in Tokyo and met professionals in the fashion industry, I gradually found out that people in fashion—mainstream fashion, that is—were reluctant to be associated with street fashion or subcultural fashion. A fashion design instructor at a fashion school said to me: "I am surprised that a professor like you who teaches about fashion at FIT [the Fashion Institute of Technology] in New York is interested in subcultural fashion." She was genuinely amazed at my research interest and that I would spend so much time and money on researching Japanese youth subcultures, which are devalued in the Japanese fashion community. She gave me the impression that, as a fashion scholar, I should be researching true fashion and not youth fashion on the streets. Indeed, I am very interested in youth street fashion. It became one of my purposes, in writing this book, to introduce to the world how creative and unique the styles are and what today's Japanese youth are thinking.

Those who belong to high fashion–related occupations, such as the journalists and editors covering French haute couture or those involved in selling upscale clothes, did not want to be identified with the world, people, and fashion of the subcultures. The youth themselves were aware that they were considered third-rate and that they were looked down on. An independent publicist who works with young designers and creators to get their clothes featured in fashion magazines said:

> These street fashion–related magazines are looked down upon by the mainstream fashion community in Japan. I would not know what to say to my clients if their clothes appear in one of those magazines. That would hurt their image and reputation. I want the major fashion magazines to cover my clients' works. Major fashion magazines are still looking to Western fashion, especially Paris fashion. If Japanese designers do not come up with styles that are similar to what the editors see on the stages of Paris collection, they will not pay any attention to their work.

Subcultures are definitely not considered products of high culture. Whether a material object is placed in the category of high culture or mass culture depends on its social context. As Crane explains:

> If music videos, which have many of the characteristics of twentieth-century avantgarde art styles (Kaplan 1987), were shown only in art museums instead of on cable television, they would be defined as high culture rather than as popular culture. The reason why Broadway theater is classified as high culture and television dramas as popular culture have more to do with differences in accessibility to the average person than with differences in content. (1992: 64)

As Crane (1992: 60) asserts, the status of the audience determines the status of the producers as well. Variations in standards occur as a result of social class differences, and when the audiences for these forms of culture are drawn from the middle and upper class, the cultural products are usually defined as high culture.

In the case of Japanese subcultural styles—although this is extremely difficult to prove at this point—the audience tends to be young, sometimes unemployed, uneducated people. Some of the girls I interviewed did not go to high school, some had eating disorders, and some were from divorced families and received no financial support from their parents. Their styles are far from high fashion or Paris fashion. However, as the subcultural fashion phenomenon begins to spread, Japanese high-fashion industries are feeling increasingly insecure. They are in jeopardy as they try to maintain the system and the institution as a whole. They would rather associate themselves with people who have wealth, status, and power—which the youth do not have.

I was invited to speak at a corporate symposium in Japan in July 2010, and I mentioned in my presentation that *Koakuma-Ageha*, one of the Japanese street magazines mentioned in chapter 7, is very different and original in its editorial makeup. My comment surprised the audience. A fashion journalist said, "When I tell my boss that I want to do a story about Shibuya or Shinjuku, he would say that our publication is not a regional paper so I need to cover a story that is more worthwhile."

However, scholars and the general public in the West have seen the power of, for example, the punk subcultures; they have seen that a subcultural style can attract the world's attention and spread globally throughout various industries. If a style is acknowledged by large numbers of people, it can become fashion. Punk fashion was conspicuous, but it was not an expression of conspicuous waste or leisure. Yet it became fashion. Punk styles began to be commercialized and filtered into mass-market fashion and even high fashion. They had a tremendous effect on British fashion, and designers such as Zandra Rhodes, Vivienne Westwood, and Malcolm McLaren incorporated punk styles in their collections. Although punk fashion, which helped establish London's reputation for innovative youth style, was primarily associated with Britain, similar developments have taken shape in other parts of Europe, Japan, and New York (Mendes and de la Haye 1999: 220).

STREET SUBCULTURAL FASHION VERSUS HIGH FASHION

Individual networks may initiate a subculture and facilitate its spread, but without institutional involvement to commercialize and expand the subcultural trend, it will not become widely popular. In order for fashion to become a genre or a category, there must be institutional and industry support and involvement, and each genre has its own aesthetic taste, producers, gatekeepers, and distributors.

Fashion is a collective activity among individuals and institutions. In order for clothes to become fashion, they need to go through a particular legitimating process. The taste in subcultural fashion is obviously far from that in high fashion, which is believed to be the ultimate expression of aesthetic taste. High fashion cannot be in bad taste. Therefore, professionals involved in high fashion, such as journalists, editors, and buyers, want to separate themselves from other, subcultural genres of fashion.

The simplest way to theoretically explain the differences between street fashion and high fashion is to describe their diffusion processes. High fashion is created by qualified fashion designers and is spread by major fashion magazines that feature semiannual fashion shows in Paris, New York, London, and Milan. Street fashion is initiated by youth and is spread by word of mouth. The industries come into the game afterward; they are always one step behind. The differences between high fashion and street fashion are shown in Table 9.1. High fashion serves a status function, and street fashion serves a symbolic group identity function.

Table 9.1: Basic Differences between Subcultural Fashion and High Fashion

Subcultural Fashion	High Fashion
Emerges from street subcultures	Emerges from professional designers
Street magazines use amateur models	High fashion magazines use professional models
Professional categories are not intact (consumers are the producers)	Professional categories are intact (producers versus consumers)
Social media are used as diffusion tools (blogs, Web sites, social networking sites, etc.)	Structured diffusion mechanism is in place (journalists, publicists, etc.)
Produces fashion from the bottom	Produces fashion from the top
Used as a symbolic group identity	Used as a status symbol

Subcultural fashion and styles that emerge out of youth subcultures are definitely not high fashion. They also are not simply different genres of fashion, and some industry professionals do not consider them fashion at all.

THE POPULARITY DECLINE IN WESTERN HIGH FASHION

A widespread notion of the nature of Japan's relationship with the West in the postwar period is that Japanese people turned to the West to learn, emulate, and adopt Western standards. There can be no denying the power of Europe and the United States in the cultural landscape of Japan in the twentieth century. For Japanese, the West has served as a model for both emulation and contrast. Nowhere is the Western cultural dominance in Japan more visible than in fashion.

In modern democratic societies, people do not want to be drastically different from others, but they do want *some* differences. One way to create slight differences is through consumption activities, and fashion consumption is a handy tool for achieving slight differences. Many Japanese women compete to purchase expensive fashion items. They have voracious appetites for Western brands.

A middle-aged Japanese buyer says:

> If you try to buy clothes that are very expensive and considered high fashion, you would buy Western brands, especially European brands. I can't think of any Japanese brands that fit that category. There is Hanae Mori or Jun Ashida, who designs for the Japanese royals, but as a consumer, if you are spending the same amount of money, you would buy Western brands.

Foreign fashion brands—European ones in particular—were the epitome of high fashion in the 1980s, along with the Japanese brands that became popular in Paris. But nowadays, many famous Western brands have closed their stores in Tokyo and are moving their headquarters to other parts of Asia, which is a sign of their declining popularity in Japan.

And there are other signs that high fashion is losing the game. The symbol of Japanese high fashion, Yohji Yamamoto, announced bankruptcy with a US$76 million debt in 2009. Hanae Mori also went bankrupt in 2004. A major Japanese apparel company, Renown, was bought by a Chinese textile firm, Shandong Ruyi, in 2010. Nigo's Bathing Ape was sold to a Chinese investor in 2011. Similarly, Tao Kurihara of Comme des Garçons was terminated in 2011 and stopped showing her collection in Paris. A number of upscale Japanese department stores are merging in order to survive, but they have not been successful. Magazines targeting high-income consumers, such as *High Fashion* and the Japanese edition of *Harper's Bazaar*, have closed down.

In some of the most popular stores in the Harajuku district, major Japanese designer labels such Issey Miyake and Yohji Yamamoto are not popular among the youth. The Japanese teens consider the internationally famous Japanese designers as too widely known. They find pleasure in discovering marginal underground designers and worship their labels as their own. Scarcity and originality are what make the street labels appealing. These brands are not sold in the United States or Europe, and they focus only on the domestic Japanese market. The teens want to wear clothes that few others wear but that everyone also will recognize as exclusive. Many street designers and stores sell only a limited amount of merchandise.

Therefore, good taste—that is, Western taste—is favored by the fashion elites. They are the ones who guide the trends in Japan. The styles that are featured in magazines and the clothing that stylists borrow for photo shoots are often Western brands. However, this paradigm began to shift in the mid- to late 1990s. Elite fashion professionals struggle to maintain consumers' taste for high fashion, but they are losing the battle. Today's Japanese youth, who may not be considered socially successful or known to have good taste, are taking over the hegemonic taste in fashion. This may lead to an overhaul of high fashion taste altogether.

INSTITUTIONALIZED STYLISTIC STABILITY

Fashion must be institutionally constructed and culturally diffused (Kawamura 2004: 1). Approaching fashion from a systemic perspective can explain how clothing may become fashionable. My previous research linked structural processes in the production of fashion to the variety of styles of clothing that are produced by particular designers and legitimated by various institutions in the system. I have argued that fashion as a system of institutions, organizations, groups, individuals, events, and practices that contribute to the making of fashion is supported by these external factors. I apply the same argument in a subcultural fashion system.

There are certain conditions that a group of people must meet in order to be considered and labeled as a subculture. During the process, the group members intentionally or unintentionally come up with certain styles that are distinct and unique. Once these styles are institutionalized and commercialized by the industries, they become a prominent image of the subculture. The styles need to be reproduced over and over again, season after season. The subculture then begins to expand geographically. The trickle-up or bubble-up theory of fashion requires the involvement of the media, such as magazines and TV programs, and major retailers. Subcultural fashion districts need subcultures to maintain the fashion image, and the members of the subcultures need a sacred place to visit and shop for their favorite labels.

FORMATION AND VALIDATION OF NEW AESTHETIC TASTES IN FASHION

Emile Durkheim talked about the different class cultures of individuals in a stratified society, and this idea was reiterated by French sociologist Pierre Bourdieu (1930–2002) in his book *Distinction: A Social Critique of the Judgment of Taste* (1984). Bourdieu showed for France what Herbert Gans (1974) had found in the United States: that there are coherent social-class differences in the consumption of culture. Bourdieu argued that people's class positions and aspirations are closely connected to how they style their lives. Fundamental life sensibilities, which Bourdieu called "habitus," are what determines one's taste preferences. It is something that is inherited both materially and through socialization. Max Weber (1968) had treated social classes as status groups with special lifestyles, and Veblen ([1899] 1957) and Gans (1974) had offered accounts of the relation between social classes and culture. Terms of status are dictated by the dominant class, and people individually and collectively employ strategies of distinction to vie for acceptance of their own worth by others.

Bourdieu's research shows that people are stratified especially by the amount of aesthetic reframing they do: the higher social classes value "sophisticated" art, which reframes ordinary objects into art, while the lower classes need a much more blatant frame of "prettiness" in order to regard something as art. Frames are crucial not only for creating different realms of human experience but also for stratifying social groups. Subcultural members are not in high socioeconomic brackets, so Bourdieu would say that they care about their functionality rather than their aesthetics. However, the aesthetic conscious-ness among members of subcultures is actually quite high. They are very much concerned about achieving their own version of the best taste possible.

Therefore, taste is not a matter of individual choice but is determined by one's class. Bourdieu analyzed taste in the arts, such as painting, books, food, and fashion. For fashion, he put forward a theory regarding the aesthetic and functional components of dress. Bourdieu does not elaborate on the aes-thetic components of the working class, but dress does serve more than a utilitarian function among the working class. It also serves an aesthetic func-tion, too, but it is a different kind of aesthetics, one that is often dismissed by the dominant class.

Throughout my research on Japanese subcultures, I witnessed a taste struggle in Japanese fashion. Individuals participate in a class-defined strug-gle for social distinction that renders status differentials legitimate, even though the terms of the contest are set by a dominant class. Stratification can be intensified by differences in personal taste and styles of entertain-ment. Consumers and producers of high fashion rely on their cultural capital to appreciate their aesthetic taste, but the new aesthetic tastes in subcultural fashion do not require cultural capital.

THE STRONG FEMALE PRESENCE IN JAPANESE SUBCULTURES

Dick Hebdige wrote (1979) that girls have been relegated to a position of secondary interest within both sociological accounts of subculture and pho-tographic studies of urban youths, and the masculine bias is still there in the subcultures. Furthermore, McRobbie and Garber asked an important question (1991: 4): "Are girls really absent from subcultures?"

> Female invisibility or partial visibility in youth subcultures takes on the qualities of the self-fulfilling prophecy. Perhaps women and girls have played only a minor role in these groupings. The exclusive attention paid to male expressions and male styles none the less reinforces and amplifies this image of the subculture as a male formation. (McRobbie and Garber 1991: 4–5)

McRobbie and Garber examine the roles of girls in motorbike, mod, and hip-pie subcultures and find that their positions within the group are marginal and subordinate. For instance, in rocker or motorbike culture, a girl's membership depended entirely on whose girlfriend she was. Mod culture offered a more complex subcultural opportunity for girls, whereby participation was wholly reliant on wearing the right clothes, having the right hairstyle, and going to the right clubs (McRobbie and Garber 1991: 11). The researchers argue that there need to be complementary ways in which young girls interact among themselves and with each other to form a distinctive culture of their own (McRobbie and Garber 1991: 11).

In Japanese subcultures, as explained in chapters 4 through 8, the key players are girls and young women, and they express their gender identity in an extreme manner. They put on a specific female identity that projects an intensified feminine image, which comes in various forms, shapes, and styles. For Shibuya's Gyaru, their sexuality and an erotic sense of self are emphasized. Harajuku's Lolita's image is cute and innocent. Maid café girls in Akihabara play a stylistically and physically submissive role of a maid that primarily serves male customers.

Masculinity and manhood are stressed in male-dominant Western subcultures, while female qualities are emphasized in Japanese subcultures. While violence is an outspoken expression of rebellion, sexuality and cuteness are nonviolent forms of rebellion. Both are ways to empower oneself by enhancing sex and gender characteristics. After all, subcultures are gendered phenomena in both Western and non-Western cultures. In Japanese subcultures, girls and young women are more present and more dominant than boys.

CONCLUSION

A sociological discussion of fashion looks at the macro-structural analysis of the social organization of fashion and also the micro-interactionist analysis of the individuals, such as designers, publicists, journalists, and editors, among many others, involved in the production of fashion, which is different from the production of clothing, dress, or costume (Kawamura 2005). It also investigates the interaction and interdependence between the organization and the individuals in the world of fashion (Crane 1997a, 1997b, 2000). Therefore, sociologists of fashion pay less attention to a semiotic analysis of the details of clothing that costume historians might engage in. Instead, sociology focuses on the social, cultural, or subcultural context in which a particular fashion phenomenon is produced, diffused, maintained, and, gradually, faded away. Fashion practice was commonly believed to start from the upper class and then was trickled down to the masses. This was known as the trickle-down theory of fashion (Simmel [1904] 1957; Veblen [1899] 1957). This theory may be valid in explaining the fashion phenomenon of the seventeenth and eighteenth centuries, but not today's fashion (Blumer 1969a), especially subcultural fashion.

By using Japanese street subculture as a case study, we can understand the group affiliations of the youth on the streets of Tokyo. Fashion emerges out of youth culture and is then commercialized to reach a wider audience to spread it as fashion. There is a strong social connection and a sense of belonging among the youth who dress in unique and original outfits, some of which are outrageous, radical, and extraordinary. As Howard Becker (1982) remarked, art is a collective activity. Fashion is also a collective activity that arises out of particular social relationships among the members of a subculture. Within every subculture, common values, attitudes, and norms bind the members, and the norms are frequently expressed visually through distinctive clothes, makeup, accessories, and jewelry. Dress is used to create a symbolic group identity.

Fashion today is not solely dictated by professional designers. The junior high and high school students who represent Japanese street culture and fashion have the power to influence other teens. They not only produce and diffuse fashion but also market and guide the industry professionals on what the next trends will be, and this influence may apply to other creative industries. Particular styles imply membership of particular social groups. The teen consumers are also the producers, and control (although not completely) the production and dissemination of fashion, resulting in a complementary relationship between the consumption and production of fashion.

Plate 1 Shibuya 109 department store; Photo by Yoya Kawamura.

Plate 2 A group of Gyaru in Shibuya; Photo by Yusuke Arai.

Plate 3 A group of Gyaru-o in Shibuya; Photo by Yusuke Arai.

Plate 4   A flyer for Yusuke Arai's retirement party.

Plate 5 A Gyaru at her retirement party in Shibuya; Photo by Aznyan_Ultimate.

Plate 6 Manami Abe in Classical Lolita; Photo by Masato Imai.

Plate 7 Sara in Punk Lolita; Photo courtesy of *Kera!* magazine.

Plate 8   Momo Matsuura in Classical Lolita (left) and Sphere in Ouji (right); Photo courtesy of Momo Matsuura.

Plate 9 Zuki (left) and Haru (right) in Twin Lolita; Photo by Momo Matsuura.

Plate 10 Haru in Sweet/Pink Lolita; Photo by Momo Matsuura.

Plate 11 Cosplayers on Jingu Bridge in Harajuku; Photo by Yoya Kawamura.

Plate 12 Cosplayers on Jingu Bridge in Harajuku; Photo by Yoya Kawamura.

Plate 13 A maid café waitress handing out flyers in Akihabara; Photo by Yutaka Toyama.

Plate 14 A waitress in a high school uniform at Cosplay Café; Photo by Yutaka Toyama.

Plate 15 Rice and curry served at a cosplay restaurant in Akihabara; Photo by Yutaka Toyama.

Plate 16 Cosplayers at Comic Market; Photo by Yutaka Toyama.

Plate 17 A cosplayer at Comic Market; Photo by Yutaka Toyama.

Plate 18 Ayumi Saito in a Ninja character in Nintama Rantaro; Photo by Sorata.

Plate 19 Otaku Lolita in Akihabara; Photo by Yutaka Toyama.

Plate 20 Black Lolita ensemble (left), Princess Decoration ensemble (center), and Mori Girl ensemble (right); Photo Courtesy of FIT.

Plate 21 A girl posing for photographers in Harajuku; Photo by Yoya Kawamura.

Plate 22 A boy posing for photographers in Harajuku; Photo by Yoya Kawamura.

Plate 23 A Lolita and a cosplayer posing for photographers in Harajuku; Photo by Yoya Kawamura.

Plate 24 A boy dressed in Ouji (Prince) lining up for a magazine photo shoot in Shinjuku; Photo by Yuniya Kawamura.

Plate 25 Silvia Nodari, an Italian Lolita; Photo courtesy of Silvia Nodari.

Plate 26   American Lolita at FIT's Lolita Tea Party in 2010; Photo by Yuniya Kawamura.

Plate 27 American cosplayer at NY Comic Con and Anime Festival in 2010; Photo by Maya Kawamura.

Plate 28 American cosplayers at NY Comic Con and Anime Festival in 2010; Photo by Maya Kawamura.

Plate 29   American cosplayer at NY Anime Festival in 2007; Photo by Maya Kawamura.

Plate 30   American cosplayers at NY Anime Festival in 2007; Photo by Maya Kawamura.

III: THE POWER OF THE YOUTH: TRICKLE-UP/BUBBLE-UP THEORY REVISITED

All of the case studies in Part II demonstrate the power that the Japanese youth have to collectively produce a new genre of fashion with a new taste and spread it. The new fashions are later recognized and picked up by industry professionals, such as designers, marketers, merchandisers, retailers, and magazine editors, who are constantly searching for ideas and items for commercialization to reach those who simply like their fashion expressions. The youth are both the consumers and the producers of fashion. Their background, qualifications, or professional experiences are irrelevant, because their sense of creativity is intuitive. Professionals in the fashion industries rely on the youth, and, as a result, individuals and institutions are in an interdependent relationship in spreading a subcultural phenomenon that comes with specific styles and fashion. They become interactive in expanding and perpetuating the subculture. Shibuya, Harajuku, and Akihabara possess the largest institutional framework for subculture-related industries to grow and prosper, with the cooperation of a number of retailers, manufacturers, and the media. Shinjuku is becoming increasingly inclusive of different subcultures as many Gyaru work in Shinjuku as Age-jo or Caba-jo, and Lolita girls also visit there to shop. Mori Girl in Kouenji is not as widespread as the other subcultures because of its lack of institutional support and involvement. It remains marginal, as do Ikebukuro, Nakano, Tachikawa. and Saitama; but their marginality may be what attracts the youth.

Classical sociologists at the turn of the twentieth century (Simmel [1904] 1957; Spencer [1896] 1966; Sumner and Keller 1927; Tarde 1903; Toennies [1887] 1963; Veblen [1899] 1957) theorized and conceptualized the notion of fashion, and they show us the sociological importance and perspective of fashion. What earlier sociologists share in their discussions of fashion is the concept of imitation. It is a relational concept that is necessarily a social relationship and, therefore, of sociological significance. These sociologists explain how fashion, which is a process of imitation, is included in understanding culture and society. Imitation, which is at the basis of analyzing fashion, is typically a view from above; it assumes that social inferiors envy superiors and engage in imitative activities to emulate their betters to gain recognition and even entry into the privileged group (Hunt 1996). For instance, for Spencer ([1896] 1966), fashion is intrinsically imitative: "Imitative, then, from the beginning, first of a superior's defects, and then, little by little, of other traits peculiar to him, fashion has ever tended towards equalization." Spencer posits two types of imitations: reverential and competitive. For instance, any modification of dress adopted by a king is imitated by courtiers and spreads downward; the result of this process is fashion in clothing. This is the fundamental principle of a trickle-down theory of fashion. Competitive imitation is prompted by the desire to assert equality with a person.

On the other hand, in the 1950s Herbert Blumer (1969a), in his famous article "Fashion: From Class Differentiation to Collective Selection," explicitly stated that the classical theory of fashion—that is, the trickle-down theory of fashion proposed by earlier scholars such as Georg Simmel, Thorstein Veblen, and Herbert Spencer—was no longer valid in explaining contemporary fashion. He proposed the bubble-up theory. While appreciating Simmel's contribution to the study of fashion, which Blumer uses to set off his argument, Blumer argues that it is a parochial treatment, suited only to fashion in dress in seventeenth-, eighteenth-, and nineteenth-century Europe within a particular class structure. It does not fit the operation of fashion in our contemporary epoch with its many diverse fields and its emphasis on modernity. While not rejecting the power of the prestige of a wearer, Blumer argues that one does not set the direction of fashion. Blumer, who defines fashion as a collective selection, takes a different perspective and argues that "the fashion mechanism appears not in response to a need of class differentiation and class emulation, but in response to a wish to be in fashion, to be abreast of what has good standing, to express new tastes which are emerging in a changing world" (Blumer 1969a: 281). He continues, "It is not the prestige of the elite which makes the design fashionable but, instead, it is the suitability or potential fashionableness of the design which allows the prestige of the elite to be attached to it. The design has to correspond to the direction of incipient taste of the fashion consuming public" (Blumer 1969a: 280).

The transformation of collective taste results from the diversity of experience that occurs in social interaction. For Blumer, fashion is directed by consumer taste, and it is a fashion designer's task to predict and read the modern taste of the collective mass. His bubble-up, or trickle-up, theory situates consumers in the construction of fashion. By investigating Japanese youth subcultures in different districts, it is evident that the fashions did not come from wealthier social classes, celebrities, or popular retailers. The fashions were born on the streets.

Since Blumer (1969a), who was probably the first scholar to explicitly negate the imitation theory of fashion, more and more fashion scholars have shared his perspective in explaining fashion phenomena. Like Blumer, Davis (1992) rejects the class-differentiation model and argues that the model used by classical theorists is outdated because, although what people wear and how they wear it can reveal much regarding their social standing, this is not all that dress communicates, and under many circumstances, it is by no means the most important thing communicated. Davis (1992) shares with Blumer the view that it is to the collective facets of our social identities that fashion addresses itself. Davis's focus is on the relationship between fashion/clothing and individual identity in modern society. According to Davis, as one's identity becomes increasingly pluralistic, the meaning of fashion also becomes increasingly ambivalent—a notion in line with postmodern thought. According to Davis, our identities are flexible and uncertain, and fashion fulfills that instability and ambiguity (1992: 17).

FASHION AS ROLE-PLAYING IN POSTMODERN CULTURES

In postmodern cultures, consumption is conceptualized as a form of role-playing, as consumers seek to project conceptions of identity that are continually evolving. Social class is less evident and less important in one's self-image and identity in contemporary society than ever before. Style differentiation no longer distinguishes social classes. There is a great deal of interclass and intraclass mobility. Social identity that used to be based on the economic and political spheres is now based on something outside. Like Davis (1992), Crane (2000) also emphasized the significance of identity construction: "the consumption of cultural goods, such as fashionable clothing, performs an increasingly important role in the construction of personal identity, while the satisfaction of material needs and the emulation of superior classes are secondary" (Crane 2000: 11). One's style of dress conveys an initial and continuing impression-making image. The variety of lifestyles available in contemporary society liberates the individual from tradition and enables him or her to make choices that create a meaningful self-identity (Giddens 1991).

According to Crane:

> Consumers are no longer perceived as "cultural dopes" or "fashion victims" who imitate fashion leaders but people selecting styles on the basis of their perceptions of their own identities and lifestyles. Fashion is presented as a choice rather than a mandate. The consumer is expected to "construct" an individualized appearance from a variety of options. An amalgam of materials is drawn from many different sources, clothing styles have different meanings for different social groups. (2000: 15)

As explained in chapter 3, the structure of Japanese society has been going through a major transformation, and with the advent of technology, fashion information is spreading from various sources through the media at an amazingly fast pace. Instead of looking for the fashionable items of the season in Paris, consumers look elsewhere, and sometimes youth subcultures create their own styles with their own definitions of fashions. I would call this another type of fashion system that appears in opposition to the mainstream high-fashion system. Fashion is being decentralized, and a growing number of younger designers worldwide are emerging out of street cultures and designing distinct street fashion, one type of which is subcultural fashion. Although there are still gatekeepers of fashion who play an intermediate role between designers and consumers, they are not an essential part of the process.

Now that the youth have the power to produce fashion, the boundary between fashion amateurs and professionals is blurring. With the manipulation of technology and the diversification of fashion trends and tastes, anyone can be involved in the production and dissemination of fashion. Chapter 10 examines the deprofessionalization of fashion-related occupations. As fashion magazines began to include pictures of youth fashion on the streets, a growing number of photographers, both professional and nonprofessional, are roaming the streets. At the same time, those with a sophisticated taste in a unique style can be selected as models to appear in magazines. For the youth, the streets are their catwalks. Anyone can become a celebrity in today's society. Chapter 11 discusses the future possibilities and limitations of the globalization of Japanese subcultures and investigates the diffusion process and the mechanism of Japanese subcultures. Although the Japanese government has subsidized the semiannual fashion shows taking place in Tokyo since 2005, the Japanese fashion industry has failed to formally establish a fashion system in Japan. I explore the Internet as a major force for the growth and spread of Japanese fashion subcultures, some of which are gaining global popularity, albeit on an individual level. In conclusion, I discuss the future of Japanese subcultures.

–10–

The Deprofessionalization of Fashion

Wearing the latest style was the privilege of the rich until the mid-nineteenth century in Europe, and, indeed, it was the rich who initiated fashion. Applying Erving Goffman's (1959) idea of the social sphere that is divided into front and back stages, it can be said that there was a clear distinction between the front stage, where fashion was exposed and shown to the public, and the back stage, where clothes were manufactured for the rich by seamstresses, dressmakers, and tailors. Once the clothes appeared on the front stage, they became fashion. The producers of fashion and the producers of clothing never overlapped.

The professionalization of occupational categories in fashion had been intact in the mainstream fashion world for centuries. In the old guild system in Europe, there was a clear division of labor, occupational categories were tightly controlled, and the manufacturing process and the use of tools and equipment were regulated. Tradesmen started as apprentices to learn the trade and acquire the necessary skills. Even after fashion became an institutionalized system in Paris in 1868 with the establishment of the first fashion trade organization (Kawamura 2004), the division of labor was fixed. The power relationship between the designer and the consumer/wearer was reversed by Charles Frederick Worth (1826–1896),[1] and trained and qualified designers rather than the wealthy were the ones who initiated the latest styles (for more detailed information on this, see Kawamura 2004). Fashion and the latest trends were now produced by designers and couturiers.

Some occupations, such as lawyers and doctors, require an official license. But even in occupations that do not require licensing, training and experience are necessary to function effectively in any industry. In the world of fashion, those who want to become designers typically attend a fashion school to learn sketching and design and to acquire basic sewing, pattern-making, and draping skills so that they are able to convey their ideas to the makers of the clothes, such as sample makers and factory sewers. Without these skills, designers cannot materialize whatever they have designed. Some schools offer courses in textile design to fashion design majors; because designers deal with textiles and fabrics, they need to have a basic knowledge of weaving and knitting. Designers need to learn everything about clothes-making, just as a conductor in an orchestra needs to know how to play every musical instrument. Fashion buyers and merchandisers often have a business background to understand procurement and selling strategies, to accurately forecast what will be in trend next season, and how to merchandise and market a collection.

However, as discussed in chapter 4, the latest phenomenon in the world of fashion, especially in Japanese subcultural fashion, is the deprofessionalization of occupational categories in the fashion industry. In the world of youth fashion, training, prior experience in the industry, and qualified skills are not necessarily required. In the new business model of fashion, such prerequisites are not important. Whoever has a different and unique idea can produce fashion, and good taste can be produced through socialization.

An industry professional said to me, "Kids are so talented and creative that we who are supposed to be the fashion professionals need to learn from them. Fashion is all about having fresh ideas, and they are the ones who have them." Japanese street fashion provides the fashion industries with a new business model of fashion that blurs and defies occupational classifications in fashion. Fashion is no longer produced by well-trained designers who know how to drape, make patterns, and instruct sewing procedures. Anyone with a great idea is in a position to produce and disseminate fashion. This new model allows the youth to be designers, merchandisers, salespeople, stylists, and models. They are the gatekeepers, as well as the agents, of street fashion in every sense. A popular salesgirl told me, "If I know in my gut feeling what will sell, I just know it. I share the same taste as the other teen girls, so I just know it." For these fashion producers, there is no logic. Salespeople are becoming the designers, merchandisers, and marketers.

TEEN READERS AS MAGAZINE MODELS

Before the street fashion phenomenon that started in the mid-1990s, fashion trends were mostly dictated by the major fashion magazines. But this is no longer the case, and the magazines no longer dictate styles to consumers. With street fashion came a new type of fashion magazine. A number of Japanese street fashion magazines, such as *Tune*, *Mini*, *CUTiE*, *Jille*, *Fudge*, and *Egg*, were published one after the other. Instead of having professional fashion models pose in famous designers' clothes, the street fashion magazines feature high school students and teens on the streets.

The deprofessionalization of occupational categories in fashion is most prominent among the models in fashion magazines previously discussed. To be a model, one typically needs to possess certain physical features, such as being tall and thin. To be hired as a professional model, many register at model agencies that represent hundreds of professional models. In street fashion, there are no agencies and there are no stylists.

Magazines undoubtedly play a crucial role in producing and maintaining subcultures and fashion. Since the emergence of many street fashion magazines that use their readers as models—known as *dokusha* models (reader models)—professional models are no longer needed. The models do not have perfect figures or perfect faces. The *dokusha* model, often abbreviated as *doku-mo*, can be a girl next door who happens to be fashionable. Some of these young women become celebrities and appear on television and in movies. These models give hope to some young readers: if they are as fashionable and as pretty as the amateur models in street fashion magazines, they can also become someone special.

The professional labor that used to require formal training (e.g., dressmaking, patternmaking, designing, modeling, etc.) is being performed by untrained but fashionable amateurs. They are the ones who create street fashion. The consumers and the magazine readers are the producers and disseminators of fashion, and, thus, the boundary between the production and consumption of fashion is breaking down. Furthermore, the mass media contribute to the elimination of the boundary between the social organization of fashion professional insiders and nonprofessional outsiders by allowing the nonprofessional viewers to participate in the professional world of fashion.

A teen described how she appeared in one of the street fashion magazines:

> I visited the editorial office at a street fashion magazine. Then they called me later and asked me if I wanted to model in the magazine. Then another magazine called me. It's a thrill to see your picture in the magazines. I think everyone wants to be in it. That's why street fashion is getting more and more exaggerated so that they would stand out and get their pictures taken.

Some of the teen models who have become well known because of the frequency of their appearances in the magazines are hired by the popular retail stores. One of the store managers in Shibuya 109 said, "We now aggressively hire teenage models who appear in the street fashion magazines as our salesgirls. It's one way to attract the teens, because they visit our store to talk to them and get to know them." Fashion does not trickle down anymore; it trickles across and trickles up.

A former editor-in-chief of a street fashion magazine said:

> Professional models were not wanted. We need someone who was half a step forward in fashion. We needed someone, an ordinary girl who is a little bit more forward in fashion than others. Retailers asked the girls to wear the clothes, or

asked the bloggers to write about them. ... Our editors talked to high school girls on the streets every day. Words they use or what they are looking for. And they always bought the magazine if their friends were in it. The editorials were emphasized on our readers' values and what they were looking for.

It is the readers who are giving direction and guidance to the magazines. The editors digest and communicate what is already happening in youth fashion on the streets.

Social recognition is what humans ultimately need after satisfying all the basic needs, such as food, sleep, and shelter. Human desires are rarely fulfilled. Once our basic needs are met, we usually want something else and something more: social recognition and acknowledgment. Although the Japanese economy has faltered drastically in the past two decades, most Japanese people still have food to eat and places to live and sleep. The youth crave intense attention and recognition, and the media oblige them by creating role models that look like their friends in school or the girls next door. Amateur models are the modern-day celebrities. They do not need to be extraordinarily beautiful; they need only average beauty and a creative taste in fashion.

THE COLLAPSE OF PRODUCTION AND CONSUMPTION BOUNDARIES

An object is almost always manufactured before it is purchased, and we therefore have a tendency to see consumption activities as the result of, or as a process secondary to, the development of manufacturing and other forms of production. However, in postmodern culture, the boundary between production and consumption is starting to collapse. For Howard Becker (1982), there is no distinction between production and consumption in the art world. The audiences are undistinguished from the artists. Everyone participates in producing and distributing their works.

The distinction between popular/mass and high culture often appears in studies of culture and the arts, and this may extend to the classification of high fashion and popular fashion. Paul DiMaggio (1992) showed in his study that, at the beginning of the twentieth century in the United States, a high-culture model was established by a distinct organizational system. He analyzed how differences in various categories were cultivated and institutionalized over time in order to maintain the distinctions. However, Crane (2000) argues that the high/low distinction is becoming arbitrary, and, thus, we have to define cultures in terms of the environments in which they are created, produced, and disseminated rather than in terms of their content.

As young consumers become increasingly fashionable and fashion conscious in modern and postmodern societies, they become the producers. Fashion was originally defined as dressing up, but the concept of dressing down began to emerge in democratic societies as class boundaries became less rigid. Street fashion began as antifashion, but, ironically, it was still acknowledged as fashion. This flow of the fashion trend is the trickle-up theory of fashion.

Since fashion defines the legitimate taste of clothing, people strive to discover what that is, and this legitimate taste, according to Bourdieu (1984), is class based, differing from one social class to another. However, more recently, fashionable styles are provided in different forms for people in different social classes so that fashionable items can reach almost every level of consumer.

Punk fashion exemplifies the breakdown of the boundary between the production and consumption of fashion. Punk first emerged among groups of unemployed young people and students in London in the mid-1970s. Punk culture developed as a reaction to unemployment and the general pessimism among youth. Punk was an anarchic, nihilistic style that deliberately set out to shock society. Punk clothing was almost entirely black and consciously menacing; it was often homemade or bought from secondhand thrift shops. Garments were frequently slashed and worn in disheveled layers. Both men and women shaved their heads, mutilated themselves, and wore dirty and torn clothes. They used makeup and hair products to produce outrageous styles. Mendes and de la Haye (1999: 222) describe the styles that shaped punk identity as follows:

> Clothes for both sexes included tight black trousers teamed with mohair sweaters, leather jackets customized with paint, chains and metal studs. For female punks, miniskirts, black fishnet tights and stiletto-heeled shoes, and for both sexes bondage trousers joined with straps from knee to knee. Jackets and T-shirts often featured obscene or disturbing words or images. Garments were festooned with chains, zips, safety-pins and razor blades. Hair was dyed in different colors, and shaved and gelled to create Mohican spikes. ... Multiple earrings were popular, some also pierced their cheeks and noses. It also challenged both masculine stereotypes and long-held ideals of feminine beauty.

Punks violated the conventions and norms that society placed upon them, and their challenging message attracted a large audience. It gave a sense of belonging to youngsters who were in search of an identity.

THE IMPACT OF ADVANCED TECHNOLOGY

The advent of technology accelerated the deprofessionalization of fashion. The world of professional photographers has become extremely competitive since the invention and widespread availability of digital cameras. Many of the subcultural members who I encountered in my research mentioned photography as a hobby; they dress in their unique outfits and then take photographs of each other. The quality of their photos was professional.

As street fashion magazines began to include photos of youth fashion found on the streets, a growing number of street photographers appeared on the scene. On weekends in Harajuku and Shibuya in particular, many photographers line the pavement looking around and waiting to take pictures of the fashionable youth. The streets are the catwalks of the youth. Some teens are regulars on the streets, and they intentionally dress creatively and uniquely so that they will get their pictures taken.

A growing number of online magazines feature street fashion snapshots, and these images do not require the high resolution that is needed to produce crisp images in print. Many teens take pictures with their smartphones and upload them to their own Web sites or to social networking sites, or they send them to Web magazines. Street snaps have become a huge industry in Japan. Countless participants in this industry are not trained in fashion or photography. They post photos of teens in Shibuya, Harajuku, Shinjuku, Kouenji, and Daikanyama and of unique window displays that change on a regular basis, and they sell the pictures on the Internet.

Fashion writing is another occupation that someone with little training can pursue. One does not need any particular qualifications or experience to critique and write about fashion and designers. Before the invention of the Internet, landing a position at a fashion magazine was no easy task. It was extremely competitive to become a fashion journalist or fashion editor. Today, anyone can create a Web site, an online magazine, or a fashion blog. One can become a self-claimed fashion critic or fashion editor instantaneously. Bloggers—some of whom are affiliated with popular magazines and some of whom are independent—are becoming very influential in spreading certain fashion trends. It used to be the privilege of a fashion professional as an industry insider—such as a fashion journalist, editor, or a buyer—to attend the semiannual fashion weeks in major fashion cities. Today many bloggers obtain passes to major fashion shows; indeed, many are so popular and influential that they get front-row seats, because the industry knows the power of the bloggers. Fashion weeks in Paris and New York that used to invite only industry professionals are now sending invitations to online fashion critics.

When I attended a fashion show in New York during the 2010 fashion week, the woman sitting to my right was a blogger from Israel, and on my left were bloggers from Germany and the United States. A blogger I talked to at the show who writes about New York youth fashion said:

> I started my blog on youth fashion in New York. Then one big sneaker company somehow found my blog and asked me to blog about their limited edition sneaker

collection that was about to be released. They sent me images and they said if I write about them on my blog, I would get some pairs of these sneakers from the collection free! Who can turn down an offer like that! And they really sent me three pairs in my size. I was impressed.

The fashion industry professionals know the power of the youth who are sophisticated technology users and who can influence their peers better than adults in the industry. Many youth surf the Internet for hours at time, looking for different and creative items. The diffusion process of fashion has changed completely since the days before the Internet and since the days when the major fashion shows were highly valued as a way to promote and distribute new fashion. Today, both amateurs and professionals have the capacity to spread fashion globally via the Internet, and the deprofessionalization process of occupational categories in fashion allows Japanese fashion subcultures to spread globally among youth around the world.

CONCLUSION

Industries are usually made up of individuals who are experienced and trained. That is how the industry is maintained, produced, and reproduced. Since occupations in fashion do not require licenses or diplomas, experience is important. But in the new model of Japanese youth fashion, including subcultural fashion, that idea does not apply. The experience, qualifications, and skills that the youth have are limited, but those who have an eye for fashion and who understand what other teens will like and want can find themselves in fashion-related occupations such as designer, marketer, merchandiser, model, editor, and journalist. The teen consumers are not simply consuming fashion; they are setting the trends, spreading them, and promoting them. This deprofessionalization in the fashion industry provides more opportunities to the youth and opens more doors to those who want to work in fashion-related industries. This trend of deprofessionalization receives much help from the Internet, since today's youth are technologically savvy. We live in an age where fashion professionals are learning from the nonprofessional youth, and the deprofessionalization of fashion is accelerating every day.

The Globalization of Japanese Subcultures and Fashion: Future Possibilities and Limitations

The development of communication technologies has made the distribution and circulation of media information, images, and texts extremely easy, and the global diffusion of cultural products, such as anime, manga, and fashion, is rapidly accelerating. It is possible—and not particularly difficult—for individuals to produce and spread cultural content to the world. This chapter explores the measures and processes that individuals and institutions are taking to publicize, promote, and raise the reputation of not only Japanese subcultural fashion, but youth fashion in general, and it examines the possibilities and limitations of the expansion of Japan's new genre of fashion.

SPREADING JAPAN'S SOFT POWER

Joseph Nye, an American scholar at Harvard University, coined the term "soft power" (Nye 2004). He defined soft power as the ability of a nation to achieve its objectives by attracting or seducing other nations to do its bidding or emulate its policies without resorting to coercion (which is "hard power"), since gains and victories achieved by military force and economic sanctions are often short-lived and provoke a backlash (1990, 2004). Hard power does not produce any positive outcomes. Nye maintains that it is more effective to inspire nations to adopt desired policies and objectives. Some scholars and analysts believe that Japan can use its popular culture as soft power.

Japanese anime and manga have proven that Japan is able to provide a high standard of cultural content that attracts millions of people around the world. Other areas of Japanese popular culture, such as fashion, music, and food, have also gained attention worldwide. The export of popular culture, which was once dominated by the United States, has been increasingly influenced by other countries, such as Japan.

It has been argued that Japan is represented and represents itself as culturally exclusive, homogeneous, and uniquely particularistic through the operation of a strategic binary opposition between two imaginary cultural entities:

Japan and the West. It was believed that Japan lacked external cultural power, which is synonymous with a postwar strategy of constructing an exclusive and unique Japanese national identity (Iwabuchi 2002: 6–7). But the Japanese government's policy has changed since 2002, and it is now aggressively promoting "Cool Japan" and making an effort to increase Japan's popular culture exports to help Japan's ailing economy and trade.[1]

Since World War II there have been massive interventions of Western fashion into Japan from Europe and the United States, and the global reach of French fashion is expansive and is hegemonic in taste. But the Japanese youth are walking away from that taste, which dominated their parents' generation. Taste in high fashion will probably continue to be centralized in Europe, especially in Paris, but Japanese subcultures and fashion can be used strategically as major vehicles of Japan's cultural expansion as a new taste in youth fashion around the globe, just as punk fashion became an accepted legitimate taste in particular segments of youth populations.

In the past, if a young Japanese designer wanted to be world famous, he or she would participate in the biannual Paris fashion collection, since that is where the annual cycle of fashion is anchored (Skov 1996, 2006). It also determines the fashion seasons to which international fashion magazines devote their pages (Moeran 2006). This is the path taken by many designers, such as Atsuro Tayama, Keita Maruyama, and Jun Takahashi of Undercover. They are conforming to a Western-dominated cultural hierarchy that governs transnational cultural flows. Japanese fashion needed Western legitimization.

However, this model is now changing. As indicated in chapter 10, "The Deprofessionalization of Fashion," technology has transformed all aspects of the fashion industry. The world is literally at one's fingertips and only a click away. The Internet has obviously been a major force for the growth and spread of Japanese fashion subcultures, some of which have become world famous and popular. For instance, there are Lolita and cosplayers in Asia, Europe, and the United States. Many American and European teens who have never been to Japan are attracted to Japanese subcultures and their stylistic expressions.

THE GLOBAL DIFFUSION: JAPANESE
LOLITA AS A CASE STUDY

Whether it is authentic Lolita or part of cosplay, Lolita fashion is beginning to take root around the world. Diffusion theories of fashion seek to explain how fashion is spread through interpersonal communication and institutional networks, and they assume that the fashion phenomenon is not ambiguous or unpredictable. Diffusion theories of fashion can focus on individuals, which can give a small-scale analysis, and on institutions, which is a systematic, large-scale approach. Similarly, fashion subcultures can be studied from the point of view of the individual, as the early psychologists indicated, or from the point of view of the structure and function of society as a whole, as many sociologists do.

Thus, we can see individuals and institutions involved in the diffusion process of Lolita. The process of fashion diffusion used to involve a highly centralized system, initially started in Paris. Innovators belong to a community where a group of individuals and organizations are involved in the production, reproduction, evaluation, and dissemination of a specific form of culture as well as subculture. Opinion leaders and gatekeepers included editors of leading fashion magazines and highly visible fashion consumers, such as society women, movie stars, and popular music stars. However, today, the centralized fashion system has been replaced by another system. As explained in chapter 10, trends are no longer set by professional designers. Fashion originates in many types of social groups and communities, such as youth subcultures, and as a result, fashion emanates from many sources and diffuses in various directions.

INDIVIDUAL EFFORTS

With technology and the Internet, it is not difficult to diffuse fashion worldwide. Teens create Web sites promoting, chatting, and exchanging information about their favorite fashions. It is not surprising that some of the Japanese street styles have migrated to the streets of New York City. In addition to manga, anime, sushi, and other cultural objects, Japan is attempting to promote the latest street fashion and is setting new fashion tastes.

Many Lolita followers who were not familiar with Japanese culture are fascinated by the Lolita image and fashion. The Internet has undoubtedly been the key tool that helps followers find information about Japanese Lolita labels, events, auctions, and chat rooms. Many are initially influenced by manga and anime.

A 22-year-old Italian Lolita who has been wearing Lolita since 2006 said, "The first time I found Lolita was on the Internet. I was looking for an image of a manga that I was reading. Then I started to get more information about this subculture, and I found an Italian forum about Lolita (gothiclolita.forum-community.net)." An American Lolita told me, "I went to a Japanese bookstore with my friends and found *Gothic and Lolita Bible* and fell in love with it. Then I started to Google to get more information on the Internet." These young women find sufficient information online about Japanese Lolita brands that they want to wear. They are familiar with the well-known Lolita brands, such as Baby, the Stars Shine Bright, Metamorphose, and Angelic Pretty.

The Italian Lolita girl continued, "My favorite brand is Alice and the Pirates, but I love Innocent World and Mary Magdalene, too. Usually I buy them through international online shops, but sometimes I also buy secondhand through European Lolita girls. I can buy them in Italy, too, but there are few shops that carry them, and their prices are really high, usually three or four times the original price in Japan so I prefer to buy them online." Lolita clothes are rather expensive, and this is probably one of the reasons that many of the followers of this style sew their own clothes.

As indicated in chapter 5, "Harajuku: The Youth in Silent Rebellion," it is not only the look that Lolita adopt but also a lifestyle. Lolita girls like to organize tea parties, so they often find their friends on Internet chat rooms or on social networking sites and get together at the parties. There is a large U.S. Lolita community on Live Journal (www.livejournal.com), a popular social networking site, and it is subdivided into smaller communities with specific Lolita interests, such as Lolita Housewife, Princess Lolita, Loli Graphics, Lolita Indies, and Lolita Pattern Swap. There is a Lolita community in almost every state in the United States. One of the largest Lolita communities on Live Journal writes:

> Welcome to The Elegant Gothic Lolita (EGL) Community! Please make sure and understand all the rules before posting! Our mission is help others share, grow, and learn in the Gothic Lolita fashion. The community discussions focus on Japanese Gothic Lolita fashion and its manifestations the world over. We hope you will enjoy browsing our community!

The community has monthly themes. For example, the theme for October is "Lolita and Literature." Participants can share their own writings, or they can post an outfit inspired by their favorite novel.

INSTITUTIONAL EFFORTS

The Japanese government systematically and collaboratively attempts to promote a wider range of Japanese popular culture. Consumers in the West take interest in Japanese subcultures and their stylistic expressions initially through anime and manga. Japanese fashion magazines are popular in East and Southeast Asia but not in Europe or the United States. Although there are Chinese versions of Japanese street fashion magazines, such as *Popteen*, *S-Cawaii*, *mina*, *Vivi*, and *Ray*, there are no English versions of them, which indicates the geographical limitation of Japan's fashion expansion.

There are several institutional efforts to spread Japanese Lolita worldwide since it appears to be one of the most well-known Japanese subcultures overseas. The Japanese government and both commercial and nonprofit organizations realize that there is significant commercial potential to Lolita style. In March 2009, the Ministry of Foreign Affairs appointed three *Kawaii* (cute) Ambassadors: Shizuka Fujioka, Yu Kimura, and Misako Aoki. They went around the world promoting Japanese *Kawaii* culture. According to the press release issued by the Japan Ministry of Foreign Affairs (2009),

> The main mission of the three ambassadors is to transmit the new trends of Japanese pop culture in the field of fashion to the rest of the world and to promote understanding of Japan by their attending cultural projects carried out by the Japanese Embassies and the Japan Foundation. Pop culture, including fashion, is an integral part of today's Japanese culture. It enjoys worldwide popularity and we witness that such people are ever-increasing. Pop culture is expected to help the people of the world have more chances to know about contemporary Japan, hand-in-hand with other traditional and contemporary cultures.

Fujioka gave a lecture on Japanese fashion at the Japan Festa in Bangkok in March 2009. Aoki, who is a Lolita model for two major magazines, *Gothic and Lolita Bible* and *Kera!*, went to the Japan Expo in Paris to promote Japan's pop culture diplomacy. She also attended the World Cosplay Summit in Brazil to introduce Lolita fashion and traveled to Italy, Spain, Korea, and Russia.

Many European Lolita visit the Japan Expo in Paris, which is one of the world's largest international events celebrating Japanese pop culture, where over 160,000 people interested in Japanese pop cultural trends gather from all over the world. There are trade fairs, fashion shows, games, and various events related to Japanese popular culture, including Lolita. The Ministry of Foreign Affairs, the Agency for Cultural Affairs, the Ministry of Economy, Trade and Industry, and the Japan Tourism Agency (JTA) collaborated to participate in the Japan Expo Paris 2010. The number of visitors has increased every year since its inception in 2000. The Lolita come from all over Europe and hold meetings at the convention.

The Fashion Institute of Technology in New York hosted a Lolita tea party in October 2010, in conjunction with its exhibition *Japan Fashion Now!* The exhibition featured contemporary Japanese fashion from world-famous designers, such as Issey Miyake and Yohji Yamamoto, as well as youth subcultural fashion, including different styles and brands of Lolita fashion. A similar exhibition on contemporary Japanese fashion took place at London's Barbican Art Gallery in 2010. A new store called Tokyo Rebel opened in New York in 2009, which exclusively sells imported Japanese Lolita fashion.

As a form of cultural diplomacy, the Japanese government has started to export Japanese pop-cultural products. To increase tourism, Taro Aso, during his tenure as foreign minister, was central in developing policies to promote manga and anime overseas. He was behind the establishment of the International Manga Award for non-Japanese manga artists in 2007.

However, does the world's attraction to Japanese popular culture, including street and subcutural fashion, contribute to Japan's economy?

A LACK OF UNITY: THE FAILURE TO ESTABLISH A SOLID FASHION SYSTEM

Japanese fashion, whether high, street, or subcultural, must be legitimated by the Japanese in Japan before seeking the legitimization and recognition of the West. However, Japanese fashion gatekeepers, if there are any, seem to lack the confidence and the ability to criticize fashion that emerges out of Japan. They wait until fashions are recognized or ignored by the European or U.S. fashion gatekeepers.

A Japanese designer who went to Paris in 1997 said to me:

> When I was showing my collections in Tokyo, people in the industry used to say that I will never make it in Paris because my taste is very feminine and cute, and Western girls always try to be sexy and seductive, not cute. Then I started showing my collection in Paris, and the same people are now saying, "Oh, you are so talented. I knew you would be successful anywhere in the world!" The fact is that these people don't know anything about fashion. Even within the fashion industry, people don't know fashion.

It's easier for a Japanese designer to go overseas and get recognition. Then he or she comes back to Japan and makes money in Japan with the extra symbolic status and value that was earned overseas.

Japanese designers continue to mobilize in Paris, permanently or temporarily, due to the structural weaknesses of the fashion system in Japan (Kawamura 2004). When Japanese designers became known in Paris, it was believed that the widespread popularity of Japanese fashion in the 1980s was a decisive factor in placing Tokyo on the list of international fashion capitals (Skov 1996: 134). It has been more than forty years since Kenzo's and thirty years since Yamamoto's and Kawakubo's appearance in Paris, but Tokyo still falls far behind Paris in the production of fashion; that is, in setting the fashion trends, creating designers' reputations, and spreading their names worldwide. Tokyo as a fashion city lacks the kind of structure and effectiveness that the French system has. Thus, the lack of institutionalization and of a centralized fashion establishment in Japan forces designers to go to Paris; that is the battlefield for designers, where only the most ambitious compete and can survive.

Since 2005, the Council of Fashion Designers in Japan has been restructured as the Japan Fashion Week (JFW) organization, and the Ministry of Economy, Trade and Industry has been investing 500 million yen (approximately

US$6.25 million) annually in the organization to reorganize the semiannual fashion show event, in the hope that Tokyo will be internationally recognized as a fashion city and attract international buyers, retailers, journalists, and editors. However, in 2010, it was announced that the ministry would stop investing in the event. One government official at the ministry who I interviewed in August 2010 said:

> We are the Ministry of Economy, so whatever they [people in the Japanese fashion industries] do, we ultimately need to see some results in Japan's economy. We would not be satisfied simply by promoting Japanese popular culture worldwide. We need to see the outcome of our financial support. But after five years, we did not see any positive results so we have decided to stop investing in the shows. But it does not mean we have given up on the Japanese fashion industry. We will continue to support them in different ways.

He insisted that it is the ministry's job to boost Japan's economy, unlike the Agency for Cultural Affairs, whose goal is to expand Japan's culture and the arts. Their goals and interests are different. There appears to be a split not only between the government organizations, but also between the government and the JFW. In August 2010, the JFW announced that it had signed a partnership deal with a major event-planning company (IMG) in New York to organize a fashion show event in Tokyo. Based on the number of participants during the Japan Fashion Week in Tokyo, it was far from successful. The organizers have failed to make Japan Fashion Week into an international event.

Table 11.1:   Number of Participants (Labels) at Japan Fashion Week in Tokyo (2005–2011)

Date of Event	Number of Participants (Labels)
November 2005	52
March 2006	44
October 2006	39
March 2007	38
October 2007	40
March 2008	45
October 2008	37
March 2009	39
October 2009	52
March 2010	44
October 2010	49
March 2011*	39
October 2011	47

Source: From www.jfw.jp.
*The March 2011 event was canceled.

In 2010, it was announced that India's Lakmé Fashion Week organization would be collaborating with the JFW organization to showcase and introduce some Japanese designers' collections to the Indian market (some of the events planned on March 11, 2011, were canceled). A Japanese journalist who wished to remain anonymous told me:

> That investment by the government was a total failure. It is a waste of taxpayers' money. People in the Japanese fashion industry have no idea how to spread our fashion globally. No one thinks Tokyo can be Paris or New York. Now JFW is tying up with people in India. India? Don't get me wrong, I like India, but in terms of fashion, they are even behind us. They started wearing Western clothes only recently. Why would they collaborate with India?

THE SHINMAI CREATORS PROJECT

Since 2009, the JFW started The Shinmai Creators Project to support new designers who are beginning their own labels. So far, twelve designer brands have been selected. Except for one winner in 2009 (Shida Tatusya, who graduated from Nagoya Modo Gauen in Japan and now lives and works in Japan), the rest of the winners were either educated and trained in the United States or Europe, or work in the United States. The implication seems to be that those who are trained to become designers in Japan are not as good as designers trained at Central Saint Martins College of Art and Design in London or at Parsons The New School for Design in New York. Young Japanese designers are not motivated to apply to this project. If the Japanese fashion system is unable to recognize and legitimate the talent and creativity of Japanese youth, the system will never stand on its own. The French system at one point was extremely territorial and allowed only the membership of French designers. While Paris is global and international, the star designer remains French as far as French fashion professionals are concerned (Kawamura 2004).

The reputation and status of a fashion school depends on its graduates' success. Kenzo Takada, Yohji Yamamoto, and Junko Koshino all made Bunka Fashion College world famous because of their global reputations, which started in Paris and then spread to other parts of the world. The selection of the winners of the Shinmai Creators Project and their schools underscores and reinforces the names of the already-famous fashion schools in Europe and in the United States. Belgian designers Martin Margiela and Ann Demeulemeester brought renown to the Fashion Design Department of the Antwerp Royal Academy of Fine Arts; John Galliano and Alexander McQueen were graduates of Central Saint Martins; and Donna Karan and Michael Kors studied at Parsons.

Table 11.2: Winners of the Shinmai Creators Project by School Affiliation and Winners' Country of Origin (2009–2011)

Year	Brand Name	Designer	School	Winner's Country of Origin
2009	NIMA	Nima Taherzadeh	Parsons The New School for Design	Iran
2009	donna sgro	Donna Sgro	University of Technology, Sydney	Australia
2009	aéthéré(e)	Ly-Ling Vilaysane and Adiren Escaravage	The Textile School of Austria and Esmod, Paris	Switzerland/ France
2009	Shida Tatsuya	Shida Tatsuya	Nagoya Modo Gakuen	Japan
2009	Sachio Kawasaki	Sachio Kawasaki	Central Saint Martins College of Art and Design	Japan
2010	A Degree Fahrenheit	Yu Amatsu	Tokyo Modo Gakuen	Japan
2010	Akane Utsunomiya	Akane Utsunomiya	Central Saint Martins College of Art and Design	Japan
2010	Fabiola Arias	Fabiola Arias	Parsons The New School for Design	USA
2010	The Individualist(s)	Luise Schwarze and Franck Pouchoulin	Esmod, Paris	France/Germany
2011	Yasutoshi Enzumi	Yasutoshi Enzumi	Central Saint Martins College of Art and Design	Japan
2011	Van Hongo	Izumi Hongo	Antwerp Royal Academy of Fine Arts	Japan
2011	Fernanda Yamamoto	Fernanda Yamamoto	Parsons The New School for Design	Brazil

Source: From www.jfw.jp.

A Japanese journalist said:

People who are involved in this contest [the Shinmai Creators Project] probably don't have the confidence themselves to choose those who have studied and worked only in Japan when there are other candidates applying from internationally famous schools like Parson and Saint Martins. There are already biases in the minds of the judges or whoever is involved in this project that those who were trained overseas are more creative. Japan has great talents, but no one can voice it loud and clear. Many people still believe in this day and age that anything from the West is better. It's about time people get rid of that mentality. It's an insult to all the great fashion schools in Japan!

Not surprisingly, the subcultural fashion community has nothing to do with the events organized by the JFW. None of the Lolita brands or Gyaru or Gyaru-o brands ever take part in Japan Fashion Week.

On an institutional level, there is no system in place that would make the worldwide export of subcultural fashion possible. Fashion or apparel export is different from anime and manga export. Many brands in Shibuya 109 or popular Lolita brands sold in La Foret have no or very limited means to export their products despite their global popularity. One American Lolita said:

> You go into their site, and many of them don't have them in English so I ask my Japanese friend to read it. But even if I send an e-mail asking about the sizes, they rarely respond. Some bluntly say that they don't send their stuff overseas. Even if you do get it, the size is too small. Many of the Lolita dresses are for petite Japanese girls. We American girls are big.

There is demand for Japanese fashions overseas but no means to meet the demand. An export system is unlikely to emerge as long as mainstream fashion professionals do not recognize the value of subcultural fashion.

CONCLUSION

To improve the image of Japan's popular culture is one thing; for it to contribute to Japan's export and economy is another. Before the Japanese government can make a further contribution to the fashion industry, whether high fashion or street fashion, a solid system needs to be in place. To date, Japan has not been successful in creating a system to export Japanese fashion. Individuals, organizations, government agencies, and various industry sectors are all working independently to satisfy their own needs and goals. Few people and institutions have a broad perspective on Japan's future in fashion. When the Japanese economy as a whole is declining, it is difficult to look outside the country. Japan has great fashion taste and talents, but in order for them to spread beyond the country's borders, there must be an established system and mechanism in place. Efforts to establish such a system have so far failed.

Conclusion: The Future of Japanese Subcultures

Fashioning Japanese Subcultures introduced and explained various Japanese youth subcultures that originated in different fashion districts in Tokyo and analyzed theoretically the continuous subcultural phenomenon in Japan while referring to various subcultural studies and theories found in the West. My intention was to fill the void in the Euro-Americentric bias in subcultural studies and the male-dominant perspectives of subcultures in general. In addition, I discuss the dimension of a taste struggle, although, at this point, I hesitate to jump to the conclusion to explicitly say that it leads to a class struggle. I also see a strong, yet ironic, correlation between the growing number of subcultural groups with distinct appearances and Japan's long-lasting recession. Structural changes in Japan's economy and labor market have contributed to this phenomenon. It has always been my conviction that wealth does not make people creative; rather, we hone our artistic abilities in a state of poverty. Japanese youth of today did not experience Japan's economic success in the 1980s and thus have limited resources, but that may be why their tastes are unique and original. They do the best they can to create new styles with whatever they can find to look fashionable and aesthetically beautiful.

The distinctive looks function as a visible group identity for the teens and become shared symbols of membership affiliation. A symbol is the vehicle by which humans communicate their ideas, intentions, purposes, and thoughts to one another. The teens are almost uniformly aware of all of their communication, which utilizes symbols that vary in the degree to which meanings are shared and intended. Therefore, these styles are functional and meaningful only within the specific territories of Tokyo among particular groups of people. Our appearance conveys messages about ourselves, and the messages in turn become our identities. We dress according to our ascribed statuses, such as class, sex, age, and race/ethnicity. We have multiple identities with different roles to perform. The Japanese youth intentionally create a new status and various identities.

All subcultures have the main determinants, such as rebellion, going against the mainstream, and creating their own value system, but my research on the Japanese subcultures finds that youth values are not always overt and outspoken. The way youth communicate can be silent and latent, but through their stylistic expressions, it is evident that the youth are not mainstream in terms of their beliefs, values, and ideologies. I confirm this through my in-depth formal and informal interviews with the subcultural members, in which the members revealed that they are very much aware of the dominant culture with which they do not associate. The Japanese youth subcultures reveal features that not only distinguish them from other conventional youth groups but also identify themselves as a distinctive community with different appearances, dress, and language, resulting in a strict conformity of behavior among the members, and these features are perpetuated among succeeding generations of youth.

Signs of cultural turmoil are everywhere. A broad social and cultural shift is taking place, and the concept of the postmodern by Crane (2000) and Muggleton (2000) captures some aspects of this transformation. The transition from modernity to postmodernity is a consequence of social, political, and cultural changes in the relationships between different social groups. Modernity presumes the existence of clear distinctions between different types and genres of aesthetic and stylistic expressions, while postmodernity no longer recognizes these categories as legitimate. It is almost impossible to define what is legitimate and what is not. Fashion emphasizes newness and change, which are the epitome of a postmodernist cultural form. Postmodernity is difficult to characterize because of its preoccupation with ambiguity and contradiction. It has no fixed meanings or has multiple meanings. Meanings are unstable, contradictory, and constantly changing. Subcultural identities that the youth create are fluid and flexible.

As I walked through different districts in Tokyo where youth subcultures are found, sat at coffee shops, listened to boys' and girls' conversations, and interviewed them face-to-face, what became evident about the young people was an evasion of any serious responsibility and the assertion of pleasure-loving attitudes in a very innocent way. The reality of what they have to face in the future to many is frightening, unpredictable, and painful. What the future holds for them should be the society's major concern, but the adults seem to be just as insecure and scared as the youth. At the same time, it is undeniably true that the youth subcultures are becoming increasingly innovative and creative as the Japanese economy declines and the youth lose a sense of belonging. Japanese fashion subcultures have never been so daring, radical, and provocative. As a fashion scholar, I am intrigued and fascinated by how the youth dress and express themselves through clothing, makeup, and accessories, and I plan to continue to follow these subcultures. Will the subcultures disappear slowly? Will they be replaced by new subcultures in the same district? Will they survive? Will they maintain the same subcultural beliefs and values? Will there be more male-dominant subcultures in Tokyo in the future? To what extent will the subcultures spread globally? I have countless questions.

My research on Japanese subcultures is not complete. There are many areas that can be covered, researched, and analyzed further. I welcome other fashion scholars as well as researchers in social sciences to develop more academic research on subcultures, Japanese youth, and fashion using my work as a departing point for debates and discussions. I also encourage scholars to investigate and explore youth subcultures in non-Western societies to discover their peculiarities and commonalities with other subcultures in the West and in Japan, since we do not hear much about them in scholarly literature and in the mass media. I hope this book can motivate other researchers, scholars, and graduate students to explore these topics.

Appendix

Table 3.1: Japan's Prime Ministers and Terms of Office since 1989

Name	Term of office (days in office)
Toshiki Kaifu	1989–1991 (817)
Kiichi Miyazawa	1991–1993 (643)
Morihiro Hosokawa	1993–1994 (262)
Tsutomu Hata	1994–1994 (63)
Tomichi Murayama	1994–1996 (560)
Ryutaro Hashimoto	1996–1998 (931)
Keizo Obuchi	1998–2000 (615)
Yoshiro Mori	2000–2001 (386)
Junichiro Koizumi	2001–2006 (1,979)
Shinzo Abe	2006–2007 (365)
Yasuo Fukuda	2007–2008 (364)
Taro Aso	2008–2009 (357)
Yukio Hatoyama	2009–2010 (265)
Naoto Kan	2010–2011 (270)
Yoshihiko Noda	2011–present

Source: Prime Minister of Japan and His Cabinet, http://www.kantei.go.jp/foreign/archives_e.html. Retrieved on June 1, 2011.

Table 3.2: Full-time and Part-time Employment in the Nonagricultural Sector in Japan (1990–2011)

Year	Number of full-time employees (million)	Number of part-time employees (million)	Percentage of part-time employees
1990	34.73	8.70	20.0
1995	37.61	9.88	20.8
1996	37.80	10.31	21.4
1997	37.97	11.39	23.1
1998	37.80	11.61	23.5
1999	36.69	12.10	24.8
2000	36.09	12.58	25.8
2001	36.21	13.47	27.1
2002	34.68	13.94	28.7
2003	34.17	14.81	30.2
2004	33.61	15.38	31.4
2005	33.18	15.77	32.2
2006	33.19	16.46	32.2
2007	33.71	17.06	33.6
2008	33.48	17.19	33.9

(Continued)

Table 3.2: Continued

Year	Number of full-time employees (million)	Number of part-time employees (million)	Percentage of part-time employees
2009	33.62	16.77	33.3
2010	33.34	16.90	33.6
2011	31.35	17.17	35.4

Note: Part-time employment includes part-timers and contract workers.
Source: Compiled from White Papers and Annual Reports released by Ministry of Health, Labour and Welfare of Japan, http://www.mhlw.go.jp/wp/hakusyo/roudou/11-2/. Retrieved on September 1, 2011.

Table 3.3: Suicide Rate in Japan (2000–2010)

Year	Total number of men's suicides	Total number of women's suicides	Total number of suicides	Total suicide rate per 100,000 people	Men's suicide rate per 100,000 people	Women's suicide rate per 100,000 people
2000	21,656	8,595	30,251	24.1	35.2	13.4
2001	22,144	8,898	31,042	24.4	35.6	13.7
2002	21,677	8,272	29,949	23.8	35.2	12.8
2003	24,963	9,464	34,427	27.0	40.1	14.5
2004	23,272	9,052	32,325	25.3	37.4	13.8
2005	23,540	9,012	32,552	25.5	37.8	13.8
2006	22,813	9,343	32,155	25.2	36.6	14.3
2007	23,478	9,615	33,093	25.9	37.7	14.7
2008	22,831	9,418	32,249	25.3	36.6	14.4
2009	23,472	9,373	32,845	25.8	37.8	14.3
2010	22,282	9,407	31,690	24.9	35.9	14.4

Source: From various documents released by the Ministry of Health, Labour, and Welfare of Japan.

Table 3.4: Men's and Women's Average Age at First Marriage in Japan (1950–2008)

Year	Man's age	Woman's age
1950	25.9	23.0
1960	27.2	24.2
1970	26.9	24.2
1980	27.8	25.2
1985	28.2	25.5
1990	28.4	25.9
1995	28.5	26.3
2000	28.8	27.0
2005	29.8	28.0
2008	30.2	28.5

Source: From various documents released by the Ministry of Health, Labour, and Welfare of Japan.

Table 3.5: Fertility Rate in Japan (1975–2010)

Year	Total fertility rate	Mother's average age at first childbirth
1975	1.91	25.7
1985	1.39	26.6
1995	1.37	27.5
2005	1.37	29.1
2007	1.34	29.4
2008	1.26	29.5
2009	1.42	29.7
2010	1.76	29.9

Source: From various documents released by the Ministry of Health, Labour, and Welfare of Japan.

Table 3.6: Divorce Rate in Japan (1987–2010)

Year	Number of divorced couples	Divorce rate per 1,000 people
1987	158,227	1.30
1988	153,600	1.26
1989	157,811	1.29
1990	157,608	1.28
1991	168,969	1.37
1992	179,191	1.45
1993	188,297	1.52
1994	195,106	1.57
1995	199,016	1.60
1996	206,955	1.66
1997	222,635	1.78
1998	243,183	1.94
1999	250,529	2.00
2000	264,246	2.10
2001	285,911	2.27
2002	289,836	2.30
2003	283,854	2.25
2004	270,804	2.15
2005	261,917	2.08
2006	257,475	2.04
2007	254,832	2.02
2008	251,136	1.99
2009	253,353	2.01
2010	251,000	2.00

Source: From various documents released by the Ministry of Health, Labour, and Welfare of Japan.

Table 3.7: Average Annual Income in Japanese Single-parent Households by Employment Status (2003)

Average annual income (in million yen)	Full-time single fathers (%)	Part-time single fathers (%)	Full-time single mothers (%)	Part-time single mothers (%)
Less than 1 (US$12,500)	0	16.1	7.9	48.3
1–2 (US$12,500–25,000)	6.4	20.2	31.7	44.2
2–3 (US$25,000–37,500)	21.3	28.2	32.4	5.0
3–4 (US$37,500–50,000)	21.3	12.1	14.1	1.2
4–5 (US$50,000–62,500)	13.8	16.1	7.7	0.2
5–6 (US$62,500–75,000)	14.9	4.0	3.5	0
More than 6 (US$75,000)	22.2	4.0	2.7	0

Note: The average annual income for single-mother households in full-time employment was 2.29 million yen (US$28,265), and the average annual income for single-mother households in part-time employment was 1.6 million yen (US$20,000). The currency conversion is an approximation.
Source: From various documents released by the Ministry of Health, Labour, and Welfare of Japan.

Table 6.1: Cosplay Events and Anime Conventions in Europe and the United States (June–November 2011)

Dates	Cosplay Events and Anime Conventions
June 11–12	DoKomi 2011 in Düsseldorf, Germany
June 10–12	A-Kon 21 2011 in Dallas, Texas
June 10–12	Anime Next 2011 in Somerset, New Jersey
June 17–19	METROCON 2011 in Tampa, Florida
June 17–19	Anime Mid-Atlantic 2011 in Chesapeake, Virginia
June 17–19	QC Anime-zing! 2011 in Davenport, Iowa
June 23–26	Port Con Maine 2011 in South Portland, Maine
June 25–26	JAFAX 2011 in Allendale, Michigan
July 1–3	Delta H Con 2011 in Houston, Texas
July 1–2	Labyrinth of Jareth Masquerade Ball 2011 in Los Angeles, California
July 1–3	AM² 2011 in Anaheim, California
July 1–4	Anime Expo 2011 in Los Angeles, California
July 1–4	Florida Supercon 2011 in Miami, Florida
July 8–10	Connecticon 2011 in Hartford, Connecticut
July 9–10	SoyCon 2011 in Chicago, Illinois
July 8–10	Ikasucon 2011 in Fort Wayne, Indiana
July 8–10	Anime Overload 2011 in Austin, Texas
July 16	SMASH! 2011 in Sydney, Australia
July 15–17	PersaCon 2011 in Huntsville, Alabama
July 15–17	Ai-Kon 2011 in Winnepeg, Manitoba, Canada
July 15–17	Anime Kaigi 2011 in Flagstaff, Arizona
July 15–17	Tokyo in Tulsa 2011 in Tulsa, Oklahoma
July 21–24	Comic-Con 2011 in San Diego, California
July 26–28	MechaCon 2011 in New Orleans, Louisiana
July 29–31	Anime Iowa 2011 in Coralville, Iowa

(Continued)

Table 6.1: Continued

Dates	Cosplay Events and Anime Conventions
July 29–31	AniMex 2011 in Monterrey, Mexico
July 29–31	Otakon 2011 in Baltimore, Maryland
July 29–31	AnimagiC 2011 in Bonn, Germany
August 5–7	Anime Festival Orlando 2011 in Orlando, Florida
August 5–7	Nom-con 2011 in Dublin, Ireland
August 5–7	San Japan 2011 in San Antonio, Texas
August 13–14	Cos & Effect 2011 in Vancouver, British Columbia, Canada
August 12–14	Otakuthon 2011 in Montreal, Quebec, Canada
August 12–14	AniMiniCon SoHo 2011 in New York, New York
August 19–21	Mizu Con 2011 in Miami, Florida
August 25–28	Fan Expo 2011 in Toronto, Ontario, Canada
August 26–28	Manifest 2011 in Melbourne, Australia
September 2–5	Dragon*Con 2011 in Atlanta, Georgia
September 2–5	AnimeFEST 2011 in Dallas, Texas
September 3–5	KumoriCon 2011 in Vancouver, Washington
September 9–11	Geek.Kon 2011 in Madison, Wisconsin
September 9–11	Nan Desu Kan 2011 in Denver, Colorado
September 24	Anime St. George 2011 in St. George, Utah
September 23–25	Erie Anime Experience 2011 in Erie, Pennsylvania
October 1	Anime Destiny 2011 in Berkeley, California
September 30–October 2	Saboten-Con 2011 in Phoenix, Arizona
September 30–October 2	Archon 35 2011 in St. Louis, Missouri
September 30–October 2	Anime Weekend Atlanta 2011 in Atlanta, Georgia
October 7–9	Tsubasa Con 2011 in Huntington, West Virginia
October 13–16	New York Comic Con & NY Anime Festival 2011 in New York, New York
October 14–16	Another Anime Convention 2011 in Nashua, New Hampshire
October 21–23	Anime Banzai 2011 in Layton, Utah
October 20–23	Bakuretsu Con 2011 in Colchester, Vermont
October 21–23	Necronomicon 2011 in St. Petersburg, Florida
October 21–23	MileHiCon 2011 in Denver, Colorado
October 28–30	London MCM Expo Fall 2011 in London, United Kingdom
November 4–6	Sugoi Con 2011 in Ft. Mitchell, Kentucky
November 4–6	NekoCon 2011 in Hampton Roads, Virginia
November 3–6	Youmacon 2011 in Detroit, Michigan
November 4–6	Anime NebrasKon 2011 in Omaha, Nebraska
November 4–6	Chibi-Pa: MOTO 2011 in West Palm Beach, Florida
November 11–13	ShadoCon 2011 in Tampa, Florida
November 11–13	IzumiCon 2011 in Oklahoma City, Oklahoma
November 11–13	Pacific Media Expo 2011 in Los Angeles, California
November 18–20	DaishoCon 2011 in Stevens Point, Wisconsin
November 18–20	Anime USA 2011 in Arlington, Virginia
November 18–20	Naru 2 U 2011 in Ottawa, Ontario, Canada
November 18–20	Kollision Con 2011 in St. Charles, Illinois

Source: "Upcoming Cosplay Events and Anime Conventions," CosplayLab.com, www.cosplaylab.com/events.asp.

Table 7.1: Most Desired Occupations among Z-Generation Girls in Japan in 2007 (*N* = 1,935)

Rank	Occupation	%
1	Singer, musician	39.5
2	Music-related	36.7
3	Retail	33.4
4	Pastry chef	30.1
5	Nail artist	28.6
6	Café waitress	28.0
7	Hairdresser	24.2
8	Nursery school teacher	23.5
9	**Caba-kura hostess**	22.3
10	Media-related	21.8
11	Designer	20.8
12	Dancer	20.3
13	Cosmetics salesperson	19.4
14	Office worker	18.0
15	Artist	17.9
16	Event planner	16.8
17	Boutique salesperson	16.1
18	Civil servant	15.3
19	Pet trimmer	13.9
20	Business owner	12.5
21	Social worker	12.4
22	Nurse	12.2
23	Dolphin trainer	10.6
24	Tour guide	10.4
25	Chef	9.7
26	Pharmacist	9.5
27	Merchandising	7.3
28	Athlete	5.7
29	Barista	2.6

Note: The list does not include high-status occupations, such as doctor, lawyer, accountant, and so on.
Source: Miura, Atushi, and Yanauchi, Tamao (2008), *Onnawa Naze Caba-jo ni Naritai no ka?* [Why do girls want to be a Caba-jo?], Tokyo: Kobunsha.

The data found in this book by Miura is based on collaborative research on "Generation Z Survey 2008" conducted by Cultural Studies Institute in Japan and Standard Press on "Generation Z Survey 2007."

Table 7.2: Most Desired Occupations among Z-Generation Girls in Japan in 2008 ($N = 1,154$)

Rank	Occupation	%
1	Actress, model	43.9
2	Singer, musician	40.6
3	Entertainer, performer	38.1
4	Nursery teacher, social worker, nurse	37.3
5	Pastry chef, baker	36.1
6	Hairdresser	30.7
7	Nail artist	30.2
8	Waitress at maid café	28.5
9	Variety store worker	27.2
10	Event planner	25.2
11	Flight attendant	20.9
12	**Caba-jo bar hostess**	20.5
13	Aesthetician	20.0
14	Designer	20.0
15	Dancer	19.8
16	Manager or waitress at coffee shop	19.3
17	Anime and movie-related	19.0
18	Mass media (TV director, editor)	18.2
19	Bridal business-related	17.7
20	Office worker	16.4
21	Cosmetics salesperson	15.9
22	Waitress at restaurant or pub	15.8
23	Fast food restaurant worker	15.6
24	Supermarket salesperson	15.3
25	Pet trimmer	15.1
26	Civil servant	14.6
27	Boutique manager or salesperson	14.0
28	Writer, essayist	13.5
29	Event companion	11.1
30	Housekeeper at hotel	11.0
31	Pharmacist	10.7
32	Chef	10.5
33	Artist, painter	10.5
34	News anchor	10.4
35	Lawyer, accountant	10.0
36	Sex industry worker	9.9
37	Veterinarian	9.9
38	Tour guide	9.6
39	Business owner, president	9.0
40	Dolphin trainer	8.4

Source: Miura, Atushi, and Yanauchi, Tamao (2008), *Onnawa Naze Caba-jo ni Naritai no ka?* [Why do girls want to be a Caba-jo?], Tokyo: Kobunsha.

The data found in this book by Miura is based on collaborative research on "Generation Z Survey 2008" conducted by Cultural Studies Institute in Japan and Standard Press.

Table 7.3: Sample Monthly Incomes of Women Who Work Full-time and Part-time as Bar Hostesses and Monthly Incomes of Their Other Part-time Jobs (*N* = 28)

Employment status as bar hostess	Other part-time job	Age	Monthly income as bar hostess (in yen)	Additional income from other part-time job
Full-time	—	23	500,000 (US$6,250)	—
	—	25	500,000 (US$6,250)	—
	—	22	300,000 (US$3,750)	—
	—	24	400,000 (US$5,000)	—
	—	22	350,000 (US$4,375)	—
	—	21	1,200,000 (US$15,000)	—
	—	20	50,000 (US$625)	—
	—	20	300,000 (US$3,750)	—
	—	19	400,000 (US$5,000)	—
	—	18	200,000 (US$2,500)	—
	—	18	300,000 (US$3,750)	—
Part-time	Salesperson	24	100,000 (US$1,250)	250,000 (US$3,125)
	Hairdresser	24	60,000 (US$750)	280,000 (US$3,500)
	Salesperson	21	180,000 (US$2,250)	100,000 (US$1,250)
	Administrative assistant	26	220,000 (US$2,750)	150,000 (US$1,875)
	Model	22	1,000,000 (US$12,500)	200,000 (US$2,500)
	Telephone operator	24	400,000 (US$5,000)	160,000 (US$2,000)
	Salesperson	20	200,000 (US$2,500)	170,000 (US$2,125)
	Bakery	23	50,000 (US$625)	130,000 (US$1,625)
	Cosmetics salesperson	21	300,000 (US$3,750)	200,000 (US$2,500)
	Nursery teacher	19	400,000 (US$5,000)	140,000 (US$1,750)
	College senior	23	300,000 (US$3,750)	0
	College senior	21	50,000 (US$625)	70,000 (US$875)
	College senior	22	50,000 (US$625)	60,000 (US$750)
	College senior	21	50,000 (US$625)	80,000 (US$1,000)
	Student at vocational school	21	300,000 (US$3,750)	0
	Student at vocational school	19	200,000 (US$2,500)	Scholarship
	Student at vocational school	21	20,000 (US$250)	Scholarship

Source: From Weiden Haus, in Miura, Atushi, and Yanauchi, Tamao (2008), *Onnawa Naze Caba-jo ni Naritai no ka?* [Why do girls want to be a Caba-jo?], Tokyo: Kobunsha.

Note: The currency conversion from Japanese yen to U.S. dollars was calculated at 80 yen = US$1 (as of June 15, 2011).

Table 8.1: Mori Girl Community Sites on Mixi (as of June 2011)

	Number of members	Launch date	Community name
1	35,698	August 24, 2006	Mori-Girl
2	25,865	September 8, 2009	Matured Mori-Girl
3	21,335	September 16, 2009	Mori Girl and Mori Boy
4	2,671	November 10, 2009	Push Mori-Girl into Mori
5	2,338	April 6, 2009	Mori-Girl (Humor)
6	1,707	November 9, 2009	Papier (formerly known as Mori-Girl Papier)
7	1,470	November 4, 2009	Mori-Girl, Mori-Lady, Naturally
8	810	November 8, 2010	OJI Girl and Mori-Girl
9	781	July 19, 2010	Direct Mail Mori-Girl
10	596	October 10, 2010	Teaching the Danger of Forest to Mori-Girl
11	352	November 11, 2009	Mori-Girl Takarajima Publishing
12	261	March 22, 2010	Socially Isolated Mori-Girl and Mori-Boy
13	234	December 11, 2009	SM2 is Mori-Girl's Gentenn
14	232	January 6, 2010	Mori-Girl Collection Notebook
15	191	April 26, 2010	I Am Not a Mori Girl
16	184	July 31, 2010	Mori-Girl (slightly chubby-kei)
17	149	February 9, 2010	Mori-Girl Who Loves Rock
18	120	January 5, 2010	Wow, I Am the Mori Girl
19	111	January 17, 2010	Dome-kei Mor-Girl and Mori-Boy
20	105	January 4, 2010	Decorative-kei Mori Girl
21	98	November 12, 2009	Mori-Girl Fashion and Style Book
22	82	December 4, 2009	Hidden Mori-Girl
23	81	December 30, 2009	Mori-Girl Valon
24	72	October 13, 2009	Real Mori-Girl
25	35	November 25, 2009	Yuru Kaji Mori-Girl
26	29	April 14, 2010	Mori Girl Nagoya
27	26	March 19, 2010	Spoon Mori Girl

Source: www.mixi.co.jp.

Notes

PART I

1. *FRUiTS* is a monthly magazine that was launched in Japan in 1997. A British publisher, Phaidon, compiled Aoki's pictures and published them as a book called *FRUiTS* in 2001. *Fresh FRUiTS* was published by Phaidon in 2006. Aoki published *TUNE*, a male version of *FRUiTs*, in 2004.
2. The English translation is by the author. The Japanese title is *Gyaru to Gyaru-o no Bunka Jinrui-gaku* (2009).
3. The English translation is by the author. The Japanese title is *Sekai to Watashi to Lolita Fashion* (2007).
4. There are pros and cons to conducting research as an insider or an outsider using ethnography as a method. "Being one of them" can put restrictions on the researcher, but it can also make a study very effective. See more in Yuniya Kawamura, "The Researcher as an Insider Versus Outsider," in *Doing Research in Fashion and Dress* (2011a: 50), and Emma Tarlo, *Clothing Matters: Dress and Identity in India* (1996: 132–33).
5. Max Weber (1864–1920), a German scholar, notes that people choose value-relevant research topics that they care about personally, but he cautions that once their work is underway, researchers should try their best to be value free. The first step of topic selection is undeniably subjective, and I do not deny that I feel very passionate about this topic, as I find Japanese subcultural fashion fascinating. But once my fieldwork began, I was aware of my role as a researcher and did my best to maintain objectivity.

CHAPTER 1, UNDERSTANDING SUBCULTURAL STUDIES: DICK HEBDIGE REVISITED

1. The Centre was closed in 2002.
2. The exhibition was so popular that the museum at FIT extended it by three months until April 2011.
3. Fieldwork may appear to be a simplistic way to research, but observation as a method is not as easy as one may think it is. It requires a deep insight into what you are studying. You become a human wall with your eyes and ears wide open. In participant observation, you are not simply observing; you are also participating and getting involved with those you are studying.

See more in Paul Hodkinson, "From Participant to Researcher," in *Goth: Identity, Style and Subculture* (2002); David Muggleton, *Inside Subculture: The Postmodern Meaning of Style* (2000: 171–72); Yuniya Kawamura, "Ethnography," in *Doing Research in Fashion and Dress: An Introduction to Qualitative Methods* (2011a).

CHAPTER 2, PLACING TOKYO ON THE FASHION MAP: FROM CATWALK TO STREET STYLE

This chapter was first published in *Fashion's World Cities* (Kawamura 2006c: 55–68) edited by Christopher Breward and David Gilbert.

1. The Colbert Committee (Le Comité Colbert) is a trade association for French luxury products that organizes promotional activities for its member companies. It was founded in 1954 by Jean Jacques Guerlain, a perfume manufacturer, and Lucien Lelong, a couturier and the former president of La Chambre Syndicale de la Couture Parisienne. There are seventy-one member companies among ten industry sectors as of January 2012.

2. The general meaning of the term *avant-garde* implies a cohesive group of artists who have a strong commitment to iconoclastic aesthetic values and who reject both popular culture and middle-class lifestyle. They are often in opposition to dominant social values and norms (Crane 1987: 1).

3. The Chambre Syndicale de la Couture Parisienne, which was officially established in 1911, is part of the larger organization called the Federation Française de la Couture, du Prêt-à-Porter des Couturiers et des Créateurs de Mode, which was established in 1973. For details, see Kawamura (2004).

4. The loose white socks were probably the first trend that the teens in Shibuya created. Unlike other street fashion, which was much influenced by Western designers, this was typically Japanese. The white, baggy knee socks are deliberately pushed down on the shin like leg warmers. This trend was started not by the fashion industry but by high school teenagers, and the marketing potential of these girls became strongly apparent. Fashion trends can no longer be dictated only by the designers or the fashion industry.

5. This is based on my ethnographical study conducted in Harajuku during January, July, and August 2005. Tokyo's distinctive street fashion is said to have begun in the mid-1990s by young teenage girls known as *Gyaru* or *Ko-gyaru*. They are known for wearing short plaid skirts that look like

their own school uniforms, knee-high white socks, and occasionally heavy makeup and artificial suntans.

6. The shops (retail tenants) inside the department store cater to Japanese teenagers. It is the fashion mecca where fashionable teenagers shop and where well-known salesgirls who have appeared in street fashion magazines work. Street fashion in Shibuya functions in conjunction with the building. These girls are the trendsetters, merchandisers, and designers.

CHAPTER 3, JAPANESE YOUTH IN A CHANGING SOCIETY

1. The Nikkei 225 is a stock market index for the Tokyo Stock Market Exchange and is similar to the Dow Jones Industrial Average. On June 9, 2011, the Nikkei 225 was 9,514.44.

2. In April 2011, the unemployment rate in Japan was 4.3 percent; it was 9.0 percent in the United States, 6.6 percent in Germany, 9.1 percent in France, 8.1 percent in Italy, and 7.3 percent in Sweden (U.S. Bureau of Labor Statistics 2011).

3. It was formerly called the Ministry of Public Management, Home Affairs, Posts and Telecommunications but was changed to the current name in 2004.

4. In 2009 Japan's suicide rate ranked second among the leading industrialized nations.

PART II

1. Gemeinschaft (community) and gesellschaft (society) are concepts introduced by Ferdinand Toennies (1855–1936), a German scholar. According to Toennies, these are two types of human association. Individuals in gemeinschaft are regulated by common mores or beliefs about the appropriate behavior and responsibility of members of the association, to each other, and to the association at large. Toennies saw the family as the most perfect expression of gemeinschaft. In contrast, gesellschaft describes associations in which the individual's self-interest is most important, and it is maintained through individuals acting in their own self-interest. A modern business is a good example of gesellschaft, in which the workers, employers, and owners may share very little in terms of values and beliefs. See *Community and Society* ([1887] 1963) by Ferdinand Toennies.

2. Kenzo Takada and Issey Miyake retired in 1999. Hanae Mori retired in 2004 after her company filed for bankruptcy.

3. As Herbert Blumer explained in *Symbolic Interactionism: Perspective and Method* (1969b), the scientific approach of symbolic interactionism starts with a problem regarding the empirical world, and it seeks to clarify the problem by examining that empirical world. It does not begin (like functionalism) with a set of hypotheses but looks at the processes by which individuals define the world from the inside and at the same time identify their world of objects.

CHAPTER 4, SHIBUYA: THE YOUTH IN OUTSPOKEN REBELLION

1. Shibuya 109 is often referred to in Japanese as *Ichi Maru Kyu*, or simply as *Maru Kyu*.

2. Kunio Soma, managing director of TMD, presented at a forum in Akihabara, August 2010.

3. The literal translation of *Ganguro* has no racial implications in Japanese. It means that their faces are tanned.

CHAPTER 5, HARAJUKU: THE YOUTH IN SILENT REBELLION

1. According to marketing expert Kensuke Kojima (2002), some of the unique characteristics of the fashion business in Ura-Hara are: (1) there is no organizational structure to the business that they operate, such as setting seasonal or annual budgets or promotional strategies; (2) they consider manufacturing or the actual making process extremely important, and much time is invested in planning and merchandising, and thus items are sold in small quantities; and (3) they are not worried about mainstream trends and are content as long as their own unique styles are accepted within their community and are sensitive to the trends within their own subculture. Ura-Hara street fashion grew out of social networks of some friends who managed to commercialize products that they like and that they think are cool and cute. See more in Yuniya Kawamura, "Japanese Teens as Producers of Fashion" (2006).

2. *Ama-Loli* is a type of Lolita style which means Sweet Lolita and is characterized by pastel colors.

3. *Hime-kei* is a combination of Lolita and Princess.

4. Shinjuku, a district in Tokyo, has taken away some of the Harajuku Lolita population since the Marui One shopping center was built in 2000 and it has stores that sell Lolita-related products. There are signs that subcultural fashion that used to be geographically confined is now diversifying to other districts and also around the world.

CHAPTER 6, AKIHABARA AND IKEBUKURO: PLAYING WITH COSTUME AS ENTERTAINMENT

1. I visited the event on August 2, 2010, which happened to be one of the hottest days in the history of Japan. It was so crowded that it took me and my photographer a couple of hours just to reach a ticket vending machine to get a train ticket to and from the site. There were tens of thousands of people looking at manga and anime, cosplaying outside the hall dripping with sweat, and taking pictures. I was extremely impressed by their passion and enthusiasm.

CHAPTER 7, SHINJUKU: GIRLS OF THE NIGHTLIFE USING BEAUTY AND YOUTH AS WEAPONS

1. Interview conducted with the editor-in-chief of *Koakuma Ageha* by a Japanese Web magazine, *Gigazine*, on July 14, 2009. See http://gigazine.net/news/20090714_koakuma_ageha/.
2. I had interviewed an editor-in-chief and a copy editor of another magazine very similar to Age-jo, and they clearly had no respect for those who work in bars and pubs. They were simply told by the company to run the magazine. It was easy to see why Nakajo's magazine was more successful than this one.

CHAPTER 8, KOUENJI AND OTHER FASHION DISTRICTS: FROM SECONDHAND CLOTHES LOVERS TO FAST FASHION FOLLOWERS

1. Every time I visited Kouenji, I could find only one or two girls who appeared to dress in Mori Girl fashion. I later found out that the Mori Girl subculture is believed to exist in Kouenji only because there are many secondhand and vintage stores that Mori Girls go to. Unlike Shibuya or Harajuku, you do not find groups of Mori Girl walking around Kouenji.

2. While membership to Mixi requires an invitation from a current member of a community, once you become a Mixi member, you can freely create your own community. On Facebook, there are 645 members for Mori Girl.

CHAPTER 9, INDIVIDUAL AND INSTITUTIONAL NETWORKS WITHIN A SUBCULTURAL SYSTEM: EFFORTS TO VALIDATE AND VALORIZE NEW TASTES IN FASHION

1. The youth gangs in Shibuya are an exception. If one leaves the gang, he or she will never be able to reenter the gang, or any other gang in Shibuya (Arai 2009).
2. Whenever I sat down with a teen who belongs to a subculture for an interview and asked his or her name, most of them asked me, "Do you want my real name or my handle name?" A handle name is a user name or a screen name that they also use as a nickname. The girls I met had names such as Alice, Sara, and Momo, which were completely different from their real names.

CHAPTER 10, THE DEPROFESSIONALIZATION OF FASHION

1. Charles Frederick Worth was known as the first couturier. He was British but had lived in France for many years before he started his own haute couture label, the House of Worth.

CHAPTER 11, THE GLOBALIZATION OF JAPANESE SUBCULTURES AND FASHION: FUTURE POSSIBILITIES AND LIMITATIONS

1. The term and the concept of "Cool Japan" was taken from "Cool Britannia," and was adopted by the Japanese government in 2002.

References and Further Reading

Adorno, Theodor, and Horkheimer, Max ([1947] 1979), *Dialectic of Enlightenment,* London: Verso.

Alexander, Jeffrey (ed.) (1988), *Durkheimian Sociology,* Cambridge, UK: Cambridge University Press.

Allison, Anne (2003), "Portable Monster and Commodity Cuteness: Pokémon as Japan's New Global Power," *Postcolonial Studies,* 6: 381–95.

Althusser, Louis ([1968] 1988), "Ideology and Ideological State Apparatuses," in John Storey (ed.), *Cultural Theory and Popular Culture: A Reader,* London: Prentice Hall.

Anderson, Mark, and Jenkins, Mark (2001), *Dance of Days,* New York: Soft Skull Press.

Aoki, Shoichi (2001), *FRUiTS,* London: Phaidon.

Aoki, Shoichi (2006), *Fresh FRUiTS,* London: Phaidon.

Appadurai, Arjun (1990), "Disjuncture and Difference in the Global Cultural Economy," *Theory, Culture, and Society,* 7: 295–310.

Arai, Yusuke (2009), *Gyaru to Gyaru-o no Bunka Jinrui-gaku* [The cultural anthropology of Gyaru and Gyaru-o], Tokyo: Shinchosha.

Arnold, David O. (1970), *The Sociology of Subcultures,* Berkeley, CA: Glendessary Press.

Aspers, Patrik (2005), *Markets in Fashion: A Phenomenological Approach,* London: Routledge.

Aspers, Patrik (2010), *Orderly Fashion: A Sociology of Markets,* Princeton, NJ: Princeton University Press.

Baizerman, Suzanne, Eicher, Joanne B., and Cerny, Catherine (2008), "Eurocentrism in the Study of Ethnic Dress," in Joanne B. Eicher, Sandra Lee Evenson, and Hazel A. Lutz (eds.), *The Visible Self: Global Perspectives on Dress, Culture, and Society,* New York: Fairchild Publications.

Barnard, Malcolm (1996), *Fashion as Communication,* London: Routledge.

Barnard, Malcolm (1998), *Art, Design and Visual Culture,* New York: Palgrave Macmillan.

Barnard, Malcolm (2001), *Approaches to Understanding Visual Culture,* New York: Palgrave Macmillan.

Barnard, Malcolm (2007), *Fashion Theory: A Reader,* London: Routledge.

Baron, Stephen (1989), "Resistance and Its Consequences: The Street Culture of Punks," *Youth Society,* 21/2: 207–37.

Barthes, Roland (1964), *Elements of Semiology,* translated by A. Lavers and C. Smith, New York: Hill and Wang.

Barthes, Roland (1967), *The Fashion System,* translated by M. Ward and R. Howard, New York: Hill and Wang.

Baudrillard, Jean ([1976] 1993), *Symbolic Exchange and Death,* translated by E. Hamilton Grant, London: Sage.

Baudrillard, Jean (1981), *For a Critique of the Political Economy of the Sign,* translated by Charles Levin, St. Louis, MO: Telos Press.

Baudrillard, Jean (1998), *The Consumer Society,* London: Sage.

Bauman, Zygmunt (1991), *Modernity and Ambivalence,* Ithaca, NY: Cornell University Press.

Bauman, Zygmunt (1992), *Intimations of Postmodernity,* London: Routledge.

Beauvoir, Simone de (1949), *The Second Sex,* translated by H. M. Parshley, New York: Penguin.

Becker, Howard ([1963] 1973), *Outsiders,* Glencoe, NY: Free Press.

Becker, Howard (1982), *Art World,* Berkeley: University of California Press.

Bell, Daniel (1973), *The Coming of Post-Industrial Society,* New York: Basic Books.

Bell, Daniel (1976), *The Cultural Conditions of Capitalism,* New York: Basic Books.

Bell, Quentin ([1947] 1976), *On Human Finery,* London: Hogarth Press.

Bennett, Andy, and Kahn-Harris, Keith (2004), *After Subculture: Critical Studies in Contemporary Youth Culture,* London: Palgrave Macmillan.

Bennett, Tony, Emmison, Michael, and Frow, John (1999), *Accounting for Taste,* Melbourne, Australia: Cambridge University Press.

Bibort, Alan (2009), *Beatniks: A Guide to an American Subculture,* Westport, CT: Greenwood.

Blake, Mark (ed.) (2008), *Punk: The Whole Story,* New York: DK.

Bleikhorn, Samantha (2002), *The Mini-Mod Sixties Book,* San Francisco: Last Gasp.

Blum, Sasha (2009), *The Gothic Subculture: An Empirical Investigation of the Psychological and Behavioral Characteristics of Its Affiliates,* Saarbrücken, Germany: VDM Verlag.

Blumer, Herbert (1969a), "Fashion: From Class Differentiation to Collective Selection," *Sociological Quarterly,* 10/3: 275–91.

Blumer, Herbert (1969b), *Symbolic Interactionism: Perspective and Method,* Englewood Cliffs, NJ: Prentice Hall.

Blush, Steven (2001), *American Hardcore: A Tribal History,* Los Angeles: Feral House.

Bourdieu, Pierre ([1972] 1977), *Outline of a Theory of Practice,* Cambridge, UK: Cambridge University Press.

Bourdieu, Pierre (1980), "Haute Couture et Haute Culture," in *Questions de Sociologies,* Paris: Les Editions de Minuit.

Bourdieu, Pierre (1984), *Distinction: A Social Critique of the Judgment of Taste,* translated by R. Nice, Cambridge, MA: Harvard University Press.

Bourdieu, Pierre (1990), *In Other Worlds,* Stanford, CA: Stanford University Press.

Bourdieu, Pierre (1992), *An Invitation to Reflexive Sociology,* Chicago: University of Chicago Press.

Bourdieu, Pierre (1993), *The Field of Cultural Production,* translated by R. Nice, Cambridge, UK: Polity.

Brake, Michael (1980), *The Sociology of Youth Culture and Youth Subcultures: Sex and Drugs and Rock 'n' Roll?* London: Routledge & Kegan Paul.

Brake, Michael (1985), *Comparative Youth Culture: The Sociology of Youth Cultures and Youth Subcultures in America, Britain and Canada,* London: Routledge & Kegan Paul.

Brandon, Reiko Mochinaga, Fukai, Akiko, Jackson, Ana, and Kurashige Tipton, Elise (2005), *Fashioning Kimono: Dress and Modernity in Early Twentieth Century Japan,* Milan, Italy: 5 Continents.

Breward, Christopher, and Evans, Caroline (2005), *Fashion and Modernity,* Oxford, UK: Berg.

Breward, Christopher, and Gilbert, David (eds.) (2006), *Fashion's World Cities,* Oxford, UK: Berg.

Brooker, Peter, and Brooker, Will (1997), "Introduction," in Peter Brooker and Will Brooker (eds.), *Postmodern After-Images,* London: Edward Arnold.

Butler, Judith (1990), *Gender Trouble,* New York: Routledge.

Cannon, Aubrey (1998), "The Cultural and Historical Contexts of Fashion," in Anne Brydon and Sandra Niessen (eds.), *Consuming Fashion: Adorning the Transnational Body,* Oxford, UK: Berg.

Chartier, Roger (1993), "Popular Culture: A Concept Revisited," *Intellectual History Newsletter,* 15: 3–13.

Chernikowski, Stephanie (1997), *Blank Generation Revisited: The Early Days of Punk Rock,* New York: Schirmer Books.

Clarke, John, Hall, Stuart, Jefferson, Tony, and Roberts, Brian (1976), "Subcultures, Cultures and Class," in Stuart Hall and Tony Jefferson (eds.), *Resistance through Rituals: Youth Subcultures in Post-war Britain,* London: Hutchinson.

Cloward, Richard, and Ohlin, Lloyd (1961), *Delinquency and Opportunity: A Theory of Delinquent Gangs,* Glencoe, IL: Free Press.

Cogan, Brian (2006), *Encyclopedia of Punk Music and Culture,* Westport, CT: Greenwood Press.

Cohen, Albert K. (1955). *Delinquent Boys: The Culture of the Gang,* Glencoe. IL: Free Press.

Cohen, Albert (1970), "A General Theory of Subcultures," in D. O. Arnold (ed.), *The Sociology of Subcultures,* Berkeley, CA: Glendessary Press.

Cohen, Albert, and Short, James (1958), "Research in Delinquent Subcultures," *Journal of Social Issues,* 14/3: 20–37.

Cohen, Phil (1972), *Sub-cultural Conflict and Working Class Community,* Working Papers in Cultural Studies, no 2, Birmingham, UK: University of Birmingham.

Cole, Robert J. (1989), "Japanese Buy New York Cachet with Deal for Rocke-feller Center," *New York Times,* October 31.

Collins, Jim (1989), *Uncommon Cultures: Popular Culture and Post-Modernism,* New York: Routledge.

Collins, Randall (1975), *Conflict Sociology,* New York: Academic Press.

Contemporary Youth Culture: An International Encyclopedia (2006), Westport, CT: Greenwood.

Cooper-Chen, Anne M. (2010), *Cartoon Cultures: The Globalization of Japanese Popular Media,* New York: Peter Lang.

Craik, Jennifer (1994), *The Face of Fashion,* London: Routledge.

Crane, Diana (1987), *The Transformation of the Avant-Garde: The New York Art World 1940–1985,* Chicago: University of Chicago Press.

Crane, Diana (1992), "High Culture versus Popular Culture Revisited," in Michèle Lamont and Marcel Fournier (eds.), *Cultivating Differences: Symbolic Bound-aries and the Making of Inequality,* Chicago: University of Chicago Press.

Crane, Diana (1993), "Fashion Design as an Occupation," *Current Research on Occupations and Professions,* 8: 55–73.

Crane, Diana (1994), "Introduction: The Challenge of the Sociology of Culture to Sociology as a Discipline," in Diana Crane (ed.), *The Sociology of Culture,* Oxford, UK: Blackwell.

Crane, Diana (1997a), "Globalization, Organizational Size, and Innovation in the French Luxury Fashion Industry: Production of Culture Theory Revis-ited," *Poetics,* 24: 393–414.

Crane, Diana (1997b), "Postmodernism and the Avant-Garde: Stylistic Change in Fashion Design," *Modernism/Modernity,* 4: 123–40.

Crane, Diana (1999), "Diffusion Models and Fashion: A Reassessment in the Social Diffusion of Ideas and Things," *Annals of the Academy of Political and Social Science,* 566: 13–24.

Crane, Diana (2000), *Fashion and Its Social Agendas: Class, Gender, and Iden-tity in Clothing,* Chicago: University of Chicago Press.

Dalby, Liza Crihfield (2001), *Kimono: Fashioning Culture,* Seattle: University of Washington Press.

Davis, Fred (1985), "Clothing and Fashion as Communication," in Michael R. Solomon (ed.), *The Psychology of Fashion,* Lexington, MA: Lexington Books.

Davis, Fred (1992), *Fashion, Culture, and Identity,* Chicago: University of Chi-cago Press.

De La Haye, Amy, and Dingwall, Cathie (1996), *Surfers, Soulies, Skinheads and Skaters: Subcultural Style of the Forties to the Nineties,* Woodstock, NY: Overlook.

Denzin, Norman K. (1970), *The Research Act in Sociology,* London: Butter-worths.

Derrida, Jacques ([1967] 1976), *Of Grammatology,* Baltimore: Johns Hopkins University Press.

DiMaggio, Paul (1992), "Cultural Entrepreneurship in 19th Century Boston," in Michèle Lamont and Marcel Fournier (eds.), *Cultivating Differences: Symbolic Boundaries and the Making of Inequality,* Chicago: University of Chicago Press.

DiMaggio, Paul, and Useem, Michael (1978), "Cultural Democracy in a Period of Cultural Expansion: The Social Composition of Arts Audiences in the United States," *Social Problems,* 26/2: 179–97.

Docker, John (1994), *Postmodernism and Popular Culture,* Cambridge, UK: Cambridge University Press.

Douglas, Mary (1978), *Cultural Bias,* London: Routledge and Kegan Paul.

Drake, Kate (2001), "Quest for Kawaii," *Time International,* June 25: 46.

Duncan, Hugh Dalziel (1969), *Symbols and Social Theory,* New York: Oxford University Press.

Durkheim, Emile ([1897] 1951), *Suicide,* translated by John Spaulding and George Simpson, New York: Free Press.

Durkheim, Emile ([1912] 1965), *The Elementary Forms of Religious Life,* New York: Free Press.

Eagleton, Terry (1983), *Literary Theory: An Introduction,* Oxford: Blackwell.

Eicher, Joanne B. (1969), *African Dress: A Selected and Annotated Bibliography of Subsaharan Countries,* East Lansing: African Studies Center, Michigan State University.

Eicher, Joanne B. (1976), *Nigerian Handcrafted Textiles,* Ile-Ife, Nigeria: University of Ife Press.

Eicher, Joanne B. (ed.) (1995), *Dress and Ethnicity: Change across Space and Time,* Oxford, UK: Berg.

Eicher, Joanne B., and Barnes, Ruth (1992), *Dress and Gender: Making and Meaning in Cultural Contexts,* Oxford, UK: Berg.

Eicher, Joanne B., Evenson, Sandra Lee, and Lutz, Hazel A. (eds.) (2008), *The Visible Self: Global Perspectives on Dress, Culture, and Society,* New York: Fairchild.

Eicher, Joanne B., and Roach, Mary Ellen (eds.) (1965), *Dress, Adornment, and the Social Order,* New York: John Wiley.

Eicher, Joanne B., and Sciama, Lidia (1998), *Beads and Bead Makers: Gender, Material Culture, and Meaning,* Oxford, UK: Berg.

English, Bonnie (2007), *A Cultural History of Fashion in the 20th Century: From the Catwalk to the Sidewalk,* Oxford, UK: Berg.

English, Bonnie (2011), *Japanese Fashion Designers: The Work and Influence of Issey Miyake, Yohji Yamamoto and Rei Kawakubo,* Oxford, UK: Berg.

Entwistle, Joanne (2006), "The Cultural Economy of Buying," in Patrik Aspers and Lise Skov (eds.), *Current Sociology,* 54/5: 704–24.

Entwistle, Joanne (2009), *The Aesthetic Economy of Fashion,* Oxford, UK: Berg.

Evers, Izumi, Macias, Patrick, and Nonaka, Kazumi (2007), *Japanese Schoolgirl Inferno: Tokyo Teen Fashion Subculture Handbook,* San Francisco: Chronicle Books.

Farrelly, Liz (2005), *Fashion Forever: 30 Years of Subculture,* Philadelphia: Trans-Atlantic.

Farrer, James, and Sinclair, Joan (2006), *Pink Box: Inside Japan's Sex Clubs,* New York: Harry N. Abrams.

Fasano, Sarah (2009), "Interview with Cosplay Champion of USA, Elizabeth Licata," in Yuniya Kawamura (ed.), *NY Street Fashion,* Summer: 10–11.

Featherstone, Mike (2007), *Consumer Culture and Postmodernism,* London: Sage.

Feldman, Christine Jacqueline (2009), *"We Are the Mods": A Transnational History of a Youth Subculture,* New York: Peter Lang.

Finkelstein, Joanne (1996), *After a Fashion,* Carlton, Australia: Melbourne University Press.

Fischer, Claude Serge (1972), "Urbanism as a Way of Life: A Review and an Agenda," *Sociological Methods and Research,* 1/2: 187–243.

Fischer, Claude Serge (1975), "Towards a Subcultural Theory of Urbanism," *American Journal of Sociology,* 80/6: 1319–41.

Fiske, John (1989), *Reading the Popular,* London: Routledge.

Flugel, J. C. (1930), *The Psychology of Clothes,* London: Hogarth.

Friedan, Betty (1963), *The Feminine Mystique,* New York: W. W. Norton.

Fukai, Akiko, Vinken, Barbara, Frankel, Susannah, Kurino, Hirofumi, and Nie, Rie (2010), *Future Beauty: 30 Years of Japanese Fashion,* London: Merrell.

Galbraith, Patrick W., and Schodt, Frederik (eds.) (2009), *The Otaku Encyclopedia: An Insider's Guide to the Subculture of Cool Japan,* New York: Kodansha.

Gans, Herbert (1974), *Popular Culture and High Culture: An Analysis and Evaluation of Taste,* New York: Basic Books.

Geertz, Clifford ([1973] 1975), *The Interpretation of Culture,* London: Hutchinson.

Gelder, Ken (ed.) (2005), *The Subcultures Reader,* London, Routledge.

Gelder, Ken (2007), *Subcultures: Cultural Histories and Social Practice,* London: Routledge.

Giddens, Anthony (1991), *Modernity and Self-Identity,* Palo Alto, CA: Stanford University Press.

Gilroy, Paul (1991), *"There Ain't No Black in the Union Jack!": The Cultural Politics of Race and Nation,* Chicago: University of Chicago Press.

Gilroy, Paul (1993), *The Black Atlantic: Modernity and Double Consciousness,* Cambridge, MA: Harvard University Press.

Gilroy, Paul (2002), *Against Race: Imagining Political Culture beyond the Color Line,* Cambridge, MA: Harvard University Press.

Godoy, Tiffany (2007), *Style Deficit Disorder: Harajuku Street Fashion—Tokyo,* San Francisco: Chronicle Books.

Godoy, Tiffany (2009), *Japanese Goth,* New York: Universe.

Goffman, Erving (1959), *The Presentation of Self in Everyday Life,* Garden City, NY: Doubleday.

Goodrum, Alison (2005), *National Fabric: Fashion, Britishness, Globalization,* Oxford, UK: Berg.

Gordon, Milton M. (1947), "The Concept of Subculture and Its Application," *Social Forces,* 26: 40–42.

Gramsci, Antonio ([1929–1933] 1992), *Prison Notebooks,* Vol. 1, New York: Columbia University Press.

Greenfeld, Karl Taro (1995), *Speed Tribes: Days and Night's with Japan's Next Generation,* New York: Harper Perennial.

Griffin, Chris E. (2008), "Understanding Youth: Perspectives, Identities and Practices," *Health and Social Care in the Community,* 16/1: 108–9.

Griffin, Chris E. (2011), "The Trouble with Class: Researching Youth, Class and Culture beyond the 'Birmingham School,'" *Journal of Youth Studies,* 14/3: 245–59.

Haenfler, Ross (2006), *Straight Edge: Clear-Living Youth, Hardcore Punk and Social Change,* New Brunswick, NJ: Rutgers University Press.

Haenfler, Ross (2009), *Goths, Gamers, and Grrrls: Deviance and Youth Subcultures,* New York: Oxford University Press.

Hall, Stuart (1980a), "Cultural Studies and the Centre: Some Problematics and Problems," in Stuart Hall, Dorothy Hobson, Andrew Lower, and Paul Willis (eds.), *Culture, Media, Language,* London: Unwin Hyman.

Hall, Stuart (1980b), "Encoding/Decoding," in Stuart Hall, Dorothy Hobson, Andrew Lower, and Paul Willis (eds.), *Culture, Media, Language,* London: Unwin Hyman.

Hall, Stuart (1992), "The Question of Cultural Identity," in Stuart Hall and Tony McGrew (eds.), *Modernity and Its Futures,* Cambridge, UK: Polity Press.

Hall, Stuart, and Jefferson, Tony (eds.) (1975), *Resistance through Rituals: Youth Subcultures in Post-War Britain,* London: Hutchinson.

Hargodd, Warren (2010), *Subculture,* n.p.: lulu.com.

Harris, Anita (2007), *Next Wave Cultures: Feminism, Subcultures, Activism,* London: Routledge.

Harris, Cheryl, and Alexander, Alison (1998), *Theorizing Fandom: Fans, Subculture and Identity,* Cresskill, NJ: Hampton Press.

Harris, David (1992), *From Class Struggle to the Politics of Pleasure,* London: Routledge.

Harvey, David (1989), *The Condition of Postmodernity,* Oxford, UK: Blackwell.

Hebdige, Dick (1979), *Subculture: The Meaning of Style,* London and New York: Routledge.

Hebdige, Dick (1986), "Postmodernism and the Other Side", *Journal of Communication Inquiry,* 10/2: 78–89.

Hebdige, Dick (1988), *Hiding in the Light: On Images and Things,* London: Routledge.

Heylin, Clinton (1993), *From the Velvets to the Voidoids: A Pre-Punk History for a Post-Punk World,* New York: Penguin Books.

Hjorth, Larissa (2005), "Odours of Mobility: Mobile Phones and Japanese Cute Culture in the Asia-Pacific," *Journal of Intercultural Studies,* 26: 39–55.

Hodkinson, Paul (2002), *Goth: Identity, Style and Subculture,* Oxford, UK: Berg.

Hoggart, Richard (1957), *The Uses of Literacy,* London: Chatto and Windus.

Holson, Laura M. (2005), "Gothic Lolitas: Demure vs. Dominatrix," *New York Times,* March 13.

Huq, Rupa (2006), *Beyond Subculture: Pop, Youth and Identity in a Postcolonial World,* London: Routledge.

Huyssen, Andreas (1986), *After the Great Divide: Modernism, Mass Culture and Postmodernism,* Basingstoke, UK: Macmillan.

Ijiri, Kazuo (1990), "The Breakdown of the Japanese Work Ethic," *Japan Echo,* 17/4: 35–40.

Imperatore, Cheryl, and Maclardy, Paul (2001), *Kimono Vanishing Tradition: Japanese Textile of the 20th Century,* Atglen, PA: Schiffer.

Inui, Akio (2003), "Restructuring Youth: Recent Problems of Japanese Youth and Its Contextual Origin," *Journal of Youth Studies,* 6/2: 219–33.

Ishida, Hiroshi (1993), *Social Mobility in Contemporary Japan: Educational Credentials, Class and the Labour Market in Cross-national Perspective,* Stanford, CA: Stanford University Press.

Ishida, Hiroshi (2000), "Industrialization, Class Structure and Social Mobility in Postwar Japan," *British Journal of Sociology,* 52: 579–604.

Ishida, Hiroshi (2010), "Does Class Matter in Japan? Demographics of Class Structure and Class Mobility from a Comparative Perspective," in Hiroshi Ishida and David Slater (eds.), *Social Class in Contemporary Japan: Structures, Sorting and Strategies,* London and New York: Routledge.

Ishida, Hiroshi, and Slater, David H. (eds.) (2010a), *Social Class in Contemporary Japan: Structures, Sorting and Strategies,* London and New York: Routledge.

Ishida, Hiroshi, and Slater, David H. (2010b), "Social Class in Japan," in Hiroshi Ishida and David Slater (eds.), *Social Class in Contemporary Japan: Structures, Sorting and Strategies,* London and New York: Routledge.

Issitt, Micah L. (2009), *Hippies: A Guide to an American Subculture,* Westport, CT: Greenwood.

Issitt, Micah L. (2011), *Goths: A Guide to an American Subculture,* Westport, CT: Greenwood.

Iwabuchi, Koichi (2002), *Recentering Globalization: Popular Culture and Japanese Transnationalism,* Durham, NC: Duke University Press.

Jameson, Fredric (1984), "Postmodernism, or the Cultural Logic of Late Capitalism," *New Left Review,* 46: 53–92.

Japan Ministry of Foreign Affairs (2009), *Press Release: Commission of Trend Communicator of Japanese Pop Culture in the Field of Fashion,* February 25.

Jeffreys, Sheila (2000), "Body Art and Social Status: Cutting, Tattooing and Piercing from a Feminist Perspective," *Feminism and Psychology,* 10/4: 409–29.

Jenks, Chris (2004), *Subculture: The Fragmentation of the Social,* London: Sage.

Johnson, Richard (1996), "What Is Cultural Studies Anyway?" in John Storey (ed.), *What Is Cultural Studies? A Reader,* London: Edward Arnold.

Jones, Mason, Macias, Patrick, Oniki, Yuji, and Horn, Carl Gustav (1999), *Japan Edge: The Insider's Guide to Japanese Pop Subculture,* San Francisco: Cadence Books.

Jones, Russell M. (2007), *Inside the Graffiti Subculture,* Saarbrücken, Germany: VDM Verlag

Kaplan, Jeffrey (2003), *The Cultic Milieu: Oppositional Subcultures in an Age of Globalization,* Lanham, MD: Rowman Altamira.

Kawamura, Yuniya (2004), *The Japanese Revolution in Paris Fashion,* Oxford, UK: Berg.

Kawamura, Yuniya (2005), *Fashion-ology: An Introduction to Fashion Studies,* Oxford, UK: Berg.

Kawamura, Yuniya (2006a), "Japanese Street Fashion: The Urge to Be Seen and to Be Heard," in Linda Welters and Abbey Lillthun (eds.), *The Fashion Reader,* Oxford, UK: Berg.

Kawamura, Yuniya (2006b), "Japanese Teens as Producers of Street Fashion," in Patrik Aspers and Lise Skov (eds.), *Current Sociology,* 54/5: 784–801.

Kawamura, Yuniya (2006c), "Placing Tokyo on the Fashion Map: From Catwalk to Streetstyle," in Christopher Breward and David Gilbert (eds.), *Fashion's World Cities,* Oxford, UK: Berg.

Kawamura, Yuniya (2007), "Japanese Designers in Postmodern Times," in Ian Luna (ed.), *Tokyolife,* New York: Rizzoli.

Kawamura, Yuniya (2010), "Japanese Fashion Subcultures," in Valerie Steele (ed.), *Japan Fashion Now Exhibition Catalogue,* New Haven, CT: Yale University Press.

Kawamura, Yuniya (2011a), *Doing Research in Fashion and Dress: An Introduction to Qualitative Methods,* Oxford, UK: Berg.

Kawamura, Yuniya (2011b), "Yohji Yamamoto: A Sartorial Revolutionary," in Ligaya Salazar (ed.), *Yohji Yamamoto Exhibition Catalogue,* London: V&A Museum Publishing.

Keet, Philomena (2007), *The Tokyo Look Book: Stylish to Spectacular, Goth to Gyaru, Sidewalk to Catwalk,* Tokyo: Kodansha International.

Kelts, Roland (2007), *Japanamerica: How Japanese Popculture Has Invaded the U.S.,* New York: Palgrave Macmillan.

Kinsella, Sharon (1995), "Cuties in Japan," in Lise Skov and Brian Moeran (eds.), *Women, Media, and Consumption in Japan,* Honolulu: University of Hawaii Press.

Koda, Harold (2003), *Goddess: Classical Mode,* New York: Metropolitan Museum of Art.

Koda, Harold (2008), *ReFusing Fashion: Rei Kawakubo,* Detroit: Museum of Contemporary Art Detroit.

Koenig, Rene (1974), *A la Mode: On the Social Psychology of Fashion,* New York: Seabury Press.

Kojima, Kensuke (2002), "Ura-Harajuku Bijinesu no Jittai wa Akinai no Genten," *Fasshon Hanbai,* September: 20–22.

Kondo, Dorienne (1992), "The Aesthetics and Politics of Japanese Identity in the Fashion Industry," in Joseph Tobin (ed.), *Re-Made in Japan, Everyday Life and Consumer Taste in a Changing Society,* New Haven, CT: Yale University Press.

Kondo, Dorienne (1997), *About Face: Performing Race in Fashion and Theater,* London: Routledge.

Koren, Leonard (1984), *New Fashion Japan,* Tokyo: Kodansha International.

Lacan, Jacques (1977), *Ecrits: A Selection,* London: Tavistock.

Lamy, Philip, and Levin, Jack (1985), "Punk and Middle-Class Values: A Content Analysis," *Youth Society,* 17: 157–70.

Lash, Scott (1990), *Sociology of Postmodernism,* London: Routledge.

Lavallee, Andrew (2011), "China to Overtake Japan in Luxury Demand," China Real Time Report, *The Wall Street Journal,* September 6, http://blogs.wsj.com/scene/2011/09/06/china-to-overtake-japan-in-luxury-demand-hsbc-says/.

Leblanc, Lauraine (1999), *Pretty in Punk: Girls' Gender Resistance in a Boys' Subculture,* New Brunswick, NJ: Rutgers University Press.

Lee, Alfred McLung (1945), *Race Riots Aren't Necessary,* New York: Public Affairs Committee.

Lemert, Charles (1997), *Postmodernism Is Not What You Think,* Oxford, UK: Blackwell.

Lévi-Strauss, Claude (1955), *Tristes Tropiques,* Paris: Librairie Plon.

Liebow, Elliot (1967), *Tally's Corner: A Study of Negro Street Corner,* Boston: Little, Brown.

Lockwood, Lisa (1995), "ICB: High Expectations in Japan," *Women's Wear Daily,* August 16: 8–9.

Lolitafashion.org (n.d.), For Lolitas of All Styles, www.lolitafashion.org.

Lovell, Terry (1998), "Cultural Production," in John Storey (ed.), *Cultural Theory and Popular Culture: A Reader,* Hemel Hempstead, UK: Prentice Hall.

Lukács, Georg (1971), *History and Class Consciousness,* London: Merlin Press.

Lyotard, Jean-François (1984), *The Postmodern Condition,* translated by Geoffrey Bennington and Brian Massumi, Manchester, UK: Manchester University Press.

MacDonald, Dwight (1998), "A Theory of Mass Culture," in John Storey (ed.), *Cultural Theory and Popular Culture: A Reader,* Hemel Hempstead, UK: Prentice Hall.

Macdonald, Nancy (2003), *The Graffiti Subculture: Youth, Masculinity and Identity in London and New York,* New York: Palgrave.

Martin, Richard, and Koda, Harold (1994), *Orientalism: Visions of the East in Western Dress,* New York: Metropolitan Museum of Art.

Martin, Richard, and Koda, Harold (1996), *Haute Couture,* Exhibition, Metropolitan Museum of Art, December 7, 1995–March 24, 1996, New York: Harry N. Abrams.

Martin-Barbero, Jesus (1993), *Communication, Culture and Hegemony,* London: Sage.

Marx, Karl (1956), *Capital,* Moscow: Progress Publishers.

Matsuura, Momo (2007), *Sekai to Watashi to Lolita Fashion* [The world, myself and Lolita fashion], Tokyo: Seikyusha.

Mayhew, Henry ([1851] 1985), *London Labour and the London Poor,* London: Penguin Classics.

McRobbie, Angela (1981), "Settling Accounts with Subcultures: A Feminist Critique," in Tony Bennet, Graham Martin, Colin Mercer, and Janet Woollacott (eds.), *Culture, Ideology, and Social Process,* London: Open University Press.

McRobbie, Angela (1991), *Feminism and Youth Culture: From "Jackie" to "Just Seventeen,"* London: Macmillan.

McRobbie, Angela, and Garber, Jennifer ([1981] 1991), "Girls and Subcultures," in *Feminism and Youth Culture: From "Jackie" to "Just Seventeen,"* London: Macmillan.

McRobbie, Angela, and Nava, Mica (eds.) (1984), *Gender and Generation,* London: Macmillan.

McWilliams, John C. (2000), *The 1960s Cultural Revolution,* Westport, CT: Greenwood.

Mead, Rebecca (2002), "Shopping Rebellion: What Kids Want," *The New Yorker,* March 18.

Mears, Patricia (2010), "Japanese Revolution," in Valerie Steele (ed.), *Japan Fashion Now!* New Haven, CT: Yale University Press.

Mendes, Valerie, and de la Haye, Amy (1999), *20th Century Fashion,* London: Thames and Hudson.

Merton, Robert K. (1946), *Mass Persuasion,* New York: Harper.

Merton, Robert K. (1957), *Social Theory and Social Structure,* New York: Free Press.

Miller, Laura, and Bardsley, Jan (eds.) (2005), *Bad Girls of Japan*, New York: Palgrave Macmillan.

Mills, C. Wright (1959), *The Sociological Imagination,* New York: Oxford University Press.

Mills, Ron, and Huff, Allen (1999), *Style Over Substance: A Critical Analysis of an African-American Teenage Subculture,* Chicago: African American Images.

Mitchell, Louise (ed.) (2006), *The Cutting Edge: Fashion from Japan,* Sydney, Australia: Museum of Applied Arts and Sciences.

Miura, Atushi, and Yanauchi, Tamao (2008), *Onnawa Naze Caba-jo ni Naritai no ka?* [Why do girls want to be a Caba-jo?], Tokyo: Kobunsha.

Moeran, Brian (2006), "More Than Just a Fashion Magazine," in Patrik Aspers and Lise Skov (eds.), *Current Sociology,* 54/5: 725–44.

Muggleton, David (2000), *Inside Subculture: The Postmodern Meaning of Style,* Oxford, UK: Berg.

Muggleton, David, and Weinzierl, Rupert (2004), *The Post-Subcultures Reader,* Oxford, UK: Berg.

Munsterberg, Hugo (1996), *The Japanese Kimono,* New York: Oxford University Press.

Nakajo, Hiroko (ed.), *Koakuma Ageha,* Tokyo: Inforest.

Narumi, Hiroshi (2010), "Japanese Street Style," in Valerie Steele (ed.), *Japan Fashion Now! Exhibition Catalogue,* New Haven, CT: Yale University Press.

Nathan, John (2004), *Japan Unbound: A Volatile Nation's Quest for Pride and Purpose,* Boston: Houghton Miffin.

Nava, Mica (1992), *Changing Cultures: Feminism, Youth Consumerism,* London: Sage.

Nye, Joseph (1990), *Bound to Lead: The Changing Nature of American Power,* New York: Basic Books.

Nye, Joseph (2004), *Soft Power: The Means to Success in World Politics,* New York: Public Affairs.

Ogunnaike, Lola (2004), "SoHo Runs for Blue and Yellow Sneakers," *New York Times,* December 19.

O'Hara, Craig (2001), *The Philosophy of Punk: More Than Noise,* San Francisco: AK Press.

Okamoto, Shigeko, and Shibamoto, Janet (eds.) (2004), *Japanese Language, Gender and Ideology: Cultural Models and Real People,* Oxford, UK: Oxford University Press.

Osgerby, Bill (1998), *Youth in Britain since 1945,* Oxford, UK: Blackwell.

Paris, Jeffrey, and Ault, Michael (2004), "Subcultures and Political Resistance," *Peace Review,* 16/4: 403–7.

Peterson, Richard A. (1992), "Understanding Audience Segmentation: From Elite and Mass to Omnivore and Univore," *Poetics,* 21: 243–58.

Peterson, Richard A., and Kern, Roger M. (1996), "Changing Highbrow Taste: From Snob to Omnivore," *American Sociological Review,* 61: 900–907.

Pilkington, Hilary (1994), *Russia's Youth and Its Culture: A Nation's Constructor and Constructed,* London: Routledge.

Pilkington, Hilary (1996), *Gender, Generation and Identity in Contemporary Russia,* London: Routledge.

Pilkington, Hilary, and Yemelianova, Galina (eds.) (2002), *Islam in Post-Soviet Russia,* London: Routledge.

Pilkington, Hilary, Garifzianova, Al'bina, and Omel'chenko, Elena (2010), *Russia's Skinheads: Exploring and Rethinking Subcultural Lives,* London: Routledge.

Piganeau, Joëlle (1986), "Le Japon travaille a devenie un cetre mondial de mode," *Journal due Textile,* October 24: 3.

Polhemus, Ted (1994), *Street Style,* London: Thames and Hudson.

Polhemus, Ted (1996), *Style Surfing,* London: Thames and Hudson.

Polhemus, Ted, and Proctor, Lynn (1978), *Fashion and Antifashion: An Anthropology of Clothing and Adornment,* London: Thames and Hudson.

Popteen (1999), "Who Is Your Role Model?" Survey, November 21, Tokyo: Kadokawa Haruki Corporation.

Prasso, Sheridan, and Brady, Diane (2003), "Can the High End Hold Its Own?" *Business Week,* June 30: 7

Purcell, Natalie J. (2003), *Death Metal Music: The Passion and Politics of a Subculture,* Jefferson, NC: McFarland.

Raha, Maria (2005), *Cinderella's Big Score: Women of the Punk and Indie Underground,* Emeryville, CA: Sea Press.

Rahn, Janice (2002), *Painting Without Permission: Hip-Hop Graffiti Subculture,* Westport, CT: Bergin & Garvey

Readhead, Steve (1997), *Subculture to Clubcultures: An Introduction to Popular Cultural Studies,* Oxford, UK: Blackwell.

Reddington, Helen (2004), "The Forgotten Revolution of Female Punk Musicians in the 1970s," *Peace Review,* 16/4: 439–44.

Reed, John Shelton (1972), *The Enduring South: Subcultural Persistence in Mass Society,* Lexington, MA: D. C. Heath.

Robertson, Roland (1995), "Glocalization: Time-Space and Homogenity-Heterogeneity," in Mike Featherstone, Scott Lash, and Robert Robertson (eds.), *Global Modernities,* London: Sage.

Sabin, Roger (1999), *Punk Rock: So What?* New York: Routledge.

Sage Dictionary of Cultural Studies (2004), London: Sage.

Sagert, Kelly Boyer (2009), *Flappers: A Guide to an American Subculture,* Westport, CT: Greenwood.

Said, Edward (1993), *Culture and Imperialism,* New York: Vintage Books.

Sainderichinn, Ginnette (1989), *Kenzo,* Paris: Editions du May.

Salazar, Ligaya (ed.) (2011), *Yohji Yamamoto Exhibition Catalogue,* London: V&A Museum Publishing.

Sato, Ikua (1998), *Kamikaze Biker: Parody and Anatomy in Affluent Japan,* Chicago: University of Chicago Press.

Saussue, Ferdinand de ([1916] 1986), *Course in General Linguistics,* La Salle, IL: Open Court.

Scardino, Albert (1986), "Mitsui Unit Gets Exxon Building," *New York Times,* December 11.

Schodt, Frederick L. (1996), *Dreamland Japan: Writings on Modern Manga,* Berkeley CA: Stone Bride.

Schwöbel, Laura (2008), *Gothic Subculture in Finland: History, Fashion and Lifestyle,* Saarbruecken, Germany: VDM Verlag.

Seidman, Steven (1994), *The Postmodern Turn,* Cambridge, UK: Cambridge University Press.

Senken Shimbun (2000), *Karisuma wo Uru* [Selling charisma], Tokyo: Senken Shimbun.

Shils, Edward (1975a), *Centre and Periphery: Essays in Macrosociology,* Chicago: University of Chicago Press.

Shils, Edward (1975b), "Centre and Periphery," in *Centre and Periphery: Essays in Macrosociology,* Chicago: University of Chicago Press.

Shils, Edward (1975c), "Charisma," in *Centre and Periphery: Essays in Macrosociology,* Chicago: University of Chicago Press.

Shirahase, Sawako (2010), "Marriage as an Association of Social Classes in a Low Fertility Rate Society: Towards a New Theory of Social Stratification," in Hiroshi Ishida and David H. Slater (eds.), *Social Class in Contemporary Japan: Structures, Sorting and Strategies,* London and New York: Routledge.

Simmel, Georg ([1904] 1957), "Fashion," *American Journal of Sociology,* 17/6: 541–58.

Simonelli, David (2002), "Anarchy, Pop and Violence: Punk Rock Subculture and the Rhetoric of Class, 1976–1978," *Contemporary British History,* 16/2: 121–44.

Skott-Myhre, Hans Arthur (2009), *Youth and Subculture as Creative Force: Creating New Spaces for Radical Youth Work,* Toronto: University of Toronto Press.

Skov, Lise (1996), "Fashion Trends, Japonisme and Postmodernism," *Theory, Culture and Society,* 13/3: 129–51.

Skov, Lise (2006), "A Japanese Globalization Experience and a Hong Kong Dilemma," in Sandra Niessen, Anne Marie Leshkowich, and Carla Jones (eds.), *Re-Orienting Fashion,* Oxford, UK: Berg.

Slade, Toby (2010), *Japanese Fashion: A Cultural History,* Oxford, UK: Berg.

Smart, Carl (1976), *Women, Crime and Criminology: A Feminist Critique,* London and Boston: Routledge and Kegan Paul.

Smith, Philip (1991), "Codes and Conflict," *Theory and Society,* 20: 103–38.

Snyder, Gregory J. (2009), *Graffiti Lives: Beyond the Tag in New York's Urban Underground,* New York: New York University Press.

Spencer, Herbert ([1896] 1966), *The Principles of Sociology,* Vol. 2, New York: D. Appleton.

Spindler, Amy (1996), "Zut! British Infiltrate French Fashion," *New York Times,* October 15: A1.

Steele, Valerie (1985), *Fashion and Eroticism,* New York: Oxford University Press.

Steele, Valerie (1988), *Paris Fashion: A Cultural History,* New York: Oxford University Press.

Steele, Valerie (1991), *Women of Fashion: Twentieth-Century Designers,* New York: Rizzoli.

Steele, Valerie (1992), "Chanel in Context," in Juliet Ash and Elizabeth Wilson (eds.), *Chic Thrills: A Fashion Reader,* Berkeley: University of California Press.

Steele, Valerie (1997), *Fifty Years of Fashion: New Look to Now,* New Haven, CT: Yale University Press.

Steele, Valerie (2010), "Is Japan Still the Future?" in Valerie Steele (ed.), *Japan Fashion Now! Exhibition Catalogue,* New Haven, CT: Yale University Press.

Steele, Valerie (ed.) (2010), *Japan Fashion Now! Exhibition Catalogue,* New Haven, CT: Yale University Press.

Steele, Valerie, and Major, John S. (1999), *China Chic: East Meets West,* New Haven, CT: Yale University Press.

Storey, John (1999), *Cultural Consumption and Everyday Life,* London: Arnold.

Storey, John (2001), *Cultural Theory and Popular Culture,* Harlow, UK: Pearson Education.

Storey, John (2003), *Inventing Popular Culture,* Oxford, UK: Blackwell.

Sumner, William Graham ([1906] 1940), *Folkways: A Study of the Sociological Importance of Usages, Manners, Customs, Mores and Morals,* Boston: Ginn.

Sumner, William Graham, and Keller, Albert Gallway (1927), *The Science of Society,* Vol. 3, New Haven, CT: Yale University Press.

Tajima, Yusuke (ed.), *Kera!* Tokyo: Index Communications.

Tarde, Gabriel (1903), *The Laws of Imitation,* translated by Elsie C. Parsons, New York: Henry Holt.

Taylor, Lou (2004), *Establishing Dress History,* Manchester, UK: Manchester University Press.

Thornton, Sarah, and McRobbie, Angela (1995), "Rethinking Moral Panics for Mass-Mediated World," *British Journal of Sociology,* 46/4: 559–74.

Thrasher, Frederick M. (1927), *The Gang,* Chicago: University of Chicago Press.

Thuresson, Mike (2002), *French Fancies,* Tokyo: SRD Japan.

Toennies, Ferdinand ([1887] 1963), *Community and Society,* New York: Harper & Row.

Toennies, Ferdinand ([1909] 1961), *Custom: An Essay on Social Codes,* translated by A. F. Borenstein, New York: Free Press

Treat, John Whittier (ed.) (1995), *Contemporary Japan and Popular Culture,* Honolulu: University of Hawaii Press.

Tsukino, Akemi (2009), *Koakuma Tachi no Ura Monogatari* [Underground stories of small devils], Tokyo: Basilico.

Turcotte, Bryan Ray (2007), *Punk Is Dead, Punk Is Everything,* Corte Madera, CA: Gingko Press.

Turner, Bryan (ed.) (1990), *Theories of Modernity and Postmodernity,* London: Sage.

Turner, Graeme (1996), *British Cultural Studies,* London: Routledge.

Turner, Victor (1986), *The Anthropology of Performance,* New York: PAJ Publications.

U.S. Bureau of Labor Statistics (2011), "International Labor Comparisons," http://www.bls.gov/fls/.

Van Krieken, Robert, Habibis, Daphne, Smith, Philio, Hutchins, Brett, Martin, Gerg, and Maton, Karl (2006), *Sociology: Themes and Perspectives,* Frenchs Forest, Australia: Pearson Education.

Veblen, Thorstein ([1899] 1957), *The Theory of Leisure Class,* London: Allen and Unwin.

Walters, Malcolm (1995), *Globalization,* London: Routledge.

Weber, Max (1947), *The Theory of Social and Economic Organization,* New York: Oxford University Press.

Weber, Max (1968), *Economy and Society,* New York: Bedminster Press.

White, Harrison (1993), *Careers and Creativity: Social Forces in the Arts,* Boulder, CO: Westview Press.

White, Harrison, and White, Cynthia ([1965] 1993), *Canvases and Careers: Institutional Change in the French Painting World,* New York: John Wiley.

White, R. D. (1993), *Youth Subcultures: Theory, History, and the Australian Experience,* Hobart, Tasmania: National Clearinghouse for Youth Studies.

Whyte, William Foote (1943), *Street Corner Society,* Chicago: University of Chicago Press.

Widdicombe, Sue, and Wooffitt, Rob (1990), "'Being' Versus 'Doing' Punk: On Achieving Authenticity as a Member," *Journal of Language and Social Psychology,* 9: 257–77.

Williams, Raymond (1961), *The Long Revolution,* London: Chatto and Windus.

Williams, Raymond ([1958] 1971), *Culture and Society,* London: Penguin.

Williams, Raymond (1976), *Keywords,* New York: Oxford University Press.

Williams, Raymond (1981), *Culture,* Glasgow, UK: Fontana Paperbacks.

Williams, Raymond ([1977] 1985), *Marxism and Literature,* Oxford, UK: Oxford University Press.

Williams, Raymond (1998), "The Analysis of Culture," in John Storey (ed.), *Cultural Theory and Popular Culture: A Reader,* Hemel Hempstead, UK: Prentice Hall.

Wilson, Elizabeth (1985), *Adorned in Dreams: Fashion and Modernity,* Berkeley: University of California Press.

Wilson, Elizabeth (1994), "Fashion and Postmodernism," in John Storey (ed.), *Cultural Theory and Popular Culture: A Reader,* Hemel Hempstead, UK: Prentice Hall.

Wojcik, Daniel (1995), *Punk and Neo-Tribal Body Art,* Jackson: University Press of Mississippi.

Wolfgang, Marvin, and Ferracuti, Franco (1967), *The Subculture of Violence: Towards an Integrated Theory in Criminology,* London: Tavistock.

Wood, Robert T. (2006), *Straightedge Youth: Complexity and Contradictions of a Subculture,* Syracuse, NY: Syracuse University Press.

Yoshinaga, Masayuki, and Ishikawa, Katsuhiko (2007), *Gothic and Lolita,* London: Phaidon.

Zielenziger, Michael (2006), *Shutting Out the Sun: How Japan Created Its Own Lost Generation,* New York: Doubleday.

Index